Building the Bay Colony

Building the Bay Colony

Local Economy and Culture
in Early Massachusetts

James E. McWilliams

UNIVERSITY OF VIRGINIA PRESS   CHARLOTTESVILLE AND LONDON

University of Virginia Press

© 2007 by the Rector and Visitors of the University of Virginia

All rights reserved

Printed in the United States of America on acid-free paper

First published 2007

9 8 7 6 5 4 3 2 1

Library of Congress Cataloging-in-Publication Data
McWilliams, James E.
    Building the Bay Colony : local economy and culture in early Massachusetts /
James E. McWilliams.
        p.   cm.
    Includes bibliographical references and index.
    ISBN 978-0-8139-2636-0 (cloth : alk. paper)
    1. Massachusetts—Economic conditions—17th century. 2. Massachusetts Bay
Company. I. Title.
    HC107.M4M52 2007
    974.4′02—dc22

                                                            2006038773

For Leila

Contents

Acknowledgments

I HAVE STOOD ON THE SHOULDERS OF SO MANY PEOPLE IN THE COURSE
of writing this book that it would take another volume to grant them the
thanks they are due. I can only hope that I have, in whatever way, shown
each of them the depth of my gratitude. As for the institutions that have
made this book possible, special thanks go to the Johns Hopkins University,
where I was fortunate enough to do my graduate work under the indefati-
gable guidance of Jack Greene; the Phillips Library at the Peabody Essex
Museum, the American Antiquarian Society, the Massachusetts Historical Society, the Massachusetts Archives, the Baker Library at the Harvard
Business School, and the Schlesinger Library at Radcliff College, where
I did the bulk of my research; and Texas State University–San Marcos,
which has provided me with first-rate colleagues and a genuinely pleas-
ant place to work. Last, but never least, there is my family. My wife, Leila
Kempner, and our two young children, Owen and Cecile, have not only
supported my work in more ways than they can imagine but shown me
that it all pales next to the love they bring to my life.

A NOTE ON THE SPELLINGS OF NAMES
This book depends heavily on account books that were kept without the benefits of double-entry bookkeeping, standardized spelling, or formal handwriting skills. While I was able to decipher the vast majority of the books I studied, the common habit of spelling a person's name in two, three, and even four different ways, sometimes within a single account, posed a particularly thorny problem. To deal with the issue of multiple spellings, I used the form that appeared most frequently.

Introduction: All Economics Is Local

MASSACHUSETTS PURITANS FACED A PRESSING ECONOMIC PROBLEM throughout the seventeenth century, a problem well beyond their control: the region's soil was terrible. Rock strewn and hard, it was incapable of supporting a staple crop.[1] With ample justification settlers disparaged the land as a "desart Wildernesse." They rightly called Massachusetts "barren beyond belief."[2] Unlike the southern colonies, and even unlike the middle Atlantic colonies (with their heavy focus on wheat production), New England would never exploit a cash crop to its great economic advantage. A diversified economy based on mixed farming and family labor would be its colonial fate. Making the economy run profitably—something much harder to do without a cash crop—was the settlers' economic cross to bear. Puritans bore the burden with dignity and humility, building farms with particular diligence and passion and conceptualizing their work as integral to the health of their families and community. No matter how hard they worked, though, the material reality was inescapable: their soil yielded its profits with stubborn reluctance.

Ironically, the Puritans' hard work and patience only added to the problem. Larger economic opportunities beyond the farm eventually emerged as farmers produced a marketable surplus of goods. Nowhere was this development more evident than in the renegade class of merchants who arose out of the farming communities to pull the region in a direction that ostensibly challenged the traditional habits of husbandry. Based on the produce generated from local farms, these men successfully integrated themselves into a high-rolling transatlantic economy that hewed to an altogether different, more acquisitive set of values than Puritans typically espoused. Within decades, Puritans, as a result of their hard work, developed a local economy that was so stable that it supported integration into the profit-oriented transatlantic world. Settlers, in short, were faced with

1

Massachusetts Bay Colony, 1650.

the fate of becoming profit-seeking Yankees because they worked so hard to be spiritually strong Puritans.[3]

The settlers who managed this economic paradox remained central to the economic development of Massachusetts. They were hardworking men and women whose lives centered on the local economy. Their work ensured not only a local supply of food, labor, and basic manufactures but also that merchants remained woven into the older patterns of local behavior as they embraced headier ventures and imported more exotic goods. The economic choices these Puritan pioneers made in a local context certainly promoted "peaceable kingdoms," but they also shaped the merchants' transatlantic decisions in a way that fostered stability amidst change. Worlds that once appeared vastly distinct thus became symbiotically connected. Massachusetts, as a result, thrived as a stable, diverse, if not wildly profitable, colony.

The connection between the internal and external economies encourages a fresh perspective on the locus of economic change. Although elite merchants were Massachusetts's prime economic movers, it was the men and women who made local decisions on the ground, on their farms, in their shops, and behind closed doors, that became the economy's hidden engine of economic growth. They were the ones who accomplished the less obvious but equally necessary requirements for large-scale economic development and systematic exportation. A consideration of the region's exports and imports throughout the century certainly provides a comprehensive overview of Massachusetts's economic progress. It obscures, however, such critical processes as developing the colony's infrastructure, establishing crucial patterns of internal commercial exchange, and fulfilling local requirements for the exportation that merchants so eagerly pursued and successfully exploited. In confronting the routine economic demands of daily life, Puritan pioneers provided the provincial economic foundation for exportation while establishing economic habits that preserved their founding values.[4] Puritan pioneers, in other words, struck a balance. Achieving this delicate balance was a century-long project that proved to be central to the region's ultimate success as a British American colony.

Several aspects of local economic behavior enabled Puritans to preserve economic traditions while supporting the merchant transition to the export marketplace. Although integrally linked with Massachusetts's emerging export economy, the local economy operated according to a more conservative set of customary expectations than those values that underscored more commercial ventures. The demands of building an infrastructure, establishing and keeping trading relationships with neighbors, and working to provide the preconditions for merchants to meet foreign markets reinforced the older values that enhanced stability and minimized risk. Both merchants and local traders were, in essence, getting and spending, buying and selling, producing and consuming. But Puritan pioneers, whether consciously or not, did so in a way that stressed economic continuity, tradition, and relative insularity. Merchants might have threatened to expose insular communities to the perceived dangers of ethnic diversity, explicitly acquisitive attitudes, impersonal economic relationships, and a range of real and perceived "foreign" values.[5] Puritan pioneers, however, quietly made daily economic decisions that collectively preserved the traditional ideological tenets that ministers, for one, feared were disintegrating. Their work, work of the most rudimentary sort, both preserved the past and shepherded the colony toward modernity.[6]

Another quality of the local economy that allowed Massachusetts to make the export transition so seamlessly was its emphasis on mixed farming. By its very nature mixed farming was the kind of economic pursuit that generated modest wealth. The decision to develop an economic regimen whereby settlers grew grain, grazed livestock, kept vegetable gardens, and practiced a trade or two meant that residents generally would not be separated by a socioeconomic gulf capable of undermining community cohesion. It also meant that Massachusetts residents would not, as a rule, accumulate enough assets to import substantial luxury goods for their own consumption, as their wealthier staple-crop-producing counterparts had done farther south. Instead they would have to provide one another with food, clothing, shelter, transportation services, small loans, and a wide variety of other goods and services. Although economically competitive, Puritan pioneers would have to cooperate. This regional interdependence fostered a modest pace of economic change, reciprocal financial arrangements that stood the test of time, multiple dependencies upon dozens of neighbors, family strength and stability, and a sense of acquisition tempered by controlled ambition. When Governor John Winthrop spoke of his people as having to be "knit together . . . as one man," he had no idea how successfully the mixed economy that the Puritans developed would support that vision.[7]

Further enhancing the Puritans' ability to manage the economic transition to a transatlantic economy was the fact that settlers' interests were neither overtly subsistence oriented nor overtly profit oriented, but rather a careful balance of the two.[8] Puritans neither disavowed the attractions of wealth nor centered their lives on materialistic accumulation. Instead, they pursued what they called a "competency," or a "comfortable independence." The idea—a purposefully vague one—suggested a standard of living that allowed families to form a settled and orderly society. This standard of living was to be "both desirable and morally legitimate." Extremes of wealth and poverty obviously worked against such a goal, and thus the notion of achieving a competency helped the colony avoid these destabilizing extremes. The concept was a powerful if amorphous cultural expectation that effectively motivated working men and women, as Daniel Vickers puts it, "to engage in petty commerce, structure inheritance practices to maintain family farms intact, claim perquisites at harvest, and even riot when their customary rights to private land were threatened." The popularity of competency, indeed its status as a customary value, enabled Puritans to deal with the challenges that arose as the colony moved into potentially destabilizing transatlantic venues.[9]

Sustained insight into something as elusive as the continuity of local economic behavior would not be possible without the account books that Puritan pioneers left behind. Seventeenth-century account books provide an unparalleled look into the most intricate processes of local economic development.[10] Common farmers, local traders, and artisans kept account books as a matter of course. Few—perhaps about twenty-five—have survived from the seventeenth century. My transcription and analyses of these fertile sources inform much of what follows. These documents are rare gems that have allowed a reconstruction of a previously hidden hive of economic activity. As sources that go to the vital core of local economic life, they record the daily exchanges that individually seem insignificant but collectively define the way Puritans did business on the periphery of British America.

What follows is a story of continuity, one that charts the persistence of inherited economic behavior. As such, it is a story of survival and triumph. As they mended fences, cleared fields, planted gardens, yoked oxen to carts, and built roads and ferries, Puritan pioneers were acutely aware that they had landed in a place that was, from their perspective, a rough wilderness demanding transformation. Seventy years of this local economic activity led them to feel something of a mastery over their environment, inspiring them to see Massachusetts as a place they could negotiate with confidence and, with merchants standing on their shoulders, exploit to their great benefit. The once ragged coast and daunting interior created impressive wealth and considerable stability. However one feels about this mastery, however one feels about this wealth, it occurred as a result of common people making common economic decisions—every day, every hour, every minute of their difficult lives. It occurred because Puritan pioneers knew full well that all economics is local.

ONE

Getting Lost in a New World

1630–1640

THE PIOUS FOUNDERS AND EAGER DEVELOPERS OF THE MASSACHU-setts Bay Colony were more than just devout Puritans committed to building a city on a hill. They were also astute businessmen intent on making a healthy profit on their investment. As a result, they reacted with palpable frustration when, during the colony's precarious first decade, settlers who were doing just fine in spiritual matters proved less capable when it came to matters financial. In their initial failure to export enough of the region's considerable natural resources to put the colony in the black, settlers in the Massachusetts Bay provoked a torrent of investor complaints, reminding us that when it came to money even Puritanical patience could run low. Although investors would not have known it at the time, their collective anger illuminated a problem that Massachusetts Bay colonists would spend the entire century working to solve, namely, how was the Bay Colony to make ends meet?[1]

While Puritans were hardly alone in asking this question, the answer they came up with was unique. Every other region of British America found a solution in the form of a profitable staple crop. After a decade of struggling to build mixed farms, Barbadians settled on sugar. The Chesapeake Bay region embraced that "stinking weed," tobacco. After two decades of searching for its staple, Carolina found rice. And while Pennsylvania and New York did not become monocultural societies in the way their southern counterparts did, they did allow wheat to approach the status of a staple product. Some combination of staples, non-familial labor, and exports became the profitable answer most colonists gave to the critical question of returns.[2]

But not the Puritans. As a regional economy, New England would eventually achieve unparalleled stability, respectable profit margins, and a strong predilection for capitalism through the exportation of a diverse range of goods, including fish, timber, whale products, rum, grain, and livestock.[3] Reaching that stage, however, turned out to be a radically different kind of project than establishing a staple crop and importing foreign labor, and it was a project that would occupy the entire century. When the Puritans thus asked what every other region eventually asked—how will we make ends meet?—they had no idea what the answer would be. Without an environment capable of supporting a staple crop, without an ample labor supply to exploit, the question nagged at them with particular intensity.

Few answers were forthcoming. "It is a very greate grievanc[e] and generall complainte among all the Merchants and dealers to New England," noted John Tinker, "that they can have no returnes." Should not "some course be taken for better payments of our returnes," he went on, "our Creditors . . . will utterly cease." Matthew Craddock wished that "some serious course might be thought of how returns may be provided." After "nine months patient wayting in expectation of some opportunity to be offered us," two other investors highlighted "our great charge and hindrance" as the withered fruits of an investment that should have flourished. Repeated pleas from Simon D'Ewes that the Bay Company pay a dividend led Governor Winthrop to respond, "There come no benefit of your money but losse." Even when a few beaver furs did make their way into London markets, they were dismissed by hatmakers as "faint stuffe" and "the worst of all" the imports. After only two years of settlement, Thomas Dudley reported that "the estates of the undertakers, who were 3 or 4000 pounds engaged in the joint stock . . . was now not above so many hundreds." These complaints mocked that fateful day when Winthrop had landed on the rocky shores of the Massachusetts Bay. When land was sighted, he later recalled with unbridled optimism, "there came a smell off the shore like the smell of a garden."[4] If the first few years of living in that "garden" were any indication, however, it did not appear to be an especially productive plot. Investors, after all, were going broke.

Settlers were not doing much better. The winter of 1630 went down as an unmitigated disaster. When Thomas Dudley visited the colony in the winter of 1631 he found "the colony in a sad and unexpected condition, above eighty of them being dead in the winter before, and many of those alive weak and sick, all the corn and bread amongst them all hardly sufficient to feed them a fortnight." In this desperate environment incoming ships became floating icons of salvation. When a much-awaited load of imports finally docked, as William Hubbard described it, "the people of the country were like the poor widow, brought to the last handful of meal in the barrel." One settler wrote home to his father that "we had bine put to a wonderful straight." He thanked God for sending a ship when he did, noting that "here we may live if we have supplies every year from Old England other wise we can not subsist." In December 1635 Nathanial Ward pleaded with Winthrop "to reserve some meale and malt" because, he insisted, "I am very destitute."[5] Too many of his fellow colonists understood. After only a couple of years of settlement no one knew how to answer the question how to make ends meet, least of all the starving men and women on the ground. How the Puritans would manage this dilemma was still anyone's guess.

EVEN WITH THE DEBACLES OF ROANOKE AND EARLY JAMESTOWN STILL freshly imprinted on the English mind, nobody expected a turn of events quite this dire. Neither unprepared nor smug, settlers of the Bay Colony firmly believed that they were providentially fated for success. The thirty thousand Puritans who migrated to New England during the 1630s came from England's middle class. They lived according to a tight set of moral, social, and economic values. Pursuing the imperatives of covenant theology, while dutifully preserving their souls for grace, Puritans embraced the related virtues of market production, commerce, and modest profit. These trends, they were proud to note, were reinforcing rather than contradictory. Modestly conspicuous economic success and inward dedication to providential theology fostered a culture of development well suited to the wilderness they believed awaited the benefit of their collective toil.[6]

The Puritans' demographic background also prepared them well for economic success. While England remained overwhelmingly rural, Massachusetts settlers hailed from market towns marked by diversified commercial activity, specialized and skilled occupations, and, in the words of one scholar, "local economies of considerable scope, scale, and sophistication." The investors who funded their migration included the empire's most noted financiers. Twenty-five out of forty-one initial subscribers to the company were well-heeled merchants holding investments in the Dorchester Company, the East India Company, and local real-estate ventures. They understood joint-stock arrangements, knew how to capitalize such operations, and possessed the social and cultural know-how to attract hard cash for speculative ventures. After gaining approval from the Council of New England in 1628 for a land patent stretching from the Merrimack to the Charles River, they immediately raised £2,940 in stock subscriptions and began planning the colony. When John Endicott and a small council sailed for Salem they understandably departed for the New World with the utmost economic optimism.[7] The future, in short, seemed ordained.

Investors in the New England Company, moreover, were a pragmatic group of men who intended to see their vision become reality. Wedded to the mercantile premise that a colony's primary role was to supply the mother country with natural resources that it would otherwise have to acquire elsewhere, colonial underwriters carefully structured their new venture to match colonial resources with international demand. They wanted to make cash, pure and simple, and their ambitious and not altogether unrealistic policies reflected that desire.[8]

Topping the investors' list of potentially exploitable commodities was fish. For more than a hundred years salted cod had served as a profitable staple of the Iberian diet. By 1620 its price had spiked as Spain's and Portugal's Catholics followed the dictum that they be fruitful and multiply. In response to this demand, the company moved to establish a full-fledged transatlantic fishing industry. Following the lead of preexisting Newfoundland models, investors living in the Bay Colony oversaw the construction of a large fish storehouse and demanded that "an inventory be daily kept of all the provisions and implements of fishing . . . to preserve [the business] from loss and spoil." The company, led by Matthew Craddock, imported lines, ropes, hooks, salt, barrels, experienced fishermen, small fishing boats, and ample exhortations to catch fish. Governor Endicott's first formal "letter of instruction" from the company noted that "we have sent five weight of salt," adding, "pray let the fishermen . . . endeavor to take fish, and let it be well saved with the said salt, and packed up in hogs heads." They were implored (as if it needed to be said) to "send it home." As far as Endicott, Craddock, and the company were concerned, John White's early assessment of fishing in New England was prophetic. White had described it as "one of the most honest, and every way profitable imployment that the nation undertakes." Investors distributed their resources accordingly, marveled over the rich cod banks off the coast of Massachusetts, and awaited healthy returns from a fish that was known to reach up to two hundred pounds and practically jump into fishing vessels.[9]

The colonists did not find these seagoing designs contrary to their mission, and initially at least, they seemed eager to fill out the blueprint. The arrival of John Winthrop in 1630 not only transformed the New England Company into the Massachusetts Bay Company but populated the colony with a group of men prepared to make ends meet with line, hook, boat, and bait. "The abundance of sea fish," Francis Higginson wrote, "are almost beyond believing . . . and in their season are plentifully taken." In 1635 the General Court, the colony's main governing body, approved a committee to "consult, advise, and take order for the setting forwards and after managing of a fishing trade" and arranged for "all charges of dyett or otherwayes, att the tymes of their meeting, to be allowed out of the fishing stocke." Hugh Peter, a prominent Salem resident, arranged for the public financing of lines, hooks, ropes, weirs, and other necessities, while the General Court granted to fishermen in Marblehead "grounde as they stand in need of" to dry fish upon extensive wooden flakes. Tax breaks offered to vessels used for transporting fish as well as exempting laborers involved in the fishing trade from military service were other incentives used to make cod the king of the colony's fledgling economy.[10]

The promise of cod returns kept investors' hopes high. Backers were similarly eager, however, to exploit an even more accessible natural resource: timber. Contemporaries, especially those who hailed from timber-stripped regions of England, gushed over the thickets that clogged New England's landscape. Here was a land, according to one visitor, "infinitely thick set with Trees and Bushes of all sorts."[11] Spruce, hemlock, white oak, pin oak, red maple, yellow birch, white cedar, and dozens of other trees struck the English settlers as added proof that God had anointed their venture into the wilderness. No longer would fuel supplies run desperately low, as they so often had back home. No longer would migrants worry much about finding material for homes, fences, barns, and meetinghouses—an essential factor in turning a wilderness into a settled civilization. But most importantly, at least as the investors saw it, the English could even export timber to meet Europe's expanding hunger for good wood. "[T]here has never been a better time for the sale of timber," wrote Craddock, before sending to Massachusetts a sawmill expert and "coopers and cleavers of timber" to undertake the arduous process of clearing and processing trees in an environment so richly endowed with them that men reported traveling several miles on a sunlit afternoon without leaving the shade.[12]

Investors saw no good reason why the settlers could not export enough timber to diminish metropolitan dependence on Scottish and Scandinavian imports. Once he felt sure that the basic requirements for systematic timber clearing were in place, Craddock instructed Endicott to "let [settlers] provide us some staves and other timber of all sorts, to be sent to us by the *Talbot, Whelp,* or the other two ships that come after." Early enthusiasm to meet London timber orders become so intense that the General Court stipulated that "no man shall fell any wood for paling but such as shalbe viewed and allowed by the next assistant." It did so in order to preserve "good timber for more necessary uses." In 1635 Edward Trelawney wrote home to England asking for "experienced men in the making and ordering of clapboard and pipe staves." Once they arrived, he explained, the settlers could then sell surplus timber "at good rates to the straitsmen [English merchants]." Like fish, timber could, if efficiently harvested, help Massachusetts do what a colony was designed to do: make the mother country richer and more independent than its competitors.[13]

Fur was the final commodity that inspired visions of grandeur among the colony's ever-hopeful investors. Beaver fur was fetching top dollar throughout Europe as raw material for carding, bowing, and planking into fashionable hats. The Massachusetts Bay Company secured a deal whereby it would control 50 percent of the trade revenue generated from furs trapped deep in the wilderness. The other half would accrue to investors who had contributed £25 to £50 apiece. Motivated by such incentives, the colony's backers devised a plan for tapping a mature and geographically intricate trade that included an established network already monopolized by Plymouth, Native American, and Dutch trappers. Contemplating the least invasive way to merge into this commercial traffic, Winthrop speculated that the fur-rich region lining the Hudson "might easily be diverted" toward the Merrimack River, a move that would direct trade to the hub of Boston while ensuring that the Massachusetts Bay Company "would not have to share [the fur trade] with Plymouth." Part of the fur trade's appeal was that the material was easily shipped and did not require processing in the colonies. All the colonists needed to do in order to make money from fur was harvest and pack it. England would take care of the rest, even the shipping.[14]

Intent on shunting the fur trade east, several adventurers explored and settled the western interior of Massachusetts. John Oldman, of Plymouth, traveled to Connecticut in 1633 to negotiate treaties with Native American trappers. He made his contacts, proffered his wampum, returned the following year to the Bay Colony, sold a modest supply of healthy pelts, and extended his commercial contacts to as far away as Weathersfield, Connecticut. Closer to home, Simon Willard started a trapping business in the Merrimack valley and by late 1634 had successfully petitioned the General Court to found Concord as a fur-trading outpost. From his home base in Roxbury, William Pynchon extended his emerging fur-trading business toward the Connecticut River, organizing a post at Agawam in 1635 and buying the land that would later become Springfield. As was the case with early fish and timber plans, the General Court promoted this commodity by repealing taxes on beaver fur, protecting exclusive trading rights, and forbidding liquor sales to Native Americans. It hoped that such measures would allow fur to join fish and timber in generating returns that investors deemed adequate.[15]

For these reasons—fish, timber, and fur—it made perfect sense for investors to expect serious dividends. Nevertheless, the reality of local economic life intervened. It seemed that the harder Puritans worked, the more their plans imploded. Throughout the 1630s the litany of despair continued. Investors inquired when "beaver, or other commodities, or fish (if you have the means to preserve it), can be gotten ready to return in the foresaid ships." If nothing else was ready for export, they pleaded for "wood, if no better lading to be had." Whatever the circumstances, investors could only reiterate that the colonists "endeavor to get in readiness what you can, whereby our ships . . . may not come wholly empty." Anything, the company pleaded, "will help toward our charge."[16] In the end, though, they got nothing. Their main reaction was to do the only thing they could do: complain. How, in light of the vast potential to exploit fish, timber, and fur, could the situation have come to this? Why had these early economic plans come to naught?

A GLIMPSE OF AN ANSWER MIGHT BE FOUND IN A SEEMINGLY IRRELE-vant incident that took place in the winter of 1631. John Endicott needed to travel from Salem to Boston for a meeting he had arranged with the governor, John Winthrop. He prepared his horse but decided at the last minute that he could make the eleven-mile journey faster by boat. After only a couple of miles of being tossed about by an increasingly rough ocean, however, Endicott reported the wind "being stiffe against us" and judged that his boat was not up to the challenge. He put ashore at Saugus and sought an alternative. "There being no canoe," he searched for a horse to rent. Not a single beast was to be found. Cold and quite late for his meeting, Endicott ultimately chose to walk, a decision that sent him into an entirely unfamiliar thicket and quickly reduced him to "an ill condition." Deciding to cut his losses, he waited for the weather to clear, found a ride back up the coast to Salem, and penned the following message to Winthrop: "I desire you to pardon me."[17]

Winthrop did. But future historians have been less sympathetic toward

Endicott's predicament. While they have traditionally proposed a couple of plausible reasons for the colony's decade-long failure to pay off its debts, Endicott's inability to make his meeting with Winthrop has never come to bear on the issue. Instead, we know that the Great Migration, which brought more than thirty thousand settlers from the middle ranks to New England, infused the colony with an "artificial prosperity" because these immigrants purchased farm produce grown by the initial settlers in cold, hard cash. As Darrett B. Rutman explains, "The newcomers brought little in the way of material goods, having transformed their possessions into cash in England. They were now eager to transform that cash into new possessions in Massachusetts. From the already established settlers, they bought the Indian corn and wheat, the timber and, particularly, the cattle needed to start life anew." As a result, the economic opportunities missed in the export market were absorbed domestically as settlers did their best to get their farms up and running. Were it not for this constant flow of fresh immigrants, the colony would have perished in a matter of two or three years. Instead, it found temporary salvation in a market that, oddly enough, found them.[18]

Numerous as these newcomers were, however, they could not, according to another common interpretation, meet the labor and capital demands required to export goods systematically enough to generate profits in European markets. The dearth of manpower, equipment, and expertise was especially evident in the fishing industry, which, because of the lack of cheap labor and small craft, developed only intermittently throughout the colony's first generation. As one historian puts it, "The very abundance of what English farmers had come to find—the land that would guarantee them the independence they cherished so highly—resulted in the most profound adjustments. For while the land was plentiful, the means of bringing it into production were not." It would require a larger pool of labor, more sophisticated (and exploitive) labor arrangements, and more substantial ships for the industry to boom, which it eventually did in the 1650s. Two decades earlier, though, despite the tireless efforts of the investors, the traditional factors of production paled next to the pervasive demand for Massachusetts's potential exports.

As carefully researched and well documented as these explanations are, they fail to account for Endicott's mishap because they tell us little about the historical implications of traveling in early Massachusetts. The reason why such implications need to be carefully considered is easily overlooked until one considers the region's infrastructure. Economists (and economic historians) generally conceptualize land, labor, and capital as factors integral to a developed or developing economic system. Rarely, however, are they required to address explicitly the infrastructural requirements of an economy that has yet to become a legitimate economy, that is, one that completely lacks the most basic rudiments of Western economic development, things like communication, transportation, finance, and provisioning, not to mention food, clothing, and shelter. Until these needs were locally met, the factors of production were impotent. Plans for economic development, in short, came face to face with the reality of geography.[19]

In Massachusetts, a quintessential settlement economy, the fundamental aspects of material life were absent.[20] "When you are parted with England," Francis Higginson wrote, "you shall meet neither with taverns, nor alehouse, nor butchers', nor grocers', nor apothecary shops to help what things you need." John Pond recognized the truth of this observation at once, writing to his father that "the countrey is not as we ded expect it."[21] Native American economic habits notwithstanding, Massachusetts was, from the English perspective, a vast wilderness lacking those elements of an economic infrastructure that the English took for granted. Reliable overland transportation and specialized domestic places of production, which were necessary for export activity, did not exist.[22] The material consequences of this dearth hardly seem like the heady stuff of economic history, much less a major cause for an economically dysfunctional environment. Nevertheless, they need to be explored if we are to better understand Massachusetts's early export failures. To appreciate how well the colony's economy eventually succeeded through the daily decisions made by the men and women who survived these difficult early years, it is important to see why these settlers initially failed. To do that, we must consider how they moved from point A to point B.

It turns out that Endicott was in familiar company. Traveling regionally, a routine task in England, became in the colonies an arduous and often life-threatening undertaking. It helped none that most settlers knew little or nothing of the local environment, which consisted of an intricate patchwork of woods, marshes, rivers, ponds, and swamps. Winthrop, for one, allotted tremendous space in his journal to stories involving overland travel mishaps. "One Scott and one Eliot of Ipswich," he wrote, "were lost in their ways homewards [after harvesting timber] and wandered up and down 6 dayes and eate nothing . . . they were found by an Indian, beinge almost senseless for want of rest." The movement of labor from one town to another proved equally unreliable, as evidenced by "a mayd servant of Mr. Skelton of Salem [who on a trip to Saugus] was lost 7 dayes and at length came home to Salem." She survived despite being "in the woods, having no kinds of food, the snow being very deep and cold." Then there was the case of an old man who "lost his waye between Dorchester and Winaguscas," during which time he "wandered the woods and swamps 3 days and 2 nights with out taking any food." The man being "neare spent," according to Winthrop, "God brought him back to Scituate, but he had torne his leggs much."[23] These mishaps, all of which occurred on short journeys, reflected more than the routine traveling hazards common in England. To the contrary, they confirmed a more disturbing truth: colonists were deeply ignorant of the region's geography, and compounding their ignorance, they lacked the transportation equipment needed to improve their condition. One of the cruelest and most frustrating realities of the New World was that traveling was an utter nightmare. How could the Puritans be "knit together in this work as one man" when they could hardly congregate in the first place?

Overland debacles were magnified by the region's weblike network of rivers and streams, many of which could only be crossed by ferry. Ferries, however, were few and far between and difficult to find, and when one did locate a ferry in the wilderness, it was often less than effective. After listening to repeated complaints from local residents, the Salem court fined Richard Graves, the licensed ferryman, "for neglecting to tend the ferry carefully." Graves, for his part, pleaded guilty as charged but informed the court that "it was necessary that he go to the mill" and have his corn ground rather than usher travelers to safety. This problem was common enough in a labor-starved environment, and Graves accordingly elicited a show of sympathy. George Carr, by contrast, evoked the bitterness of his neighbors when, in addition to failing to keep the ferry open and running (for no good reason), he stood accused of "suffering people to stand waiting at the waterside three hours, to the prejudice of their health." It did not help his case that when Carr's ferry was open he was known for "taking 4d a head for cattle swimming over the ferry, he not offering them his help." Before levying the fine, the court told Carr that his license required that "he find a sufficient horse boat"—a prescient reminder with license renewals coming up.[24]

Ferrying horses across rivers, however, could not have been too common a concern, primarily because there were so few horses to ferry. Although colonists certainly owned horses from the settlement's outset,

Massachusetts inventories recorded between 1636 and 1645 fail to confirm ownership of a single one. References to horses in literary accounts are equally rare. One indication that these sources speak accurately comes from William Hubbard, who wrote that the colony established its system of quarterly courts in 1635 in order "to prevent the traveling of the inhabitants many miles from their places to obtain justice; long journies of that time being, for want of horses and other means of transportation, very difficult to any sort of person." Overland transport instead relied heavily on plodding oxen yoked to rickety carts. Essex County inventories during the first decade show a rate of ownership of 16 percent for oxen, 10 percent for carts, and 12 percent for the gear needed to link the two. This mode of transport, however, was less than ideal because the beasts and carts had to be preserved for the more burdensome demands of plowing fields and hauling dirt, dung, and hay. As the disheartening stories of lost souls wandering cold forests suggest, the transportation situation left many people to go about their business on nothing more technologically advanced than their own two feet.[25]

Settlers who could afford to travel by horses or oxen and cart encountered a haphazard system of roads that created more confusion than direction. In 1635 the General Court, responding to "a complainte made to this court that many highe wayes in the country are inconveniently laid out," ordered local courts to "rectify those that are amiss." Local courts did their best to comply, but efforts to improve roads proceeded glacially. The first fine for an inadequate road was issued in 1638, and over the next two years only ten fines for defective highways followed, each one allowing a generous three months for the necessary repairs to be made. Magistrates presented evidence for the ten defective roads at four court sessions, burying them under a slate of more pressing legal matters, while admitting that the repairs would be next to impossible to enforce. Given these logistical problems, it is no wonder that in 1638 two men living in Watertown (just outside of Boston) complained that "it [Watertown] is so remote from the Bay, and from any towne, we could not see how our dwelling there could be advantageous to these plantations." Throughout the first decade, dismal road conditions, despite valid efforts to improve them, rendered once routine trips into painstaking treks to be avoided if at all possible.[26]

The sea was an even less forgiving mode of transport. Unfamiliar swells and eddies, strange and unpredictable weather shifts, ambiguous points of entry, and new, often hastily built vessels combined to make coastal travel a difficult experience. In the summer of 1632 a Salem man "carrying wood in a canoe in the South River was overturned and drowned." Such accidents happened frequently during the first decade of adjustment to the ragged contours of the Massachusetts coast. When six Salem men "went fowling in a canoe," a strong current overturned them near Kettle Island, sending five of them to a watery grave. Winthrop recalled an incident in which "a man almost drowned here in the narrow river in a canoe" after having "laden his canoe so deepe with dung that she sunk under him, scarce anything surviving." When two men and their two children tried to maneuver their "small boat," which was "overladen with wood," around Noddles Island, "they were cast away in a great tempest." One midnight in July 1634, a man "putt much goodes in a small boat in the Charles River [and] overset the boat . . . so as they were all drowned."[27] Settlers quickly developed a healthy respect for the turbulent sea, but that respect hardly eased passage across its tempestuous surface.

Accidents, of course, occur everywhere, all the time, in every setting. These examples, however, indicate that such mishaps resulted from conditions specific to a settlement society. William Hubbard, a man who seemed especially sensitive to the causes of the Bay Colony's frequent transportation problems, attributed one particular mishap to "want of experience and judgment in things of such a nature." Two fishermen drowned in the Massachusetts Bay "for not being acquainted with the channel." After visiting the colony during its early years, Sir John Clotsworthy mentioned to John Winthrop that if colonists expected to ever see profits materialize in "this wicked land," they would have to find "a man who had experience in transporting," adding rather snidely that "all hopes will be little enough."[28] If Winthrop took offense, he still had to agree with Clotsworthy's assessment.

Clotsworthy's skepticism was hardly diminished by the Bay Colony's mercurial climate. English expectations of what they assumed would be conditions similar to England's were dismayed by erratic weather patterns. "Of all the preconceptions English people brought with them to New England," writes one of the few historians to address weather as an explicit topic, "perhaps none was so important or so mistaken as that about the American climate." Settlers familiar with prevailing weather patterns in England or even southern France and Spain arrived in New England to find a place not only "in the grip of a Little Ice Age" but also burdened by summers that were baked by a more intense heat than they had ever before withstood. It helped little that the most recent report on the bay's climate was William Wood's not inaccurate assessment that the anomalous winter of 1629–30 "was a very milde season, little Frost, and lesse Snow, but cleare serene weather." The very next season, and the others that followed, brought the customary freezing rain, sleet, and snow.[29]

Colonists' information regarding waterways was similarly skewed and incomplete. Conventional wisdom regarding the Bay Colony's navigability came from John Smith's *Description of New England*. After a careful mapping of the coast, Smith surveyed in rich detail the bay's intricate network of harbors, islands, forests, rivers, fish banks, fowl coveys, and Indian population. Like any cartographer at the time, he exposed his personal biases, especially his hope that future settlers would exploit the southern region, taking advantage of its dense fishing banks. Intentionally or not, this goal predisposed Smith to portray the southern area as a navigable and well-protected harbor, or as Smith himself put it, "the strangest fishpond I ever saw."[30] With his concerns centered solely on a viable export trade, Smith left it to the settlers themselves to discover the more challenging obstacles constricting the region's coastal and internal waterways. They did so, as we have seen, at great risk to life and limb.

Central to that peril was wind. Wind patterns daunted traders and travelers who struggled to negotiate the rock-strewn, cross-currented coast. Winthrop reported "a great shallop cominge from Pascataqua in a N. E. wind," explaining that "the skillfulness of the men" cast it "upon the rocks and lost 100 li [pounds] of goods." During another violent swirl of wind and snow "a shallop of William Lovell laden with goods to Salem worth 100 li was put into Plim; and coming out the men went aboard a small barke by the waye and their shallop broke loose and was lost." On a day when "the winde came n.w. very stronge," three of Winthrop's servants "coming in a shallop from Misticke were driven by the winde upon Noddles Island and forced to stay there all night without fire or food." With considerable disappointment, Winthrop complained how "the company sett forth a pinace to the parts about Cape Cod, to load for corne" only to have the mission undermined by "contrary windes."[31]

Contrary winds could be more than a nuisance: they could be deadly. When a group of men ventured to Noddles Island "to fetch wood in a small boat, and none of them having any skill or experience," they were "cast away in a n.e tempest as they came home in the night." They were never found. During a summer trip along the coast to Connecticut "2 shallops laden with goods . . . were taken in the night with an easterly storm and cast away upon Brownes Island and all the men drowned." Isaac Allerton felt lucky to be alive after a powerful gust catapulted his boat into a archipelago of rocks that "beate out all her kele," following which Allerton laboriously mended his boat only to have the keel "beate out all again" by another patch of submerged boulders. Although he returned home "without provisions," Allerton did have his life, for which, given the fate of so many of his neighbors, he must have been thankful.[32]

Traders and travelers had even less success managing the region's ice and snow. Winthrop recalls how "3 men had their boat frozen at Bird Island, so as they were compelled to lodge there all night." Not until the next afternoon did "they [come] over the ice to Noddles Island and thence to Molton's point in Charlestown and thence over the ice . . . to Boston." These men were fortunate; during the same freeze "6 other men were kept a weeke" from their destination. Throughout that entire weather spell there was "no open place between the Garden and Boston, neither was there any passage at Charleston for 2 or 3 days." On a journey to Agawam one Mr. Watson "met such a snow (knee deep) as he could not come back for –– days" (dashes in the original) since the only viable boat in the area "was frozen up in the snow." Traveling alone in this new land was ill-advised, as one gentleman discovered after being "21 days frozen upon plumme island and found by chance frozen in the snow, yet alive and did well." In a letter sent to his son in England, Winthrop routinely lamented how "winter hath begun early with us" and then launched into one sordid weather tale after another. "We had a snow last week," he wrote in December 1634, "much deep in many places, it came with so violent a storm, as it put by our lecture [sermon] for that day." What the colony needed, Winthrop pleaded with his son, was that "in your return [to Massachusetts] you could observe the winde and weather every day that we may see how it agrees with our parts." In other words, Winthrop understood the need for a systematic record of weather trends to foster the safer movement of colonists in a strange new world where waterways did not freeze as predictably or as reliably as they had back home.[33]

AS THESE EXAMPLES SHOW, ENDICOTT'S FAILED ATTEMPT TO MAKE HIS meeting with Winthrop was no isolated incident. Instead, it reflected one of the harshest and most common realities of life in the Bay Colony's first decade: traveling was beset with often insurmountable burdens. In light of Endicott's aborted venture, the colony's inability to generate returns necessary to keep its investors happy makes a bit more sense. A tight labor market and the welcome cash infusion of the Great Migration undoubtedly diminished Massachusetts's export production of fish, timber, and fur during the colony's first decade of existence. In appreciating these causes, however, we must not overlook the more mundane logistics of settling four thousands families in a region lacking even the most basic economic infrastructure. Unlike in England, settlers' difficulties with traveling overland, maneuvering unfamiliar boats through strange waters, and dealing with a weather system they misunderstood were concrete environmental factors, obstacles to the movement, preparation, processing, and packaging of exports. Settlers showed every sign of appreciating the potential worth of fish, timber, and fur, but their primitive economic environment required them first and foremost to construct an economic foundation to suit their radically simplified society. This construction had to occur before they could even consider exploiting their environment's resources, transporting its goods, and profiting from the rich bounty of its wilderness.

It would have been human nature, of course, to want to return home. From Roanoke to Jamestown, recent history was rife with fresh colonial ventures gone sour under conditions not altogether unlike those endured by the Puritans. Driven by their deep faith that God "will provide a shelter and a hiding place for us and ours," however, the Puritans defied human nature, reaffirmed the course that they had chosen, and persevered.[34] In fact, the difficulties they confronted had the paradoxical effect of furthering their determination to make Massachusetts work as a cohesive society. "All other churches of Europe," explained Winthrop, "are brought to desolation." In Massachusetts, however, "God has provided this place, to be a refuge for manye, whom he means to save out of the general destruction." The uncultivated environment that this chosen people committed themselves to cultivating would only yield to the covenanted community the Puritans so optimistically sought once its inhabitants got to the business of building the Bay Colony. "When a man is to wade throughe a deepe water," Winthrop wrote, "there is required tallnesse."[35] Rather than quit this unprecedented venture into the wilderness, the Puritan pioneers who settled the Massachusetts Bay Colony reached for heaven by digging into the soil.

TWO

Mapping the Landscape

1630–1640

F OR ALL THE MISHAPS, THE MASSACHUSETTS BAY COLONY'S FOUND-
ing decade had its moments of hope. At times genuine optimism
pulsed beneath the surface of suffering that plagued the 1630s. As recent
settlers struggled to transform the forests and seas from a sprawling wilderness into a manageable society, they came to understand that their venture would, with patient forbearance, ultimately succeed.

Settlers gradually realized that they were slowly making significant
internal improvements. William Wood, after acknowledging the region's
early economic problems, recognized that necessary steps had to be taken
before *any* settlement society could start paying off its debts with respectable export returns. Colonists and investors eager to balance the books
right away, he insisted, were being unrealistic. They would simply have to
wait "till by their labors [farmers] had brought the land to yield its fruit."
Men and women naive enough to expect "walled towns, fortifications, and
corn fields, as if [these] could have built themselves," were doomed to per-
ish in "so rude and unmanaged a country." The American environment
posed considerable challenges, but the fact remained that those settlers
who were "industrious enough . . . shall not need to fear want." The fruits
of industry took time. The colonists were not only well aware of this
difficult and unavoidable reality but eager to overcome it.[1]

Wood's call for patience was one voice in a chorus of sympathy. Richard Saltonstall stressed the inevitable "time of liberty from building and
for enclosing grounds" as a necessary prerequisite for more productive export endeavors. Once the crucial chores of building a local infrastructure
were completed, he continued, "we shall raise good profit not only by our
fishing trade . . . but by hemp, flax, pitch, tar, potashes, soap ashes, masts,
pipe staves, clapboards." Francis Higgenson likewise knew "this country to
be a wonderment"; the "hopeful commodities" the colony was pressured

to produce were items that "time will teach [us] to make good use of." Thomas Dudley reassured his friends in England that the colonists would only rely on outside help "till time and industry produced them here."[2] Settlers who ventured to New England during the Great Migration encountered an environment beset with economic obstacles. Nevertheless, they understood the inevitable delay required to minimize those obstacles before exploiting a region endowed with ample, if currently elusive, natural resources.

Puritan pioneers confronted the harsh physical reality of their new world with an attitude that stressed patience. It did not take long for them to appreciate that the new environment, with its less than explosively productive soil, was well suited to small-scale family farming. Mixed farming, in turn, with its limited potential to generate excessive wealth, was especially conducive to the covenanted community Puritans hoped to establish. Farm building was an activity that tempered greed while reinforcing the dictates of "moral capitalism." There was nothing wrong with making a decent profit in the export market, but the soul (as well as the infrastructure) had to be in order before Puritans ventured forth to test their mettle against the grander temptations of mammon. In this way, the region's natural limitations reinforced the ideology that would guide Puritans throughout most of the century. In the short term it helped them negotiate the mundane hardships of settlement.[3]

Inspired by the dictate that work "was a child's performance by which He wants to give his gifts in the fields," Puritans quickly embraced the idea that profiting from exports meant making the most of local resources.[4] The fact that the Bay Colony settlers categorically failed to export goods throughout the 1630s, concentrating their efforts instead on establishing small-scale farms, hardly meant that they remained indifferent to economic improvement. To the contrary, New England's first generation confronted the inevitable obstacles to economic progress with a coordinated effort to meet immediate material needs. In shaping their environment to address the short-term demands of material life, Bay colonists pragmatically built an infrastructure while laying the foundation for what would eventually become a successful export trade in local commodities. That this future trade would produce the kind of wealth that would challenge Puritan ideology would not have crossed the mind of even the most prophetic Puritan. If it had, though, he might very well have taken solace in his conviction that the communitarian values that solidified while settlers built an infrastructure would become lasting ones that framed the local economy throughout the seventeenth century and, in so doing, helped account for its continued stability.

The process of building a familiar local economy started with proper organization. Settlers mapped the landscape to accommodate specific economic developments. They did so while pioneering a pragmatic and flexible legislative system to nurture these plans.[5] Achieving this balance was a crucial element of the foundation they hoped to establish. Through well-designed acts and policies, colonists were able to close their ears to investor complaints, put explicit export concerns aside, and pursue the critical task of achieving basic stability through local economic decisions. Angry investors, in turn, learned to sit tight, take a deep breath, and put their faith in the settlers' ability to mold the environment into a place marked by social cohesion and agricultural productivity.

STRUCTURING THE LANDSCAPE INTO CLEAR ZONES OF ECONOMIC ACTIVity was an endeavor that settlers accomplished with a deep appreciation of the extensive land that sprawled before them. Thomas Cooper would later reflect this sentiment when he wrote that "the staple of America . . . consists of land, and the immediate products of land." Organizing that land, however, was an immediate necessity whose considerable benefits never registered on official balance ledgers. Nonetheless, controlling the environment, which settlers did primarily by building English-style farms, became a vital aspect of the region's internal development.[6] Settlers began the process of ordering the landscape the minute they landed, and they did so, not surprisingly, with livestock. As the decade progressed, Bay colonists helped increase the production of subsistence-oriented commodities by keeping crops and livestock as far apart as possible. Livestock came to dominate the New England economy more than it ever had back home, and in light of its obvious importance, the General Court left it to towns to pass policies that enhanced their chances of surviving in a new environment. Towns, for their part, jumped at the opportunity.[7]

They focused first and foremost on livestock safety. In 1633 William Wood complimented the settlers' judicious decision to send cattle to nearby islands, explaining that "the inhabitants . . . put them in these for safety, viz. their rams, goats, and swine when corn is in the ground." If a town lacked easy access to islands, it held cattle on plots of pastureland owned in common by the town's inhabitants. In order to "secure [cattle] from the wolves," Lynn residents placed them on a "store of good ground, fit for the plough," thus showing their willingness to place cattle preservation ahead of growing corn. Settlers in Newtown were said to be "well stored with cattle of all sorts," so much so that they set aside a pasture with "one general fence, which is about a mile and a half long, which secures all their winter cattle from the wild beasts."[8] Simple and efficient, these initial responses to the region's modest but burgeoning cattle supply worked well enough as long as land remained abundant and the population of people and cattle relatively manageable.

But as settlers poured in, isolating cattle on islands or specifically designated public space for grazing gave way to other measures. Wealthier residents hired private cow keepers to take cattle off the farm in the morning and return them by evening. A few Dorchester settlers paid Nicholas Stover "9 bushels of meals or of Indian corne or 9 li of beaver" in exchange for his "keeping of their said cattle." Seeing the logic of this plan, Dorchester's selectmen granted one young man "6 acres of planting land neere the mill" so long as "he shall keepe Cowes or young Cattle at such rates as the Tenn men shall agree with him." Settlers unable to afford a private cow keeper often rented space in a "cowyard" at rates set by the town. Newtown, for example, granted twenty-eight such plots, which ranged from a half-acre to four acres, in 1633 alone. Applications increased steadily throughout the decade.[9] In 1633 Dorchester granted twenty-one cowyards, allotting twenty-eight square feet per cow. Private cow keepers and the rental of cowyards initially complemented and eventually replaced the more burdensome task of trucking cattle to an island or leaving them alone in a wide pasture. In these ways settlers adjusted their cattle population to the growing human population.

But the press of the Great Migration continued. By the middle of the decade an increase in settlers had forced residents to devise more sophisticated arrangements to accommodate the rapid rise in cattle and land under tillage. The colony-wide attempt to plant and tend crops, catch and dry fish, and transport timber while maneuvering around haphazardly penned cattle proved increasingly troublesome and necessitated further improvements in livestock organization. In addition to taking up space on potentially tillable plots of land, livestock rammed the soil into hard clay, occasionally eluded shoddily built fences to destroy grain, vegetable gardens, and drying flakes of fish, and called upon precious family labor for their upkeep. Towns began to systematize their cattle policies by appointing cowherds to remove an entire town's cattle supply to lush pastures and away from agricultural areas. From April to November a town's keepers left the common by six in the morning (signaled by the blowing of a horn) and returned a half-hour before sundown. The keeper's job earned him a decent wage of £20 a year, but it came with stipulations. For one, the threat of a fine of 3d. per cow helped ensure that a cowherd did not retire for the evening until every cow he tended was returned to its owner. Similarly, if he lost a cow, the cowherd owed the owner 10s. a day until he caught the wayward beast. If he chose to leave too late in the morning, disrupting local business, or too early, before all cows had been delivered to him, he also suffered a fine. For the most part, though, cowherds appear to have run smooth operations. Penalties rarely show up in the records, and to compete for business, cowherds would frequently offer specialized services, such as encouraging reproduction (for an impregnation fee of 10s.), as well as veterinary care and branding. The size of a typical cowherd business is suggested by records for Newtown, which entrusted more than five hundred cattle to nine cowherds in the years 1635–40.[10]

Cowherds further focused their businesses by working with town magistrates to designate certain areas appropriate for holding specific types of cattle at specific times of the year. Whereas many cowherds accepted any and all cows into their fold, others preferred milk cows, dry cattle, or calves. Recognizing the economic benefit of such specialization, towns might decree, as Newtown did, that "there shallbe no dry cattle kept on this side of the river" with the exception of those "cows neer calving." Draft cattle had to be stored "beyond Bar[ett] Lampsons Planting field between the cow common Ray[le] and the Charlestown Rayle." The town assigned space "for the Milch Cowes to lyein on nights," adding that "now othere cattell whatsoever go there." Boston adopted comparable measures, requiring that a carefully specified plot of land had "to be fenced for draft cattel to be put in," while "all barren cattell and weaned calves 20 weekes and weaned mayle kids shalbe kept . . . off the neck." Dorchester went so far as to list the ratios of cattle types that belonged on certain plots of land, specifying "10 kidds to one cowe; two yearlings to one cow . . . one woking ox to a cow, one mare and colt to two cowes, 4 calves to one cow," and so on.[11] These small decisions on the part of every town helped struggling colonists squeeze as much milk, beef, grain, and vegetables as they could from a frontier economy that was starting to feel remotely familiar.

After cattle came swine. Pigs posed special problems in the overall quest to control livestock. These "weed creatures," as they were called, combined an undiscriminating palate with a virile enthusiasm for reproduction to render domestication a foolhardy task. The General Court nonetheless laid down the law in 1631 when it declared, "All swine that are found in any mans corne shalbe forfeit to the public." Colonists heeded the word and abruptly took enthusiastic and evidently accurate aim at wayward hogs, quickly prompting the court to clarify the point that they had to deliver forfeited swine *alive* to collect the bounty. The hog population proliferated to the point that swifter action was in order. The General Court reassessed the issue and added that in addition to forfeiting the animal, the owner of an errant hog "shall satisfie for the damages his swine shall do in the corn of another." Evidently neither of these stipulations had much effect, for a year later the Court conceded that a settler was at leisure to "kill any swine that comes into his corne."[12] Predictably, they fired away, and just as predictably, the problem persisted. Until the knife cut their throats, hogs were accustomed to having their way, and they were admirably successful in going where they wanted to go.

Once again, town policies proved most effective. As they did with cows, towns combined private and public initiatives and resources to help get a handle on hogs. Settlers began by employing hogreeves and keepers to supplement private initiatives. Salem ordered that "all swine shall goe under keeper; or be kept up, and that all swine taken abroad without a keeper it shall be lawful for any man to pounde them and to have for every swine 2s 6d before they be taken out of the pound." After appointing a hogreeve and requiring that any hogs ringed "shall be ringed by W[illia]m Wilcok," Newtown required citizens either to ring their swine, hire a hogreeve to keep them, or remove them to the town's pound. It was not uncommon, after a hog had destroyed a garden, for example, for disputes to arise over the quality of the ringing. Had the ring been deficient? Had the ringer been negligent? Had there been witnesses to the escape? If the ringer was found guilty, magistrates delivered a fine of 6d. Dorchester went so far as to order private pig sties demolished, after which it built a public pig pound and asserted that "none shall keepe any swine to let them runne in the Commons without sufficient yokes and rings within one mile of any corne field." Boston demanded that anyone who found a pig rooting through crops could avoid the hassle of finding its owner and simply "send a note of them to the foldkeeper" by tacking a note to the whipping post.[13] To be sure, swine still roamed, rooted, and destroyed, but towns fought back by establishing well-designed local measures to minimize crop destruction while maximizing their precious pork supply. While these decisions rarely qualify as explicitly economic ones, they are precisely that. In fact, it is hard, in light of the conditions endemic to a settlement society, to see them as anything but basic economic decisions made by regular settlers facing routine problems in a new environment.

In addition to tightening their grip on animals, Massachusetts Bay colonists spent the first decade making substantial improvements to the region's transportation facilities. It would be easy, especially given what we saw in chapter 1, to dismiss this effort as a failure, but in a new settlement road quality was relative. The General Court turned the responsibility of road maintenance and construction over to the Court of Assistants in 1634. This transfer of authority had little practical impact, and throughout the early 1630s roads connecting towns were either nonexistent or impassable. By 1638 the court had taken stock of the region's roads and concluded that "the highways in this jurisdiction have not bene layd out with such conveniency for travellers as were fit, nor was intended by the Court."[14] This report should not imply, however, that individual towns were doing nothing to improve the quality of their byways. Local tasks such as moving cows from commons to pastures, transporting hogs to pounds or islands, and hauling timber to construction sites required, at the least, adequate pathways. Towns, in response, worked diligently to provide them.

More often than not, towns took the logical step of linking road improvement to private economic concerns. Newtown, for example, granted Andrew Warner a "licence to fetch aylwives from the weir" under the expectation that he would oversee the construction of a highway to that weir. John Banjaman received a grant of land that required him to allow access to "Windmill Hill" via a cartway that he was to build. Simon Bradstreet enjoyed a substantial land grant from Salem under the stipulation that he "make a sufficient cartway along by his pales and keep it in repair 7 years." Richard Ingersoll and Lawrence Leach were told to "be sure to leave roome for high ways for cartes to bring wood." After allowing Isreal Stroughton rights to build a water mill, Dorchester ordered that "there shall be a sufficient cartway . . . made to the mill at the common charge."[15] The first roads in Massachusetts thus wisely merged local initiative, individual interest, and basic economic needs.

Towns further worked to improve local roads by linking annexation to private road building. Dorchester's George Hull would receive the "meadow that lyes before his door where he now dwells" so long as he made "a sufficient way for passidge." When a Mr. Holland applied to enclose a marsh adjacent to his land, Dorchester approved his request but demanded that "a little part of marsh" be left open for "a sufficient high way." Jonathan Gellet's grant to fence off a plot of land required that he first build "a sufficient cartway" around the land to be fenced. When four neighbors in Boston went to build fences around their properties, the town intervened to demand that they "preserve a path way, of a rod breadth, between payle and payle."[16] These small but significant measures, once again, strategically connected the local quest for economic security with the towns' long-term transportation needs. They also ensured that the daunting task of moving goods and people throughout the colony became more manageable.

What exactly constituted a road was open to interpretation. While towns could not actively monitor the quality of all roads within their jurisdictions, they could formulate policies intended to preserve the integrity of roads already built. Salem issued a warrant for "mending of high ways" in 1637, requiring "every working man upon the 7th day of the month" to clear and repair roads that passed through his property. Newtown ordered all citizens to keep all passageways "in good and sufficient repaire" under the threat of a fine for "every rodd so repaired for him." With families preoccupied with home and fence construction, and given the region's growing demand for fuel, the most common problem with roads was fallen timber. "Noe person whatsoever," ordered Newtown, "shall fell any tree neer the town within the path wch goeth from Wattertow[n] to Charlestowne upon the forfeiture of five shillings for every tree soe felled." Salem reminded settlers that "who soe ever hath or shall cutt any trees and leave [them] in the paths about the town to the disturbance of carts, cattle, or passangers not being moved within fifteen days shall forfeit five shillings for such offence."[17] The earliest roads did not foster travel and trade between distant New England towns. However, in responding as they did to local transportation needs, they provided a pragmatic model for a cohesive system of roads between towns. In 1639 the General Court took over the project of developing that model. It could never have done so, through, had the task not been persistently pursued on the local level, where basic needs were most evident and thus directly addressed.

Another aspect of the early effort to control the local environment was building and maintaining fences. Few structures reflected English conceptions of land use as deeply as the rail and picket borders that designated who owned what.[18] Towns dealt with fences through several methods. In the most general terms, they required settlers to fence their own fields as well as the town's common ground. "For as mush as divers of our town are resolved to some English grain this spring," wrote Salem's townsmen, "it is therefore ordered that all common and particular home fences about the town shall be sufficiently made up." They added that a townsman who refused to comply "shall forfeit his sayd lot." Whereas rules governing swine generally required the beasts' owners to keep track of their own animals, several towns enacted fence regulations that placed an equal burden on fence owners. Boston leaders declared that "upon paine that if any losse doe come for defect therein, that damage shall be satisfied by such upon whose fence the breach shall be" unless the damage had been caused by "unruly cattell." Dorchester similarly ordered that "if any hoggs commit any tresspasse in any of the corn fields within the plantation . . . the owner of the Pall where they breake in shall pay the on[e] halfe of the tresspasse." Refusing to place sole responsibility on fences or livestock, these towns encouraged settlers to keep both in order.[19]

As with roads, popular conceptions of a solid fence varied. After establishing fencing regulations, towns listed increasingly stringent specifications that settlers had to meet before a fence could be considered legitimate. Newtown initially demanded that fences be only of post-and-rail design rather than the less secure crotched model. Boston began under the vaguest instructions, declaring that fences had to be "a doble rayle with mortesses in the posts, of 10 foot distance from each other." By decade's end, however, it now sought to "see to the making of such styles and gates as may be needful for every field." Newtown demanded that a fence be set in a furrow at least two feet deep and reach at least four feet above the ground. The town issued a fine for "every rodd of fence that is faieling" instead of doling out a fine for the fence as a whole. Dorchester followed suit, judging fences inadequate unless "they be well set and bound at least 4 foot above the ground."[20] If a fence surrounded larger plots of corn, rather than garden plots, the town required that the structure have at least five sturdy rails. These provisions helped settlers judge what in fact made a fence a fence, an altogether crucial definition that allowed cows and crops to coexist peacefully with each other, not to mention with settlers.

As specifications become more intricate, towns appointed fence viewers to enforce regulations. These men routinely surveyed fences within a carefully specified jurisdiction. Boston fence viewers, to cite a well-documented example, were responsible for anywhere from 83 to 187 fences. When a viewer deemed a fence defective, he could either repair it himself and charge the owner or report the defect at the next town meeting, whereupon the owner incurred a fine as well as an order to repair it promptly. Fence viewers were rarely prominent members of the community, but like modern-day traffic cops, they could command attention when necessary. After a series of repeated incursions by Braintree residents, the town's fence viewer in 1634 decreed that "fences be made sufficient before the seventh day of the second month; and they to be looked at by our brother Hudson for the new field." The fence viewer in Newtown required that "all generall fences about the house lotts . . . be made by the first day of March on the penalty of 5s for each default" and that "Wm Moody [et al.] shall lay out the general fences in the town that are to be made, as likewise ten yard between man and man, for garden plots."[21] These directives were neither made casually nor taken lightly.

Settlers may not have exported fish, fur, and timber during the first decade. They may have lost their way on rough ocean inlets. They may have contemplated a permanent return to the homeland. Nevertheless, their decision to organize cows and pigs, build roads and fences, initiate such services as those of cow keepers, hogreeves, and fence viewers proved essential to the more pressing demands of meeting basic needs in a settlement society currently more concerned with safe passage than with balancing transatlantic ledger books. Settlers undertook these tasks to give the region's nascent infrastructure a familiar organization as they replicated inherited traditions. Relative to future development, the immediate benefits were small. But they were not insignificant, and thus they were noticed by settlers doing local business on a daily basis.

COMPLEMENTING THE LITERAL LANDSCAPE WAS THE LEGISLATIVE ONE. One of the Bay Colony's most distinguishing features was its ability to conjoin local, individual actions with official policies that reflected customary attitudes about those actions. Indeed, buttressing the colony's concerted effort to control the local environment was a series of economic policies that helped settlers meet subsistence needs in a place that proved to be radically foreign to their experience. Magistrates recognized that before a thriving overseas trade could ever develop, the local economy had to be able to foster economic stability. Massachusetts leaders were nothing if not economically savvy. Just as critically, they had experienced firsthand the region's primitive conditions. From an economic perspective, they knew very well that undeveloped markets provided fertile ground for usury, that inflation was a dire threat, and that settlers arriving after 1633 had the means to return home if the spirit moved them to do so. A series of local economic measures therefore followed to defuse these potentially devastating consequences.

Most notably, the General Court set down a series of price valuations and wage controls. Neither stringently drawn nor actively enforced, the measures served more as temporary guidelines than as permanent limits. Almost immediately, however, the court moved to restrict the daily wages that carpenters, joiners, bricklayers, sawyers, and roof thatchers could collect from desperate clients, thereby checking price gouging in an environment where almost every family needed at least some help building a house. By 1631 these restrictions seemed to have achieved their intended affect. Accordingly, the court replaced the measures with the suggestion that workers set wages "as men reasonably agree." This decision, however, proved premature when a handful of skilled laborers took reasonable agreement to disagreeable levels by capitalizing on the intense demand for their services. These infringements prompted the court to reinstate wage caps and add clapboard cutters, tailors, wheelwrights, and mowers to its expanding list of regulated occupations. These wage controls remained in effect until September 1635, when the court once again repealed all laws restricting wages. At that time the court turned the issue over to towns under the condition that "if a bargaine proves not equall . . . it shall be lawful for the towne to appoint three men that shall set an equal rate thereon." This decentralized approach was becoming an endemic aspect of local economic life, and it lasted throughout the second half of the decade, contributing to the regulation of services that were in dangerously high demand.[22]

A similar kind of flexible control characterized the court's handling of commodity prices. Rather than legislating specific prices for all essential goods, the court instead demanded that "noe persons shall sell to any of the inhabitants within this jurisdiction any provision, clothinge, tooles, or other commodities, above the rate of four pence in a shilling more than the same cost as might be bought for ready money in England." The way the court dealt with the cost of corn typified its approach to setting commodity rates overall. While the price of corn hovered in the excessively inflated range of 10s. per bushel in 1630 and 1631 (it would later stabilize at 3s.), the court artificially deflated its price by securing the rate at which the government would accept corn as payment for taxes, fines, and services. Technically, this rate of exchange only applied to governmental transactions. In reality, though, it provided an accurate benchmark against which traders could threaten unscrupulous merchants with the damning charge of usury.[23]

Local economic measures also focused on controlling exports and imports in order "to prevent a world of disorders." Soon after Endicott's arrival in 1629 a few renegade planters, perhaps inspired by the Virginian example, began to plant tobacco. "We trust in God," an exasperated Governor Craddock explained when he heard the news, "other means will be found to employ their time," insisting that these planters "employ their labors otherwise." Craddock and local authorities, based on economic grounds, opposed planting tobacco. "It doth," he wrote, "hardly produce the freight and custom . . . there being such great quantities made in other places." More profitable commodities, of course, included fish, fur, and timber. Authorities accordingly monitored these goods with legislative vigilance. Salem selectmen ordered that no timber of any sort "be sold or transported by any person or persons . . . unless the said clapboards or other wood be offered to the thirteen men" who would determine whether the town needed the timber before it was shipped off. As for beaver skins, settlers initially enjoyed "liberty to dispose of their part . . . at their own will" as long as they paid the company a specified share and promised not "to trade with interlopers." Six year later, however, Winthrop explained how "the trade of beaver [and wampum] was to be farmed out and all others to be restrained from tradinge," a monopolistic maneuver that prompted one settler, John Oldham, to protest the decision. Winthrop, intent on using governmental fiat to structure the fur trade, sniffed that Oldham was "a man altogether unfit for us to deal with." And thus, as promised, he was studiously ignored.[24]

The local effort to minimize disruptions in the provincial economy extended to the sale and distribution of imported goods. "[With] the ship arriving," Edward Johnson explained in 1633, "the godly governors did soe order it that each town send two men aboard her, who took up her town's allowance, it being appointed beforehand." The rationale behind this plan was that "some might not buy all, and others be left destitute of food." To prevent the purchase of high-priced luxury goods at the expense of more necessary provisions, Governor Henry Vane ordered that "before [all ships coming in] offered any goods to sale they would deliver an invoice and give the Governor 24 hours liberty to refuse." Roger Clap described how "when a ship came laden with provisions, they ordered that the whole cargo should be bought for a general stock; and so it was, and distribution was made to every town, and to every person in each town as every man had need."[25] In such ways the government directed local consumption in a nascent community seeking to establish permanent roots in what was still a strange new world.

If necessary, colonial officials resorted to outright subsidization to control the movement of incoming commodities. Winthrop recounted how when the aptly named "Charity of Dartmouth, of 120 tons, arrived here laden with provisions, Mr. Peters bought all the provisions at fifty in the hundred, (which saves the country of £200) and distributed to all the towns, as each town needed." Colonial leaders often extended their policies to shape England's export patterns to the colony's advantage. In 1634 a group of magistrates calling themselves "The Planters of New England" petitioned Charles I so that "merchants and planters may have privilege to freight ships for the said plantations without any license, tax, or penalty whatsoever." In addition to seeking these breaks, the planters also asked that "all goods and merchandise for the supportation and encouragement of the said planters may be free of all customs and imposts exportable and importable from the same."[26] In their effort to control the flow of goods, these measures might smack of an antiquated economic system out of sync with the emerging capitalist ethos that was coming to dominate the early modern world. In actuality, however, they were simply provisional attempts to stabilize a local economy that sought order under otherwise precarious conditions. They were, in other words, commonsense solutions to predictable problems.

The final element in the colony's early attempt to stabilize the local economy involved recruiting skilled labor. The New England Company lobbied actively for Thomas Graves to migrate, touting his "skills in many things very useful" while encouraging Endicott and company to "take his advice." Graves, speaking on his own behalf, promoted his qualifications "in the discovery and finding out of iron mines, as also of lead, copper, mineral salt, and alum., in fortifications of all sorts . . . in surveying of buildings and of lands, and in measuring of lands, in describing the country by map, in leading of water courses for mills, or other uses, in finding out all sorts of limestones and materials for buildings, in manufacturing, etc." The colony's founders naturally sought men with Graves's abilities, albeit men with more defined talents. They worked from the premise that "all persons resident upon our plantation [should] apply themselves to one calling, or other, and no idle drone be permitted to live amongst us."[27] The Massachusetts Bay Company sent, among others, Richard Waterman, "whose chief employment will be to get you good venison," six shipwrights, a master carpenter, a sailor, a master fisherman, and a cooper. Recruited labor enjoyed special financial incentives. The sailor, a man named Richard Clayton, benefited from the company's promise of three shillings a day and a guarantee that "what shall be wanting the company will [furnish.]" "We hope," the investors wrote to Endicott, "you will be careful to see [imported skilled labor] so employed as may countervail the charge." They also suggested that "you appoint a careful and diligent overseer to each family, who is to see each person employed in the business he or they are appointed for."[28] Such oversight would never have been possible in such a labor-strapped place, but the expressed intention nonetheless speaks powerfully to the underlying intention of this comprehensive regulation.

SETTLERS MAY NOT HAVE EXPORTED FISH, FUR, AND TIMBER DURING these trying years. They may have floundered on unfamiliar rivers and turbulent coastal passages. They may have lost their way in dense forests between neighboring townships. Nevertheless, migrants to the Massachusetts Bay Colony not only bought, divided, granted, and brought under cultivation the land along the coast of Massachusetts Bay; they also organized what once had seemed a totally unfamiliar landscape into recognizable and replicable zones of economic activity. Separating livestock and fields of grain, building roads and fences, providing essential services, and initiating and enforcing a series of provisional regulatory policies hardly helped the Bay colonists balance the company's books. These wise measures did, however, provide a critical infrastructural foundation. Puritans had every reason to be cautiously optimistic. The landscape they had mapped was directing them in a more familiar and more profitable direction.

THREE

Founding Industries: Fish and Timber

1630–1650

T HE BAY COLONY'S IMPROVEMENTS, HOWEVER SUBTLE, DID NOT GO
unnoticed. As early as 1636 Winthrop commented with great delight
that "cattle were grown to high rates," corn was abundant, and "much
rye was sown with the plow this year, about thirty plows were at work."
Assessing the economic situation in Ipswich, Edward Johnson similarly
swelled with pride, noting the rapid increase in cattle and corn. His friend
William Hilton praised "the extraordinary convenience that your plantation hath . . . for the keeping of swine." One James Cudworth found occasion to "blesse the Lord" in 1634 for "at least 50 bushels of corne which
is worth some 12 li so that I think I shall not need but shall have enough
until next harvest." Lynn had "cattle exceedingly multiplied," according
to Johnson, while Newbury enjoyed a "store of cornland in tillage" surrounded by more than four hundred head of healthy cattle. Thomas Welde
wrote home to England to assure his former parishioners that "blessed be
God . . . here is plenty of corn," noting that "cattle of all do thrive and feed
exceedingly." Johnson, moved by the material improvement in his midst,
concluded, "The Lord . . . hath caused to thrive much in these latter days
than formerly." While his contemporaries would hardly have downplayed
the Lord's role in their fortune, they most certainly would not have for-
saken their own decisions to build fences, lay pathways, and regulate the
movement of livestock. It was in such small ways, after all, that settlers
began to carve an economy out of a wilderness.[1]

Impressive as these accomplishments were, they went well beyond improving the region's meat, dairy, and grain supplies. While the Bay Colony
failed miserably at meeting foreign demand for fish and timber in the early
years, it was especially successful at meeting *local* demand for these highly
valued items. In fact, while a great deal of economic theory leads us to
think that exportation primarily shaped the economic nature of frontier

economies, the opposite was the case during the early years in the Massachusetts Bay. Local consumer demand, especially during the founding decade, played a more powerful role in structuring the early fishing and timber industries than foreign demand ever did.

As thousands of settlers reached the shores of the fledgling colony, they proved to be especially hungry consumers for fish and timber. Not surprisingly, Puritan pioneers organized concrete efforts to meet these needs. Although fish and timber would eventually become the basis of the region's export economy, they began as items integral to the ongoing process of building a stable infrastructure. Investors might have chafed at the almost complete emphasis on local production, preferring that any and all fish and timber be exported, but settlers consuming these essential items would not have had the time to differ.[2]

The quest to catch fish and fell trees expanded the traditional notion of mixed farming while strengthening the communal bonds central to the Puritans' covenanted ideals. It did so because the expansion of the fishing and timber industries reiterated that it was indeed possible for Puritans to venture beyond their small farms without severing the ties fostered by families and communities striving for a godly life on earth through farming. Many Puritans initially feared that these endeavors could pull their communities into the transatlantic world too quickly, distract them from the virtues of husbandry, lead to unhealthy levels of profit, and become "a prison and constant calamity" as a result of the individual's spending his life "in doing little good at all to others, though he should grow rich by it himself." Thus the Puritans' foray into these industries tested the time-honored belief that traditional farming was akin to preaching in the Puritan hierarchy of callings. Fishing and timber production were initially not, after all, on par with farming as a calling "most useful to the public good." The local focus of this work in the Massachusetts Bay, however, helped these endeavors become legitimate enterprises in the context of conventional husbandry. The seamlessness with which the Puritans integrated fish and timber into mixed agriculture precluded potentially disruptive problems, and in time the fish and timber trades proved themselves to be practical endeavors that helped stabilize their venture.[3]

Settlers pursuing fish and timber for sale in local markets avoided the problems that hindered more elaborate attempts to reach distant venues.[4] Lack of competition, low operation costs, and proximity and reliability of demand enabled fishermen and timber suppliers to develop a decentralized system of supplying fish and wood in a variety of local contexts. With cod fish "in such multitudes," according to William Wood, that it "is al-most incredible," the task would not require an especially extensive effort. This supply, in turn, led to a healthier group of settlers who enjoyed sturdy shelters, a reliable source of fuel, strong fences, better boats, sound stables, and sturdy carts—all of which, yet again, might not have appeared in the ledger books of any merchant but were absolutely essential to on-going local economic development. Whereas other colonies poured their resources into finding staples to export as soon as possible, Massachusetts began by exploiting commodities for local consumption. This difference—best manifested in fish and timber—had critical consequences for the col-ony's future.

LOCAL DEMAND FOR FISH NEVER SLACKENED DURING THE FOUNDING decades. Within days of arriving, settlers took to the ocean to seek sus-tenance. Hunger gripped the colonists in June 1630, and Winthrop re-called their reaction matter-of-factly: "we heaved our hookes and took 26 coddes, so we all feasted with fish that 3 days." When a rare scarcity of corn tried the patience of Puritans who had otherwise provided quite well for themselves, they "lived well with fish and the fruit of their gardens." After complimenting the colonists' willingness to make do during trouble-some times, Edward Johnson admired how, "in the absence of bread," they "feasted themselves with fish." In 1634 Winthrop explained that when food ran low, "fish, cod, bass, and herring supply us." Roger Clap, on one occa-sion, remembered that "fish was good help unto me and others" during the precarious early years of settlement. Later, he recalled how settlers were "supplied only by clams, mussels, and fish" because "flesh of all birds was a rare thing." Consuming fish became a dietary habit that left adults "sweetly satisfied," while rendering their children, according to one ob-server, "cheerful, fat, and lusty."[5]

The practice of fertilizing cornfields with fish further enhanced local fish demand. As Native Americans well appreciated, decaying fish effectively fertilized stubborn New England soil by fixing it with added organic matter and an extra dose of nitrogen. One colonist wrote home explaining how most families quickly "set an ack [acre] of eindy [Indian] wheat," adding that those farmers "who set it without [fish] . . . have but a pore crop." A vocal proponent of Indian corn in general, Edward Johnson described how settlers caught "many thousands" of fish "to put under their Indian corne," a practice whereby "five or six grains doth produce six hun-dred." Edwards was almost certainly exaggerating (he had a habit of doing so), but the underlying truth was strong enough to bear overstatement: corn thrived in fish-laden soil. Later in the century, John Winthrop Jr. delivered a veritable treatise on the matter to the Royal Society of London. In his talk, which left many a proper Englishman befuddled, Winthrop referred to the "Countrey Rule" of "the coming up of a fish called Aloofes [i.e., alewives] into Rivers and Brookes for the time to begin planting." William Wood wondered how "the Indians who are too lazy to catch fish" could possibly "plant corn eight or ten yards in one place without it" and still yield "very good crops." The practice became so popular in Ipswich that residents passed an ordinance requiring dog owners to hobble their pets during the weeks after farmers set the ground with fish.[6]

Abundant as the fish supply was, catching fish was a time-consuming endeavor. Nevertheless, the pervasive demand inspired concentrated efforts to meet it. Salem led the way, with twenty-one men applying to obtain "fishing lots" on Winter Island. The collective background of these applicants says a lot about the shape that the early fishing industry assumed. In general these men worked independently of merchants, capitalized their own very small ventures, shared equipment, caught and dried their own fish on their own property, and sold or bartered their own catch. Although they were fishermen in name, fishing was not their sole calling. Most owned land and farmed it as a sort of by-employment to complement their fishing activity. Of the fourteen fishing-lot recipients that can be positively identified in the court records, nine owned property—twenty to eighty acres' worth—in addition to their half-acre fishing lots. Ownership of farmland helped keep fishermen tethered to their communities. It did so, moreover, despite the stereotypical portrayal of the New England fisherman as living against the grain of Puritan mores. Eight of the fourteen recipients served on a jury or grand jury, five held government-appointed positions, and seven served as witnesses in court. None of these men ever incurred the ubiquitous charge of drunkenness. Fisherman such as Pasco Foote, George Williams, and Richard Moore participated in community life, owned land, farmed, raised cattle, stayed on the right side of God as well as the law, and throughout it all caught fish. In successfully maneuvering between land and sea, the Bay Colony's first fishermen practiced an occupational fluidity not uncommon in settlement societies. They did so even as they partially specialized their calling to provide their families and neighbors with fish.[7]

Striking a balance between mixed husbandry and fishing was an ongoing challenge. Men who caught fish during the colony's first couple of decades went to sea only for the day, not every day, and rarely left sight of the shore when they did so. The land was a magnet, beckoning them to return promptly in order to keep up with farming duties, family, town government, and biweekly sermons. Salem granted to John Peach, identified as a "fisherman" in the court records, the right to fence five acres of Marblehead land in order to "improve the said place for building and planting." The grant confirms his attempt to balance the demands of farming and fishing. Similarly, Joseph Young and Thomas Fryar received fishing lots from Salem alongside ten-acre grants of fertile ground. Henry Swan accepted his half-acre fishing lot in addition to a "10 acre lott, neere the pond by Mr. Blackleesh his farme." Matthew Nicks, also labeled a "fisherman," received five acres "by the hogsstyes in the forest" to pen his cattle. Such applications among fishermen became common enough for Salem to allow "that such as have fishing lotts about Winter Harbor and the Hand shall have libertie to fence in their lotts to keep of the swine and goats from their fish, soe they leave it open after harvest is in." Even when the Salem court attempted to limit landownership among fishermen (to further concentrate their efforts on fishing), it still had to link fishing-lot grants with space in "the common of woods neere adjoining for their goats and cattle."[8] Little evidence suggests that fishermen were eager to leave their farms, families, and communities. By building businesses that responded to local demand, Massachusetts Bay's fishermen still had the time to participate in other sectors of an infant economy—namely, the more traditional aspects of mixed farming.

But more than cultural factors were at work in shaping these decisions. The modest scope and scale of the early fishing industry had as much to do with relative lack of equipment as with farming needs. Even if fishermen wanted to focus exclusively on fishing, they most likely could never have done so during the first decade of settlement. Men who fished from Winter Island did not own vessels capable of making long-term voyages. Local merchants, for their part, had yet to gain access to larger ships to lease to fishermen for that use. John Berenton experienced this limitation firsthand when his crew "has pestered our ship with so many Cod fish" that they "threw numbers of them overboard." The growing size and convenient proximity of the local market, however, allowed fishermen to exploit other options. The use of weirs, for example, was common. Fishermen routinely set nets along internal waterways during high tide and then paddled out in small boats to collect their catch after the tide receded. With characteristic exaggeration, William Wood described how "in two tides [fishermen] have gotten one hundred thousand of those fishes," adding that "this is no small benefit to the plantation." In Dorchester, Israel Stroughton enjoyed "the privaladge of the weir at Naponset [River]," as well as a court order that "none shall cross the river with a nett or other weare to the prejudice of the said weare." This monopoly stayed valid as long as Stroughton agreed "to sell the alewives there taken to the plantation at 5s per thousand." One Mr. Ludlow, after checking his nets at the Isle of Shoals "in a small pinnace, as he had done for many years," proceeded to "sell his fishe at Markett." In Cambridge, John Gibson was granted "the use and profit of the weare, and the weare land for two yeare ensuing, upon condition that he serve the town with fish at nine pence per thousand." Up in Ipswich, John Spencer and Nicolas Easton received permission "to build a mill and a fish weir upon the river . . . on the condition that they sold their fish to the inhabitants . . . as the market price varied." Fishermen hauled their catch to shore, took a measure of local demand, and sold their catch. It became a common local activity well integrated into the routines of mixed farming.[9]

Another method of catching fish involved dropping anchor at the precise spot where a river hit the sea and tossing a net over the side. "At the head of this river," Wood observed of the Mystic, "are great and spacious ponds, within the alewives pass to spawn." Recognizing these locations as "noted places for that kind of fish," he remarked that "the English resort thither to take them." Venturing into coastal waters offered yet another option. Winthrop commented that "there was much store of exceeding large and fat mackerel upon our coast this season, as was a good benefit to all our plantations." These benefits could be spread generously when "some one boat with three men would take, in a week, ten hogsheads." Again, it was to the local markets that they returned.[10]

Consistent with the simplified equipment available, fishermen undertook these ventures in small boats and flimsy canoes. Recalling that "fish was a good help to me and others," Roger Clap indicated the questionable seaworthiness of local craft when he explained how "we did quickly build boats and some went a fishing." Wood described fishermen who "crossed these rivers with small canoes, which are made of whole pine trees, being about a foot and a half over, and twenty feet long." Not only did settlers use these boats to navigate rivers but they often trusted them to negotiate the Atlantic, traveling "sometimes two leagues to sea." Needless to say, canoes and quickly built boats were hardly conducive to gathering hundreds of thousands of fish to meet foreign demand. While efforts to build larger ships were in the works, they were nowhere near complete by the early 1640s. If Winthrop's early assessments are any guide, the canvas, cordage, nails, and carpentry skills required for serious shipbuilding slowly trickled in, while local efforts to supply shipbuilders with pitch, tar, and timber competed with more immediate timber demands, like home building. Joseph Howe tellingly remarked that he and his fishing crew "agreed to go to sea—when they heard the school had come in they were the first boat that went out and took the first fish." The 1630s was an era when men waited for the fish to come to them. Rare was the fisherman who could afford the labor and equipment to chase them across the region's expansive fishing banks. This geographical reality further kept fishing tied to the other, more customary demands of mixed farming.[11]

The consistent interest in an ample local fish supply often led settlers to evaluate property solely in terms of its proximity to fish. "This bay is a most hopeful place," one writer opined. He praised the fish and then provided a review of the available options: "skate, cod, turbot, and herring we have tasted of; abundance of mussels, the greatest and best that we ever saw; crabs and lobsters in their time, infinite." Another settler, describing a specific plot of land, mentioned that "there is a very sweet brook that runs under the hillside . . . and in this brook much good fish." John Winthrop profited handsomely when the colony granted to him Conant's Island, "with all the liberties and privileges of fishing and fowling . . . for the term of his life."[12]

As far as the fishing industry went, the reality throughout the 1630s and early 1640s was clear: settlers did not systematically export fish. Hindsight, however, tells us that routine trade with overseas clients stood just over the horizon. A few signs might indeed have been hopeful harbingers for anxious merchants. "The blessing of heaven [was] so increased," wrote Samuel Hubbard, "that within a few years the inhabitants were furnished with not only enough for themselves, but were also able to furnish other places therewith." Settlers were indeed soon catching more fish than they could consume. This abundance boded well. Merchants were eager to truck it to Connecticut or Virginia in exchange for corn or cattle. Every now and then—it was rare, but it happened—merchants would collect enough salted fish to justify a trip to the West Indies, where they sold cod to masters eager to keep slaves minimally nourished. Even Winthrop, who understood the limitations on the ground better than anyone else, started to contemplate the potential of the future fish trade. "Dry fish," he explained, "are the only commodities [for the West Indies]." This would soon be the case. Nevertheless, during the first decade the local market was so powerful, and the industry itself so weak, that the most earnest fish promoter of them all, Hugh Peters, had to admit that "fishing would not yet serve our purpose."[13] Settlers enjoying a fresh supply to feed themselves and fertilize their crops would politely have disagreed. It did, after all, serve a purpose we have constantly overlooked: it fed them and their communities.

As with fish, local demand for timber—another product that would eventually incorporate Massachusetts into the Atlantic world—burgeoned throughout the 1630s and early 1640s.[14] And as with fish, this growth inspired a concerted local response that incorporated timber harvesting into the routines of mixed farming. Roughly four thousand families needed timber to build homes. Upon arrival, many settlers had no choice but to build their domiciles with canvas tents or resort to dugout homes. Others built Native American wigwams. Eventually, however, all families constructed freestanding homes, and they did so with clapboard walls, hewn oak frames, thatched roofs, and broad board floors. The typical dwelling, as one carpenter put it, was "one framed house 16 foot long and 14 foot wyde with a chamber[,] floor finisht[,] the roof and walles clapboarded on the outssyde[,] the chimney framed without daubing[,] to be done with timber."[15] In other words, an enormous amount of wood. Given the size of this demand, it is no surprise that the timber industry, like the fishing industry, initially developed in direct response to the basic task of trying to bring the wilderness under control rather than to the seductive pull of foreign demand.

Strong as the wood was, the first domiciles were testaments to slipshod construction. Problems therefore arose that further enhanced demand for wood. Winthrop, for example, described an unfortunate evening during which a gust of wind "overturned some new, strong houses." Unlike in England, where bricks and mortar fireproofed chimneys, Bay settlers built homes with timber-lined chimneys daubed with clay, which, along with thatched roofs, turned homes into virtual tinderboxes. Winthrop recorded in his journal that "the chimneye of Mr. Sharpes howse in Boston tooke fire (the splentes being not clayed at the toppe), and taking the thatch burned it down, and the winde being n.w. drive the fire into Mr. Colburnes howse [which] burnt down also." Edward Johnson observed that settlers had built enough homes "to intertain such as come over, with houseroom and other refreshings, while they built and made provisions of their own lotts."[16] The building—and rebuilding—of these structures helped keep the region's timber close to home.

The need for sound fences placed added pressure on the region's timber supply. Traditionally, an Englishman might just as likely have built fences with hedges as with wood. However, the vast supply of chestnut, cedar, and oak being what it was, and with livestock multiplying so rapidly, fences became not only customary but, as we have seen, legally proscribed structures. In addition to thousands of private lots, miles of common space had to be fenced with post-and-rail structures. Boston, for example, demanded that eleven common areas be fenced in the years 1634–40, while Dorchester called for thirteen, and Newtown, five, during the same time frame. Towns often linked land grants to specific requirements regarding fence construction. Salem granted "Ensign Reed" a plot "provided that the wood shall be preserved for the maintaining of the fence from the mill to Mr. Endocott's farme."[17] Expansion and subdivision, which increased throughout the first century, entailed felling more trees for more fencing. With fences generally built of ten-foot rails and six-foot posts, the push for locally provided timber remained at a premium.

Boat building further taxed local timber resources. Fishermen building small vessels, merchants engaged in regional trade, and English investors betting on future export activity pushed the colony to exploit its most conspicuous natural resource to build modest-sized craft capable of navigating the region's rough waters. Although ships over fifty tons have attracted the most attention, the vast majority of boats built during the first decade were simpler vessels designed for river and coastal travel. The humble canoe, in fact, was the most commonly built vessel. Armed with an adze, settlers—like the Native Americans—carved out the soft pulp of a pine tree, deemed the shell seaworthy, and tested the waters. They used canoes to ferry timber between islands and coastal towns, to transport small commodities over rivers and on coastal waterways, and to move passengers between towns. As we have seen, these tasks entailed considerable risk, so much so that at one point some members of the Essex County court moved to make canoes illegal. Settlers, however, protested. Canoe use became so popular that Salem eventually instituted a licensing system in order to prevent settlers from traveling in shoddy craft. In any case, the popularity of canoes pushed settlers to fell hundreds of pine trees that stood about twenty feet tall and a few feet wide, simultaneously absorbing them into a local market while keeping them from going abroad.[18]

The construction of small pinnaces similarly required considerable timber. Pinnaces were generally about thirty feet long and five feet deep, weighing about four tons. Local trading routes suggest that traders routinely built and used these versatile vessels to accomplish basic commercial transactions. Exchanges of corn, cattle, and fish between Boston and points north required easy access to pinnaces, and as Winthrop's correspondence indicates, these journeys became routine. "Mr Godfrey a merchant came from Pascataqua in Capt. Neale his pinnace and brought 10 hhd of corne to the mill," Winthrop wrote in a typical journal entry from the 1630s. Long Island and Connecticut were popular destinations for Bay Colony traders, who took pinnaces there often to trade local produce for wampum. In Plymouth they swapped livestock for beaver fur and found regional trade partners in the towns lining the Connecticut River, a body of water "not to be gone into but by small pinnaces, having a barre offeringe but 6 foote high water." Winthrop recorded that "the *Rebecca* came from Narigansett with 500 bz of corne" and the *Thunder* "now returned bringeinge ccorne and goats from Virginia." He explained to his sons that pinnaces traveled daily between the Massachusetts Bay and Richmond Island.[19] His remarks highlight the systematic trade that had evolved to such an extant that settlers were routinely braving unfamiliar rivers and coastal passages and, in so doing, voraciously consuming local timber supplies.

Vessels designed for transatlantic voyages and lengthy periods at sea emerged more slowly in a frontier economy because capital and labor requirements were comparatively steep. Nonetheless, even the modest number of grand ships that were built significantly tapped the region's supplies. Stephen Innes writes that "[e]ven the most primitive shipyard required a building slip or two, docks, [and] storehouses," not to mention shipwrights, an ample iron supply, joiners, and insurance companies. While all these were hard to come by, timber was not. Matthew Craddock and a handful of other investors began building a 100-ton vessel in 1633 with local white oak. By the end of the decade the colony had in the stockyards "6 sayle of ships at least if not more belonging to the plantations." Given that a single large vessel demanded about two thousand mature trees—as well as masts, spars, resin, turpentine, and tar—Salem and Marblehead, coastal towns that abutted vast forests, became bustling centers of shipbuilding and ship repair. "The seamen," William Wood explained, "having spent their old store of wood and water, have many supplies from the adjacent islands, with good timber to repair their weather beaten ships."[20]

Considering the nature of travel at the time, their case could not have been an isolated one.

Legislation reflected the strong demand for local timber required to build homes, fences, and boats. Throughout the 1630s towns restricted access to timber in order to ensure that wood remained readily available for domestic needs. Timber laws passed by town governments stressed the prevalent concern that precious wood supplies might be plundered by English merchants eager to ship it overseas. During the 1630s alone, Boston passed five separate timber ordinances, while Dorchester passed six. Salem noted that "we have found by experience that the transporting of boards and clapboards from our plantation hath not only bared our woods verye much of the best timber trees of all sorts but bereaved also our inhabitants of such boards and clapboards whereof they stand in need." The last thing the colony wanted was for a few merchants to enrich themselves at the expense of the colony. Accordingly it ordered in 1634 that "no sawyer, clapboard cleaver, or any other person whatsoever shall cut down, saw, or cleave any boards or tymber within our limits and transport them to other places." Later that year it added that one expanse of land "shall be reserved for the commons of the towne to serve them their wood and timber." Dorchester went so far as to require that no one "shall fell any within the Commons of Dorchester for any use to make sayles" without paying 5s. for "every tree so felled." To take down a tree in Newtown actually required a warrant from "the major part of the townsmen."[21] These legislative measures helped keep timber production tied to internal needs while preventing unscrupulous merchants from undermining the ample timber supply.

Meeting the internal demand for timber did not require the same level of labor concentration that the fishing industry needed. Collecting timber, in fact, appears to have been done haphazardly, with settlers generally meeting individual requirements on an ad hoc basis. Boston recorded that "the wood upon the neck of land toward Roxburie hath this last winter been disorderly cutt up and wasted, whereby many of the poore inhabitants are disappointed of relief." Salem's town records suggest that settlers gathered timber for personal use in a less than organized fashion when they stipulated that anyone could "fell tymber or wood trees within the liberties of Salem" so long as they removed the tops of the trees with the trunks. It was common, as this legislation indicates, for settlers to block cartways with the dregs left behind after cutting down trees. "All the wood, as left yet upon the necke of land towards Roxburie shall be gathered up," the town added, "and layed or heaped in pyles from fo[u]ling the ground." As the colony's population increased, it became more common for settlers to poach timber on nearby private property. "Noe man shall fell trees that stand at the corner of Mr. Newberye's lott on the rock," wrote a Dorchester decree in 1634, "also the trees neere William Horsefords house are to remain to his use." Citing "some differences betweene some neighbor townes and ourselves about wood and timber," Newtown magistrates asked the General Court to run "a lyne between us and watertown . . . for the settlement of peace and quiet among us."[22] Timber collection evidently wreaked a noticeable level of havoc.

Carpenters imposed some coherence on the confusion. The pressing demand for their services prompted many of them to leave England for Massachusetts. Once there, these skilled workers played a critical role in coordinating the stages between clearing timber and building products for local use. Whenever a client hired a carpenter to build something—be it a boat, a fence, a house, or a barn—the carpenter contracted out the tasks of gathering and preparing wood. This ongoing involvement with day laborers and sawyers pulled carpenters into the vortex of the evolving timber industry. Thus we find Edward Tomlins, a Lynn carpenter, on location as "Goodman Edwards felled a tree and requested Deacon's boy to cut it up," which allowed Tomlins to later testify against that wood's dubious condition. John Scobell, a carpenter hired to build a cowhouse, "worked with one of [the client's] servants in the woods in Dorchester bounds in sawing and squaring off timber and boards." Richard Carter and Matling Knight, day laborers under contract to a local carpenter, undertook "to fell and cutt out the wood growing in a swamp of Nicholas Parkers at Rumney Marsh . . . to place them in heaps fit for carriage and reasonable burdens fit for a man to carry."[23]

Carpenters further helped ease the transition from raw timber to finished product by investing in local sawmills. Isaac Cole found himself in court "for not performing certain articles in a covenant about the eight part of a sawmill." Through these relatively modest investments carpenters played a critical role in the spread of sawmills throughout the colony during its first decade. Ownership in a mill motivated carpenters to pay special attention to where settlers felled wood, how well they cleaned up after themselves, and where that wood ultimately went. A group of carpenters in Boston revealed their concern with such matters when they testified that "all the timber in the market" would be "taken away before the next meeting day," or as soon as they could find storage space for "our brother Everell" for the "timber he may rowle upon the march, provided he keep a faire passage for other men to passe with the wood." John Emery, a well-known carpenter who eventually became Newbury's market clerk, could often be found "at the coastal site where the boat came up to trade goods," handling bills of lading and distributing wood supplies to local carpenters.[24]

Carpenters also played a role in spearheading and overseeing the construction of public structures. Court records capture John Emery leading the effort "to build a school at Newbury" while initiating "a petition against [architectural] changes made to the meeting house in Newbury." Carpenters often testified about a structure's location and quality with an eye toward getting a contract to fix it. Edward Tomlins's testimony led the court to order John Deacon "to make up the half fence between Mr. Willes, John Deacon, and others of that field." Tomlins later filed suit against a fence owner whose fence he had deemed in need of repair, claiming that "Cp. Hawkins owed him for 200 ton of square and saw, timber at 17s per annum . . . and 3 hundred of two inch plank."[25] These cases were good news for local woodworkers.

The loose order that carpenters imposed on the hectic quest to acquire local timber came together slowly. Nonetheless, coordinated efforts to place an organizational framework on such a widely practiced activity enabled the Massachusetts Bay Colony to do more than meet immediate needs. In fact, settlers were soon able to take the significant step of trading processed wood intraregionally. Boston's situation initially inspired a response from towns north. One of Boston's "greatest wants," according to one observer, was wood, a situation that forced residents to "fetch their building timber and firewood from the island in boats" because Boston "being a necke [was] bare of wood." Thus in Hingham, according to Edward Johnson, "the people have much profited themselves by transporting timber, planke, and mast for shipping to the town of Boston, as also cedar and pine board to supply the wants of other townes." By the end of the decade trade had expanded in the opposite direction, even to points north of the Merrimack River. Thomas Lechford recorded "articles about a bargain between Lieutenant Richard Morris [of Roxbury] and Mr. Parker for 7000 of clapboards and pipestves at 18 li p. mille, to be delivered at Pascattaquay."[26] Again, the occasional parcel of clapboards and pipe staves even made its way to Virginia or the West Indies in the late 1630s. By the decade's end, though, the vast majority of this trade remained—as it was intended to remain—a locally based aspect of the overall quest to meet immediate needs.

THE PIECEMEAL DEVELOPMENT OF THE FISHING AND TIMBER INDUS-tries during the Bay Colony's first two decades of settlement highlights yet two more ways in which settlers ordered the economic landscape to meet local needs. The production and consumption of these basic commodities helped transform what had once seemed a daunting wilderness into what Puritan pioneers considered to be a relatively civilized environment. The myriad and tedious workaday activities that consumed the vast bulk of the settlers' time, labor, and capital throughout the first decade—building homes, fencing land, penning livestock, planting corn, establishing graz-ing areas, catching fish, building boats, hauling timber—contributed to an environment that gradually came to seem more settled, more familiar, more controlled. The Massachusetts Bay Colony initially failed to achieve systematic overseas trade—its infrastructure remained too weak for that activity—but its more astute observers recognized that the colony's cau-tious optimism was gradually proving to be well warranted. To be sure, settlers were living very simply by metropolitan standards. But by any standard, they had contributed to an astounding level of basic economic development in just a decade.

By satisfying the local market before endeavoring to reach more profit-able export venues with these valuable commodities, Puritan pioneers set an important precedent: they would fully meet local needs first. This deci-sion, perhaps more than any other, shaped the contours of Massachusetts's seventeenth-century economic development. It made what we might call "persistent economic localism" a customary, and quite fertile, Puritan value.

FOUR

The Persistence of Tradition

1638–1650

THE EARLY FAILURE TO REACH EXPORT MARKETS MAY HAVE BEEN A blessing in disguise for the Massachusetts Bay Colony. Ordering the affairs of local farms, organizing the landscape into discrete zones of activity, and initiating the fishing and timber industries were local endeavors that reinforced community bonds while establishing long-term preconditions for economic growth. The deferred dream of exportation provided the necessary time for hardworking Puritans to organize nucleated towns, homogenize their ideology at biweekly meetings, participate in civic affairs, and forge the initial elements of a provincial identity. It was, in fact, this propitious window of opportunity—a window propped open by the considerable task of building an infrastructure—that led later generations of colonists to admire the first generation's "common experiences . . . and common patterns of life and behaviour." The first generation, unburdened by the immediate demands of exportation, forged its corporate memory in the crucible of the Massachusetts wilderness. Under great duress they built a society.[1]

It hardly seemed fair, then, that the accomplishment was undermined just when this society was starting to take shape. Improved economic and political conditions in England diminished New England's main source of labor and capital at the very moment when the farms, roads, fences, bridges, and homes that settlers had built would have allowed them to make long economic strides. In 1640 the Puritans were beset by a depression. The unfortunate timing of this downturn was evident to everyone, especially John Winthrop, who wrote that "merchants would sell no wares but for ready money," little of which settlers possessed. "Men could not pay their debts," he continued, and "prices of lands and cattle fell soon to the one half and less, yea to a third, and after, one fourth part." The General Court spilled considerable ink over the fact that "many men in the plantation are in debt, and heare is not money sufficient to charge the same." Creditors in England remained coldly unsympathetic, complaining, as John Tinker did, that "it is a very greate greivanc and generall complainte among all merchants and dealers to New England that they can have no returns." His grim and not altogether unrealistic prediction that trade would "utterly cease" was a prospect that inspired many settlers to consider quietly the question that Thomas Hooker contemplated out loud: "Why should a man stay until the house fall on his head . . . where in reason he shall destroy his subsistence?" Whether Puritans saw their situation as the result of God's wrath or of economic forces beyond their control, the question was one that many of them, no matter how devout, began to ponder.[2]

It was also a question that settlers seemed prepared to answer. With the most basic elements of a local economy firmly established, it made perfect sense for the colony to think seriously about exporting fish and timber. A systematic interaction with export markets stood out as the most logical solution to the problem posed by the sudden constriction of cash. In 1640 a merchant managed to ship 8,500 pipe staves from Boston to Málaga. Samuel Maverick followed up in 1641, instructing an English agent to sell a load of staves for Spanish cash and fruit. At least seven ships set sail from Boston to the Wine Islands in 1642, selling peas, wheat, fish, and pipe staves in exchange for cash and credit with English merchants. Five more New England–built ships followed suit in 1643, and four more embarked on the high seas in 1644. In 1647 a merchant from Charlestown initiated a relationship with the Wine Islands by sending 13,500 "good sound and merchantable white oak pipe staves" alongside two hundred bushels of "good and merchantable rye corn." In 1648 a Bristol-owned ship left New England carrying 60,000 white oak staves, which it unloaded in Portugal for £1,200. Records for 1650 show a Charlestown merchant shipping 10,326 pipe staves, 800 hogshead staves, and 165 quintals of dried fish to Madeira.[3] By no means was this trade ample enough to effect an economic recovery from the depression. Nevertheless, it does reveal a telling tendency on the part of at least one portion of the population to seek salvation in overseas trade.

Merchants pursued West Indian markets with equal enthusiasm. The first recorded trip to Barbados took place in 1641 and involved a New England ship returning with cotton and "letters from Barbados and other islands in those parts, intreating us to supply them with ministers." A 1645 voyage had a ship taking wine, sugar, and salt purchased from a merchant who had just returned from the Canary Islands. It sold these goods "at Barbados in exchange for Africoes." Winthrop mentions a 1648 trip to the West Indies during which "one Bethzaliel Payton . . . comminge from Barbados in a vessell of 60 tu, was taken in a storme of winde and rayne."[4] Again, while New England merchants were obviously pushing to reach markets in the West Indies, the available evidence in no way suggests that these efforts were successful enough to account for the region's economic recovery by 1650. The fact that the colony overcame the depression and established itself on sound economic ground within the remarkably short span of a decade, combined with the fact that the sporadic exportation that did occur could not have exclusively saved the economy, raises a critical question: How *did* the region recover from the depression?

Answering this question requires developing two aspects of a single argument. First, in order to allay doubts that the export transition might indeed have shouldered the turnaround, a consideration of export-related economic conditions within the Massachusetts Bay Colony must rule out the possibility that the limited evidence mentioned above is reflective of a larger trend. That is, we must eliminate the possibility that the extant examples point to a vast, undocumented export trade that helped the region recover from the depression. Second, an equally careful consideration of the local economy as it operated on the ground in Massachusetts throughout the 1640s provides an alternative explanation for the region's recovery, one that calls for a careful consideration of something that Puritans had come to take for granted: local and inherited economic behavior.[5]

Investigations of these related themes uncover a picture of seamless economic continuity. Massachusetts Bay colonists survived the depression by pursuing local economic activities not altogether different from those they had pursued throughout the 1630s (and earlier in England).[6] The years 1640–55 were a time when Puritans relied on the familiar strategies of internal economic development to weather the economic depression that held settlers in the grip of desperation. Being Puritans, they relied on something they knew and trusted: tradition.

Ideology helped foster this continuity. Much of the Puritans' fortitude derived from their prevailing belief that challenges were to be confronted with faith and hard work. One did not quit when God tested a covenanted community with hardship. Instead, one invoked the powerful image of a "personal or generall calling" and "employed [his talent] to the best advantage," whatever the extenuating circumstances. The customary cultural standard of work provided the moral preparation to pass God's test. The Puritans' response to the depression—a continuation of infrastructural development—evoked recent history. When Winthrop and the initial band of settlers encountered Massachusetts for the first time, one settler recalled Winthrop's actions in terms that confirmed the scripted Puritanical response to hardship. "[A]s Mr. Winthrop was landed," he wrote, "perceiving what misery was like to ensewe through theire Idleness, he presently fell to worke with his own hands, and thereby soe encourged the rest that there was not an Idle person then to be found in the whole Plantation."[7] What had worked then was bound to work now. Puritans thus kept their noses to the familiar grindstone. They developed the infrastructure, acquired and distributed fish and timber, and, as always, practiced traditional mixed farming. By the late 1640s the depression had lifted. The connection, as we will see, was more than coincidental.

Local limitations to export expansion remained considerable as the depression strangled the fledgling colony. Much as unfamiliar rivers, inlets, and pathways had once nagged settlers throughout the 1630s, the ocean continued to plague them with equally unpredictable ferocity in the 1640s. Merchants went to sea in search of distant markets to sell the colony's produce with newfound hope and enthusiasm. But as they ventured into this new territory, the sea struck back. For every successful overseas journey Winthrop recorded in his journal, there is mention of a categorical debacle on the high seas. The mishaps were often so mysterious that nobody could figure out exactly what had happened. In January 1647 Winthrop described how "a small pinnace was sett out for Barbados" from the Massachusetts Bay "with persons and store provisions." Significantly, it was "her first voyage," a fact that helps explain why the shallop ran aground down the coast in Scituate. Whatever tragedy actually transpired, attempts to explain it were confused when several men found the shallop with "the goodes in her, but not a man, nor any of their clothes." This incident was no anomaly. A year earlier, after praising God for the successful fishing season, Winthrop had beamed over the news that Marblehead fishermen, in one venture, "had taken about 4000li worth of fish." Moving these fish down the coast, however, proved harder than pulling them from the ocean. Immediately after his optimistic assessment, Winthrop admitted that "the Lord was still pleased to Afflict us in our shipping" as he pondered a report that the ship full of fish, "goeing out of the River," had become entangled in a crosscurrent and been "forced up on shore." On the banks, "much of the goods spoyled: to the loss (as we estimated) of neere 2000li."[8] It was, unfortunately, business as usual.

Maritime inexperience continually compromised potentially successful trading voyages. The case of John Turner, a Roxbury merchant who entertained ambitious plans to establish a West Indian trade, further proves the point. In 1642, equipped with a "small pinnace of 15 tons," he made a voyage to the Caribbean and returned with "great advantage in indigo, pieces of 8, etc." without notable incident. For whatever reason, though, Turner's accomplishment withered under the rumor that he had achieved such "great advantages" not "by trade" but rather "by prize," which is to say, plunder. Undaunted by the skepticism swirling around him, Turner forged ahead and "prepared a bigger vessel" that, unlike that on his first voyage, "was well manned." On this trip, however, despite the additional manpower, the new vessel got the best of him, and he "was forced in again 3 times: 1. by leak, 2. by a contrary wind, and 3. he spent his mast in fair weather." After a stop in Cape Ann to replace his mast, Turner "lost it by the way, and, so by these occasions and by the frost, he was kept in all winter." Having soured on the prospect of becoming a globe-trotting merchant, he cut his losses. As Winthrop concluded the story of Turner's short and unhappy trading career, "[h]e gave over his voyage and went to Virginia, and there sold his vessell and shipped himself and his commodities in a Dutch ship to the West Indies," where he planned to stay.[9]

The lack of large trading vessels directly contributed to these seagoing disasters. In the early 1640s the Bay colonists initiated a shipbuilding industry that drew heavily on the region's supply of white oak. Throughout the decade this industry, as it were, only managed to turn out a few substantial vessels capable of battling the swells that tossed ships like matchsticks in a whirlpool. The regular production of large trading vessels did not really take off until the end of the century. Thus, most of the overseas trading that did occur in the 1640s usually depended on poorly built, undersized pinnaces that led sailors toward predictable fates. "There was a shallop with eight men to go from Pascataquack to Pemiquid about the beginning of the frost," Winthrop recounted in a not altogether unusual entry. "They were taken with a N.W. tempest and put out to sea 14 days." The result was sadly familiar: "Four of them died with cold, the rest were discovered by a fisherman a good time after, and so brought off the island."[10] These limitations and mishaps would diminish noticeably throughout the century, especially as colonists began to acquire seaworthy vessels after

1650. For the time being, though, they represented tangible limitations to mobility.

Smooth sailing, however, did not necessarily come as a result of owning a large, seaworthy ship. In November 1641 the *Charles of Dartmouth*, a 400-ton ship "lying a Pascataquack to take pipe staves," came unanchored by a fierce storm and was "driven upon the rocks." Its three masts snapped like twigs, and the ship repaired to port until carpenters could build new ones. In the meantime a thin shallop of only three tons effortlessly cut its way through the same storm. Larger ships built in the Bay Colony, at least early on, also suffered from inexperienced craftsmanship. Winthrop, for example, described a ship called the *Make Shift*, so named because "she was build of the wreck[age] of a greater vessell." While negotiating "a voyage to the southward," the recycled craft was "cast upon the ledge of rocks near Long Island," upon which it splintered into shreds. While "the goods were all lost," the men lived. Shortly thereafter a ship called the *Coach*, which was heading south from Salem, "sprang a leak, so as in the morning they found her hold half filled with water." With the ship going down, the seamen "betook themselves to their skiff, being a very small one, and the wind then growing very high." The ship sunk, but again, the men lived. Frustrating as it must have been for merchants trying to tap markets overseas, Puritans paddling for shore in the foreground of a sinking vessel became a common image for New Englanders guiding old ships through new waters.

Poorly constructed trading vessels and the lack of the requisite knowledge to sail them through turbulent seas were not the only infrastructural limits to a fruitful embrace of the export trade. Another factor was the dearth of local industries supporting the large-scale production of exportable commodities. Conventional economic theory holds that the emergence of export products quickly inspires "spread effects" that collectively support the proliferation of that product. The evolution of a serious export trade in fish and timber, for example, would naturally emerge alongside sawmills, wharves, salt houses, and shipyards. An overview of several town records, however, reveals scant evidence of these necessary developments. This dearth of evidence, in turn, further suggests that something else besides the systematic exportation of fish and timber was releasing the Bay colonists from the depression's grasp. Other forces had to be at work.[11]

In the face of depression, settlers were slow to embrace export-oriented changes on the local level. Ipswich residents did not erect a sawmill until 1649, and throughout the decade it never altered its requirement that "no man shall fell any timber on the common to make sale of." The town's first shipyard grant did not occur until 1668, when the town allotted land "for a yard to build vessels and employ workmen for that ends." The infrastructure surrounding the fishing industry matured with equal indifference. Despite the town's having established a Committee of the Furthering of Trade as early as 1641, a salt house failed to materialize until 1652, and a wharf was not built until 1656. Neighboring Rowley similarly showed few signs that settlers successfully responded to the pull of export activity. A shipwright did not show up in the town records until the 1670s, and a wharf was absent from the records until 1681. One sure sign of frequent sawmill activity was the presence of dam regulations in town records. Such stipulations, however, did not appear in the Rowley town records until 1681, when the town decreed that "the water must be let out of the mill pond in the Spring."[12] The prerequisites for exportation, in short, appear too late in the records to explain an export-led recovery as early as the 1640s.

Even a town as wedded to the fishing trade as Marblehead experienced few fundamental infrastructural changes in the 1640s. Although modest shipbuilding activity was evident, these ships—such as the *Desire,* a 120-ton vessel built in 1636—spent much of their time ferrying passengers between England and New England rather than trading commodities in the West Indies and Wine Islands. When the *Desire,* for example, did venture to Barbados, which occurred only rarely, it exported Pequot Indian boys in exchange for slaves. As the nature of the trade suggests, Massachusetts suffered chronic labor shortages. For this reason, potential Marblehead fishermen more often than not chose to receive land grants and to practice traditional mixed farming rather than to spend their lives working full time as deckhands. Historians have often made much of the fact that Marblehead fishermen sold a documented £4,000 worth of fish in 1647.[13] It would be more appropriate, however, to point out what a small amount of fish that actually was. More than anything else, it accurately reflected the economic reality that Bay Colony settlers were doing something very different with their working hours than building the necessary preconditions for an export trade.

AS IT TURNS OUT, THEY WERE LARGELY DOING WHAT THEY HAD DONE throughout the first decade of settlement—building a local infrastructure, developing the local economy, organizing their farms, dividing the landscape into zones of activity, and generally placing the immediate needs of the moment ahead of long-term economic goals. While tentatively moving into export markets in Barbados and the Wine Islands with moderate results, the Bay colonists as a whole chose continuity over change, tradition over novelty, the familiar over the unknown. Economically speaking, they relied on what they already knew to weather the storm generated by the depression.[14]

Marblehead offers another strong case in point. In 1648 residents of this coastal community finally managed to convince the General Court to grant them a jurisdiction separate from Salem. The town's first meeting after the official break serves as a poignant reflection of the economic concerns preoccupying settlers who had been living in Marblehead for well over a decade. The issues slated for discussion that afternoon were a cattle tax, fence regulations, warden appointments, land divisions, cow keepers' roles, deed restrictions, and common land regulations. As this list of concerns suggests, Marblehead settlers focused their attention on the resources and needs most integral to local economic life. Little did they seem to care about explicitly fostering the factors needed for transatlantic trade. The settlers' managing of Marblehead's local resources as they had done throughout the 1630s and early 1640s suggests that restructuring the town's economy to deal with the depression was not among their pressing concerns. More immediate tasks beckoned, and Puritans responded, as they had done for over a decade, with pragmatic solutions entirely consistent with their short history in the Massachusetts Bay Colony.[15]

Cows and wood (not fish and ships) preoccupied settlers dedicated to shoring up an infrastructure supportive of a viable local economy. Marblehead residents continued to arrange their growing supply of livestock to maximize production. Selectmen ordered that two appointed cow keepers, an expert and an apprentice, were to remove cows from planting grounds every day from the first of April to the end of November. After announcing their rates (4s. and 6s. per week), the keepers agreed "to sound a warning horn at sunrise and take herd to Walshingham Chillson's house by a half hour after sunrise." Afterwards, "the herd was to be taken past the first bridge . . . and returned to the first bridge an hour before sunset" with "another blow of the horn to give notice." Cow keepers vowed to be "especially careful in wet weather."[16] These measures hardly seem like economically advanced policies, but again, in a developing local economy they had a direct impact.

Next came wood. Fishermen who had established operations on the shore required a steady supply of timber to build and maintain their flakes. While Marblehead's leaders hardly wanted to hinder the town's nascent commercial fishery, they did not want to provide fishermen unregulated access to the region's timber supply. The measure they passed required fishermen to seek formal approval before harvesting wood, a decision that reflected both "the increase of non-fishing interests at the plantation" as well as the actions of "foreign" fishermen who came into the plantation each year "and gathered wood to construct flakes and use for firewood and stages" and then left. In the end, resident fishermen found themselves paying 10s. a year to the town "for their wood flake stuff," a requirement that ran counter to the prospect of a community primarily concerned with the exportation of natural resources to overseas destinations.[17]

Roads followed. After choosing "two way wardens" for the year, the town warned that "whoever so shall neglect to come out such times at they are warned" to help repair the town's roads "shall pay 2s 6d every day they shall be absent." In addition to linking land development to road maintenance, the town also chose several men "to order the affairs of the plantation," a task that required them to "stint the commons for the inhabitants . . . and make a rate for the repair of the . . . town way." The ongoing demands of road maintenance—in addition to other basic tasks of farm formation, such as planting crops, building fences, and organizing livestock—combined with the region's stagnant labor supply to help ensure that Marblehead, for one, remained a place better suited for "yeoman and tradesmen" than for fishermen seeking foreign trade.[18] This situation would, of course, change in time, but not in the 1640s. The burdens of building an infrastructure were as yet too substantial.

Marblehead was not alone in its continuation of a local economic behavior. The demands of a settlement society were equally evident in Rowley, which Ezekial Rodgers settled between 1638 and 1645. The blueprint that the town followed was drawn by settlers who had organized the region's earliest towns. Rowley's first recorded act involved making plans for a road that would cross the town without winding through private properties teeming with crops or jammed with livestock. Stipulating that "every town shall choose 2 or 3 men who will join with 2 or 3 of the next town . . . to lay out highways where they may be most convenient," Rowley selectmen appointed way wardens and established a few key prerequisites for the road's construction. Settlers agreed to "lay out ways wider, as 6 or 8 or 10 rods, or more in common grounds," making sure to avoid "any extraordinary damage on improved grounds." In other words, they needed to find a way to build the road without "puling downe any man's house, or laying open any garden or orchard . . . or any corne ground."[19] Whatever their transatlantic concerns at the time, Rowley residents evidently understood that laying the foundation for a functional town economy ranked first among its priorities.

Rowley was a quiet town that enjoyed especially extensive access to natural resources. Its coastal location afforded settlers access to fish, while its rich hinterland was heavily stocked with mature stands of timber. One might rightfully expect the "Bay Road," as Rowley called its main artery, to have extended to the relatively commercialized centers of Boston and Salem. Instead, settlers built it to stretch inland into Ipswich, Wenham, and Newbury, providing the town with access to gristmills and other services that it lacked. In addition to the bridge Rowley's men built over the Ipswich River at the border between Ipswich and Rowley to facilitate access to Ipswich's very active mill, they built another bridge over the Parker River for Rowley children to cross to attend Newbury's schoolhouse. Cattle destined for trade or slaughter often joined children to cross the bridge, as Rowley had agreed that the bridge attendant could collect 2d. for "every horse, cow, oxe, or any other great cattle, and also one half penny a piece for every hogg, sheep, or goat that shall pass over the said bridge."[20] In such ways did these bridges respond first and foremost to the ongoing push of local needs.

Integral to the process of farm formation was the establishment of small-scale industrial operations. Rather than building ventures related to the processing of fish and timber, as settlers would have done to feed an export trade, Rowley established industries more appropriate for supporting a local economy. Settlers cut their wood by hand in saw pits instead of building a readily accessible sawmill capable of processing exportable quantities of timber. Wanting to reduce its dependence on Ipswich, the town built its first mill, a corn mill, in 1638 under the requirement that the owner "do make his mill fit to grynde corne, and do so maintain and keep a man to grind." Few situations, after all, were more frustrating than hauling corn to the mill only to find that the mill owner had taken the afternoon off to till his own fields. Other modest industrial ventures followed. Edmond Bridges set up a blacksmith's shop in the early 1640s, and a tanyard emerged under the rule that "no butcher, currier, or shoemaker should be a tanner, nor should a tanner be a butcher, currier, or shoemaker." As for wool production, Winthrop complained of "our supplies from England failing much," but with the help of a fulling mill built and operated by John Pearson in 1643, Massachusetts soon was able to diminish its wool imports.[21]

Lynn, Massachusetts, offers another example of the ways in which local economies stayed attuned to local demand, favoring the tasks of farm formation over explicitly export-related work. The discovery in the 1630s of rich iron bogs throughout the town led several leading Lynn citizens to seek English capital to initiate an ironworks. The efforts came to fruition in the early 1640s and went on to powerfully shape local economic decisions. The considerable transportation demands sparked by the need to haul coal and bog iron throughout the region led developers to spend substantial capital on roads, waterways, and bridges. In order to regulate the Saugus River, the architects of the ironworks designed and built dams that provided settlers a chance to construct mills along the river's banks. Residents jumped at these opportunities. Joseph Jencks quickly built a mill to construct farming equipment, while Thomas Dexter yielded some of his riverfront land to the ironworks on the condition that it build a cart bridge over the river to connect his plot with his neighbor's. The deal also required that the ironworks "allow sufficient water in the olde river for the Alewives to come to their weirs before the grantor's house."[22]

In addition to building the ironworks, Lynn residents continued to pursue activities central to the process of farm formation and the strengthening of local economic and community endeavors. In 1648 the General Court allowed Lynn £20 for repairing the "Great Bridge" over the Saugus River, with a yearly contribution of 30s. for upkeep. Although Joseph Armitage had been running a respectable ordinary (a tavern of sorts) for over a decade, the town decided that another one was in order and noted, "Whereas Mr. Downings farm, in the way between Lynn and Ipswich, is a convenient place for the relief of travelers, it is ordered that Mr. Downings tenant shall have liberty to keep an ordinary." Lynn was a coastal town, but like Marblehead, it remained oriented around the basic tasks of farming. In a 1645 petition to the General Court to have its taxes lowered, the town explained, "We would not envy our neighboring towns [Salem and Boston], which are of the rising hand by trading; we rather wish their prosperity; but for ourselves, we are neither fitted for nor inured to any such course of trade, but must want God's blessinge done upon our lands and cattle."[23] Much more than the exportation of fish and timber, land and cattle, in addition to the local consumption of fish and timber, were what continued to structure the development of coastal towns throughout the Massachusetts Bay Colony.

Farther down the coast, Cambridge followed the pattern established by Rowley, Marblehead, and Lynn. Land grants, cattle regulations, fence maintenance, and timber policies continued to dominate local economic concerns throughout the 1640s. Sixty percent of the laws Cambridge passed in 1640 dealt with land allotments to new arrivals, probably migrants from other towns. The other 40 percent responded to what were by now familiar issues. For cows, the town "agreed with Richard Beckeels to keep the heard of milch cows for this yeere" and arranged "with Goodman Oaks for his man to keepe the drie heard on the other side of the water." To regulate hogs, town leaders agreed that "what ever Hogges shall be found either in streete or common without a keeper not sufficiently yoaked and rung they who are the owners of such hogs for every default are to pay 6d and if found in corne or gardens they are to pay the damage." Fence upkeep also reflected policies from the 1630s. "All fences belonging unto the necke," the town leaders declared, "shall sufficienty be kept as was ordered that last yeare by the townsmen."[24]

Cambridge paid special attention to its local timber supply. The town passed rules to keep timber within the town's boundaries, making it readily available for local uses, such as home construction and fence building. It decreed that anyone "who cutt out or take away directly or indirectly any wood or timber on this side of the path which goeth from the mill to water towne . . . shall forfeit for such load, be it timber, five shillings per load, and if wood, 2s." Rights to take wood from the common had to be obtained through an elaborate bureaucratic process, leading to entries such as the following: "liberty granted to Mr. Pellum and Bro Jackson to fell soe many tres as may serve to fence between them on the backside of Bro Jacksonne house." Cambridge protected fences by requiring swine to be "well and sufficiently ringed" and, during harvest, kept "at home in a close yard or else send them off with a sufficient keep."[25] These modifications appear throughout Cambridge's records. They indicate that these seemingly minor adjustments to local economic life were, for the settlers making them, quite monumental.

Ipswich also reflected the common trend toward traditional economic activity. Town meetings centered on issues such as swine control, with residents appointing George Giddings to make "a pound on the south side of the river near the mill." Magistrates made sure that "Mr. Herman" was sufficiently compensated for "work on town's bridge" and that "fines for fallen trees" were dealt out to the deserving parties. In September 1641 residents agreed that "no dogs were to come into the meeting house" and then proceeded to berate several homeowners for erecting the wrong kind of fence. Throughout the early 1640s, when the depression was in full swing, Ipswich continued to deal with appointments, land distribution for basic agricultural tasks, commonage rights, maintaining the "highway to Chebacco," and regulating access to timber.[26] The only major transition that the town initiated was the establishment of a school.

Salem, after Boston the most commercialized town in New England, reveals a similar emphasis on local concerns. Two hundred and twenty entries registered in the town records between 1640 and 1644 include 145 land grants, 10 cattle regulations, 22 fence regulations, 11 transportation-related regulations, 28 appointments of jury members, surveyors, and fence viewers, and 5 regulations to assist small industries. The remaining entries have to do with miscellaneous internal matters. Only two deal explicitly with the export trade, one proclaiming that Captain Trask "hath leave to set up a tide mill upon the North River, provided hee make passage for a Shallope from halfe flood to full sea," the other demanding that those who "have felled timber trees within two miles of the towne of Salem, and any timber trees within one mile of Marblehead that are fitt for shipping" be paid accordingly.[27]

THE CONTINUITY OF BASIC TASKS GEARED TOWARD BUILDING LOCAL INfrastructures during the depression is entirely consistent with the region's ongoing local needs and export capabilities. Although suffering under a painful depression, settlers working to make a life for themselves in the wilderness did not alter their economic behavior in appreciable ways to grapple with the depression in their midst. Instead, they weathered the depression by doing what their environment and their inherited economic ideals demanded that they do. They kept developing the essential preconditions for mixed farming and local trade. As farms improved, exchange became more fluid, cattle lived longer, fruit trees matured, and trade networks solidified, the region recovered its balance and found salvation in the slowly increasing economic security. It was a security nurtured by settlers who mapped the landscape into organized economic activities, turned their attention inward to consider immediate needs, and established the basic industries to help fulfill those needs. It was a security, moreover, that would remain essential to the region's stability as profound changes on the horizon began to take shape.

FIVE

Founding Forge: The Impact of the Lynn Ironworks

1650–1665

IN 1650, WITH THE DEPRESSION EFFECTIVELY OVER, SYSTEMATIC transatlantic trade was still a world away. But the daunting distance of this goal mattered none to Edward Johnson. Surveying with pride the literal ground that Massachusetts had covered since its troubled founding twenty years earlier, he marveled that Dorchester, for one, was flush with "orchards and gardens full of fruit trees" and thriving upon "plenty of Corne land." Nearby Roxbury might have been young and relatively undeveloped, but it too contained "very goodly Fruit-trees, fruitful fields and gardens, their Hearde of Cowes, Oxen, and other young cattle of that kind about 350." Ipswich was "very good land for husbandry, where rocks hinder not the course of the plow." Anywhere one went, in fact, there were to be found "Orchards and Gardens full of fruit trees, plenty of corne-land."[1]

It is tempting to interpret these optimistic assessments as exaggerations designed to lure wavering migrants to a new world. At the time when Johnson sung his praises, after all, immigration to the Massachusetts Bay had screeched to a virtual halt, with economic conditions in England providing few reasons to leave home.[2] Families in New England were reproducing at a healthy rate, but no longer were colonists enjoying the ceaseless influx of English immigrants armed with cash and eager to purchase local produce. The commonly assumed claim that merchants had finally tapped overseas markets with enough force to generate real profits and thus to bail out the colony was in fact unlikely in light of the local infrastructure's immaturity. All these factors speak powerfully to Johnson's potential duplicity, offering sound justification to dismiss him as a huckster of compromised real estate.

A wealth of other evidence, however, suggests that Johnson's optimism was genuine. For one, the Massachusetts Bay Colony was flush with local produce. This prospect, reflecting the related prospect that the local economic policies that towns had spent twenty years hammering into shape were working, is suggested by the goods that colonists were lading onto English ships in exchange for much-needed manufactured products. After anchoring in Boston in 1645, for example, the *Edmund and John* picked up at least three thousand bushels of peas, wheat, and Indian corn, while the *Dolphin*, another English ship docked in Boston, loaded seven thousand bushels of these goods. Given that family farms, constricted by a limited labor supply, were small, these figures mean that thousands of farmers were successfully producing a surplus of meat, grain, and garden produce for English ships to trade in the West Indies. Darrett Rutman estimates that the commonwealth exported no less than twenty thousand bushels of grain in 1645 in exchange for more than £4,000 worth of English goods. During that decade, fish and timber were far less vital to the region's economy than were grain and livestock, which were precisely the goods that "profited the farmers that produced them," thus justifying the critical early years of infrastructural development and unwavering emphasis on agriculture.[3]

Wills and probate inventories further portray a region that had mastered the art of local production. Records from 1650 to 1664 show that farming families produced an abundance of grain, livestock, dairy products, and beer. In all wealth categories, almost every family owned cows. Most of them had some capacity to produce beef. The price of cattle confirms its abundance. When settlers poured into the colony during the 1630s, the cost of a cow rose to a prohibitive £20. By the late 1640s, however, William Knight owned "one heifer and a calfe," valued at £4 1s., while Thomas Mighill purchased five cows for £23 and Elinor Tressler owned three cows, valued at £12. Pigs proliferated as well, with more than 75 percent of the inventories sampled showing evidence of swine. Pigs and hogs were cheap throughout the 1650s, selling for 6s. and £1–£3, depending on their size. Swine were, as always, active and voluminous breeders. Their numbers ran so high that many inventory takers threw their hands up in frustration and guessed at the number of swine on the farm, entering the vague notation "swine" alongside an estimated worth of the inventory. Clearly, though, cow keepers, hogreeves, town policies, sturdy fences, and greener pastures—all factors owing their existence to decisions made by settlers during the first two decades—contributed to this increasing supply of livestock.[4]

Grain flowed freely from family farms into local, regional, and international markets. Inventories confirm this abundance as well. Variations in wealth did not significantly influence grain ownership. With more than two-thirds of all households sampled showing ownership of Indian corn or wheat, either in storage or "in the ground," it is unlikely that many families went wanting for grain. With the exception of unusually wealthy merchants, settlers typically owned three to four bushels. Wheat appeared more often in inventories of the wealthy than in those of the poor, while Indian corn was most popular in inventories of middle-income settlers. Over time, though, as wealthier families became more comfortable with Indian corn, and as they "Anglicized" it by incorporating it into bread and beer, all Massachusetts Bay settlers came around to Indian corn, producing and consuming it prodigiously. They did so in spite of the commonly held perception in England that it was, first and foremost, grain best fed to pigs.[5]

The ubiquity of products basic to daily sustenance is even further confirmed by the frequency with which colonists traded these goods internally. John Patch, in a standard agreement, signed a contract to build a house for John Norman at a cost of £45, "one half in corn and cattle at or before the house was raised and the remainder at the next wheat harvest." When William Beale, a Marblehead miller, leased a house from Ipswich's William Paine, he did so under the stipulation that "rent would be paid by Beale in fish, corn, cattle, or money, fourteen pounds yearly." As a payment to his budding apprentice, Frances Skerry promised "ten pounds at the end of his time in corn and cattle." Cows were even used to secure a man's place in court. Debt payments frequently centered upon these local products. Thomas Marshall accepted payments from Joseph Armitage in "an ox to be paid in 4 years at 3 li" and "the hire of two yoke of oxen." Zerobaball Phillips "assigned to Mr. Nathanial Rogers and others a debt due for Isaac Cummings, Sr., and a cow in the hands of John Rise of Dedham as security for Phillips appearance at court." Exchanges such as these abound in the colony's court records. Cows, corn, and oxen were, in a sense, interchangeable with cash. They were integral in keeping the web of local trade strong and thus suggest the widespread presence of these goods in the colony as a whole.[6]

Given the ubiquity of grain and meat, it is likely that Johnson was not exaggerating when he praised the settlers' impressive capacity for farm production. In the 1650s the Massachusetts Bay Colony continued to make increasingly successful forays into the export market as the fish and timber industries started to overcome chronic labor problems, generate more capital investment, acquire more sophisticated equipment, and forge merchant contacts overseas.[7] These economic decisions, however, paled in importance next to the more routine decisions to grow grain, raise livestock, and trade these products locally. All of which raises questions about this pivotal moment in the development of the Massachusetts Bay's economy: If immigration had halted, and if exportation was not yet systematic enough to transform the economy into one dependent on the external market, how did the colony sustain its modest economic growth? How did it continue to take steps toward balancing the books? Why, given the macroeconomic context, did it not stagnate, wither, and die, sending Puritan pioneers back to England as many predicted would happen? How, only a decade later, could the economy integrate itself into the transatlantic world and become British America's most stable and diversified economic region?

The answers might very well have to do with a business best known for the fact that it ultimately failed: the Lynn Ironworks. Traditionally, historians have viewed the ironworks as a classic case of managerial disaster and inadequate capital accumulation on the colonial frontier. True enough, these factors—as well as the chronic labor shortage—contributed to the failure of colonial America's first genuine effort to establish a manufacturing endeavor on an international scale.[8] To leave it at that, however, would be to miss the subtle ways in which the ironworks sparked local economic development from 1648 to 1655, a critical period in the region's economy when the ironworks, not coincidentally, happened to be running at full tilt. The brisk trade in provisions that helped buttress Massachusetts while the depression ran its course kept settlers revolving within a relatively tight circle of exchange. The emergence of the Lynn Ironworks, however, broke this cycle and expanded it by widening the extent, quantity, and range of goods exchanged locally. As a comparatively well capitalized and technically complex industrial operation pulsing at the center of the Massachusetts Bay Colony, the ironworks became a voracious local consumer dependent on the maturing internal economy for its fundamental operating needs. From 1648 to 1655 it tapped the local economy consistently enough to generate profitable results for Massachusetts Bay's economic development. It did so, moreover, at a time when the economy desperately needed a boost to keep settlers productive while merchants moved decisively into the transatlantic market.[9]

When the ironworks' founders settled on Lynn as the site for their forge, they paid special attention to the area's preexisting infrastructural conditions—the very conditions that settlers had spent two decades building.

Richard Leader, the venture's manager, "found a spot which had been over-looked in Winthrop's survey but which clearly had distinct advantages."[10] Many of these advantages were natural. Low-lying meadows and swamps oozing with rich ore dominated the surrounding landscape. The high tides of the Saugus River provided consistently navigable loading points. Adequate water poured forth from a "natural elevation rising above the riparian plane." Other advantages were man-made. Leader praised the quality of the main road between Boston and Salem, as well as the sturdy bridge traversing the often turbulent Saugus. In January 1640 he purchased surrounding land from Thomas Dexter, citing "twoe convenient Cart wayes" as a major benefit of this location. The ironworks site, not incidentally, also enjoyed proximity to a preexisting gristmill and a weir.[11]

Once the ironworks lurched into operation, the local economy leapt to meet its needs. These needs proved to be substantial, ranging from primary resources such as the raw material to operate the mine to the tools with which to work the materials and efficient transportation sources to obtain food and clothing. The full impact of this press on the local economy cannot be precisely quantified, but the sheer breadth of the ironworks' influence becomes evident through a detailed examination of the company's records (which survive because of the claims filed against the company when it collapsed). By helping to provide and transport raw material, make clothes and supply food, and clear roads and make tools, settlers worked with the ironworks' permanent staff of imported Scottish workers not only to boost the level of iron produced by the Lynn forge but also to spark the local economy in a way that the export trade in the 1640s never could. In the end, the Lynn Ironworks, despite its ultimate failure as an early industrial venture, played a critical role in developing Massachusetts's local economy and society.

THE LYNN IRONWORKS NEVER IMPORTED RAW MATERIAL. AS WITH local economic life in general, the seemingly simple task of producing and trucking goods from one location to another remained central to the ironworks' success. While the forge was in Lynn, the materials required to operate it had to travel from surrounding locations stretching from Andover to Boston, and often from as far away as Reading or Hingham. The managers of the ironworks tended to rely heavily on local farmers and artisans to obtain and deliver these goods for the entire company.[12] The furnace depended most heavily on coal for fuel, and in 1651 alone the company paid at least forty-eight men to cut and cart more than forty-five hundred

TABLE 5.1   Raw-material production and transportation, Lynn Ironworks, 1651

Product	Number of workers	Amount	Cost
Wood	48	4,537 cords	£251 8s. 10d.
Coal	10	1,885 loads	£118 6s. 11d.
Rock	14	1,517 loads	£998 7s.
Bog ore	7	884 tons, 545 loads	—

Source: Lynn Ironworks Papers, 1651–1653, Baker Library, Harvard Business School, Boston, MA.

cords of wood, at a cost of more than £250, to a charcoal processing center that fed the furnace (table 5.1). These deliveries occurred throughout the year, with the average delivery consisting of about seventy-five cords. The company paid laborers about 4d. per cord of wood carted and about 2s. per cord of wood cut. Thus, for example, we can find William Tingle credited £3 for carting two hundred cords of wood and, on another occasion, receiving more than £5 for "44 cord cutting and carting." The work of supplying and hauling wood, however, was more than the imported labor could possibly handle. The company, therefore, regularly entered credits for tasks such as Richard Smith's "2 days cutting with Scots" and Richard Greene's "cleaving wood after the Scots and carting 26 cords."[13] As E. N. Hartley notes, "This work was carried out . . . by neighboring farmers and assorted craftsmen employed on a part-time basis."[14] The case of Samual Bennett provides a sense of this task: the company credited him for "carting 64 loads from Henry Stich . . . 282 loads from Henry Tucker; 232 loads from Richard Greene . . . 16 loads from John Francis . . . 86 loads from John Lock."[15] Carrying wood between farms was, of course, nothing new to colonists living in the Massachusetts Bay, but the ironworks significantly widened the scale and scope of this preexisting activity.

The production and transportation of coal to the furnace and forge was the next step in the long process of supplying the ironworks' raw materials. Producing coal was a laborious procedure. It was for good reason that the company dedicated nine Scotsmen to the job on a full-time basis. The first step was to build a level coal "pit," which involved clearing a space thirty to forty feet in diameter to hold about twenty-five cords of wood. Next, residents who were hired as day laborers hauled wood to the site and stacked the trunks into an intricate cone over the pit, not unlike a bonfire. Workers then drove a pole into the center of the woodpile and built a makeshift chimney on top of it, so that the chimney stood well above the heap of stacked wood. With the chimney built, colliers filled in any large gaps in the woodpile with handfuls of wood scraps before daubing the entire pile with a thick coating of leaves and dirt. When the pit was ready to be fired, a worker climbed the heap and fed hot coals into the chimney. As the fire charred downward, he made sure that the accumulating heat remained within the mud-covered stack of wood and that all holes that formed were quickly repaired. After several days the coals were cooked, cooled, and ready for carting to the ironworks.[16]

Once the coals were finished, local residents once again became essential. Evidence of their activity dominates the ironworks' records. In 1651 ten workers produced and hauled 1,885 loads of coal (see table 5.1). Thomas Locke charged £28 for "his share making of 207 loads of coals," including "setting one of the cutters and fireing the wood." Edward Baker earned £10 for "his share in carting 100 loads of coal from John Francis," and Henry Tucker took in 5s. for "his share cooling of 2/3 loades of coales." One problem that colliers often faced was the marshy ground around the pit. Their response, as usual, was to rely on local labor for a solution. Thus we find Samual Bennett, a Lynn carpenter, "carting boards, hurdles, and planks for the colliers."[17] In general, charcoal production demanded highly skilled workers and paid more than any other task at the ironworks. The process, however, was equally reliant on settlers, who showed up with their own oxen and cart ready to make some extra cash and willing to move the goods to the furnace no matter what the weather or road conditions.[18]

Acquiring and hauling bog also required the ironworks to tap local labor and transportation capabilities. Workers mined bog ore while sitting in small boats on shallow swamps or trudging on foot through low-lying areas that had once been pond beds. They gathered the ore by strenuously dragging the beds with instruments called floating shovels, produced for the company by local blacksmiths.[19] As with the other tasks, both full-time employees and local farmers and artisans worked to pull bog from the swamps and haul it to the furnace. As a more precious resource than timber, ore required workers to look far and wide, traveling to regions they might not otherwise have visited. The ironworks records show employees venturing as far away as Reading to dig up piles of the black mush. This distance elevated transportation costs, but the company still paid local transporters 6s. to 7s. a load and in 1651 doled out more than £300 for the hauling of more than a thousand tons of bog. Samual Bennett, the carpenter, completed the lion's share of this work, earning an astounding £131 for "carting 424 loads of mine."[20]

In order to yield quality iron, raw ore had to be mixed with a fluxing agent inside the furnace. Traditionally, ironworkers used limestone to create a more pliable slag, thus enabling ironmasters to maximize the amount of iron they could extract from their ore. In the absence of this material, however, the company turned to a denser rock quarried on the nearby peninsula of Nahant.[21] Mining this deeply embedded rock required considerable muscle and patience. Workers had to hack away at the rock to pry it from the quarry and then haul the weighty material from the ocean shore into Lynn, where they then "roasted" it and shaped it into workable sizes. Workers for this task came mostly from the ironworks staff, earning 1s. for every ton mined and transporting the rocks either by cart or by boat at a rate of 1s. 4d. per ton. Like the colliers, the rock miners placed substantial and consistent demands on the local economy. Records include debts for "going to Nahant and carrying of tools to break the oare," "18 cord wood to burn the ore at Nahant," and "carriage of 16 ton of mine from Nahant."[22]

Raw-material production and transportation thus linked the Lynn Ironworks to the local economy. These, however, were only the most obvious demands that the ironworks placed on the region's resources. In addition to providing wood, coal, bog mine, and rock, local residents regularly supplied the ironworks with food, drink, clothing, tools, farm services, transportation, and a range of other skilled and unskilled labor. These services, which almost exclusively involved local residents who were not permanently employed by the company, provide even more insight into the ways that the ironworks sparked and spurred the local economy, pulling residents into consistent patterns of exchange.

TRADING MODEST QUANTITIES OF FOOD AND DRINK WITHIN THE BAY Colony was already an integral aspect of local economic behavior. The ironworks, in turn, relied exclusively on this preexisting network of exchange to keep its several dozen permanent employees well supplied with food and drink. The company bookkeepers routinely recorded the employee, the supplier of his diet, the length of time he was supplied, and the cost. As a result, we find examples such as Charles Phillips earning £8 5s. for "33 weeks diet" to Nicholas Pinnion, the company's forge carpenter. Charles Hook collected £3 for "12 weeks diet" for Quinton Pray; and Goodman Osbourne provided Robert Grossman "18 weeks diet" for £4 10s.[23] Company bookkeepers later resorted to listing the collective cost of provisioning the Scotsmen with food and drink. Over the course of eight months in 1651 the company spent £301 13s. on food and drink for the Scotsmen. At this rate, the company would spend more than £450 per year obtaining food and drink for its employees. Beyond these well-documented examples of spending, purchases such as "drink for workmen," "10 bushels of oats," and "liquors given at the draying of the furnace beams" are scattered throughout the company's accounts.[24] The local economy literally fed the ironworks.

Bay colonists provided the company with the same kind of food and drink that they were already producing and selling to one another at home, within their towns, and up and down the coast. From June 26 to October 24, 1652, the company purchased food for ten Scotsmen: 4 pounds of hops, 4.5 bushels of malt, 11 hundredweight of bread, 5 hogsheads and 1 barrel of mackerel, 3.5 bushels of wheat, 3 bushels of peas, and 1 barrel of pork. In August and September 1653 the company bought the following goods:

August 8: 5 bu. wheat, 49.5 lb. pork
August 15: 2 bu. wheat, 1 pk. peas
August 22: 3 pk. wheat
August 23: "to Good. Keaser for 1 bush of malt"
August 29: 2.5 lb. hops
August 31: 1 bu. and 1 pk. malt, 2 bu. wheat, 1 pk. peas, and 44.5 lb. pork
September 3: 13 lb. fresh beef, 1 bu. wheat, 1 pk. malt, 1 pk. peas

As the quantities and products indicate, the company tapped local networks of exchange on a regular basis. In doing so, it inevitably furthered local development.[25]

The company also depended heavily on local residents for the daily transportation of other items besides the forge's raw materials. Much more comfortable and familiar with the environment than the Scotsmen were, residents capitalized on their knowledge and access to equipment. Joseph Jencks, who owned the local mill, charged the company for "expenses for voyages to Braintree and Waymouth myself and horse" and "wharfage and carriage of boards."[26] George Adams earned 6s. for traveling to a town several miles away to pick up clothes made for the workmen; Goodman Pinnion charged more than £2 for "fraight of boards from Waymouth." Thomas Wiggins took in £1 16s. for "4 days work with team [of oxen] and man bringing the furnace beam to the works." Later he earned another 10s. for "one days work with 8 oxen about the said furnace beam." These kinds of transactions were the company's bread and butter.[27]

Keeping passages cleared and in decent repair also fell to local residents. Wiggins, in addition to hauling goods for the company, charged it for "making a bridge in the woods." George Adams entered a credit for "mending the ways," as did John Sanders for "mending the ways for carting coals."[28] The company, moreover, regularly paid residents to repair and maintain transportation equipment. Debits appear in the company's records for services such as "mending the boat," "oats for the horses," "shoeing the horses," and "mending the carts."[29] Thomas Chadwell charged the ironworks for "trimming two boats belonging to the works and building a small new boat."[30] Given the range of its mobility as well as of its needs, the company demanded these kinds of services constantly. Local residents responded by incorporating these jobs into their preexisting routines of economic exchange, routines that they had been developing for more than two decades.

The Lynn Ironworks relied exclusively on local households not only for food but also for textiles. Joseph Armitage earned more than £3 for "making of clothes, expenses paid at his house," while the company paid Thomas Hartshorn more than £1 for "making a suite for Charles Hook" and "3 pr shoes to Ch. Hook from 5th of Jan to 24th Dec." Among the credits for clothing is one of the few places where women appear in the developing system of local exchange between the ironworks and the residents. The company paid Goody Hart for "making shirts and bands," "mending shoes several times," and "for a hat and making a suit." Residents generally provided the company with basic items of clothing, including stockings, shirts, britches, and boots. Occasionally, however, tailors specialized their services and produced items specific for iron making, as one resident did when he made "20 aprons" for the company. Accounts could be for a single item, such as "drawers for John Adams," but there are also several cases of residents producing clothes on a much grander scale than they had ever been accustomed to before. John Poole, for example, earned credits for "72 shirts at 5s each" and received "92 skins for making the clothes."[31]

Maintaining and improving its relatively extensive facilities was a time-consuming endeavor, and the ironworks regularly hired carpenters from the local economy to assist. The Scotsmen lived in wood cottages surrounding the forge, and the company employed local carpenters to build and repair these rickety structures. We find credits for "the glazer of

Salem glazing the house windows," "hewing and setting up 300 clapboards about Wm. Tingles house," "making the celler oven and back two hearths, at the Scots house," and "clapboarding and other work."[32] As with clothing, supplies could also reach unprecedented levels, as when Goodman Redkapp provided "3600 clapboards" and Henry Tucker sold them "5444 ft boards."[33] The company relied on carpenters from England to build the furnace and forge, but it turned to local carpenters for the upkeep. Nicholas Pinnion earned more than £4 for "6 months carpenters work at the forge," John Parker earned 8s. for "mending a furnace sieve," and John Vinson charged the company for "dressing the finery bellows." The furnace beams, which dried out and cracked every few months, required extra attention. The company had first to pay for "helping Francis Perry making and fitting the furnace beam . . . being 4 weeks work," then to compensate another for "sundry days work in getting the furnace and hammer beam to the works," and finally to pay Roger Tiler for "2 days work about the furnace beams which proved defective." Other chores included "making the furnace hearth new and the help of his man 8 days and making clear the furnace" and "breaking up the furnace hearth."[34] Finally, carpenters could always find miscellaneous jobs at the ironworks, as Goodman Perry did when he collected £23 for "framing and finishing the cow house" and as another resident did when he earned 15s. for "6 days of himself and man in mending the flood gates and dam."[35]

The company proved to be a steady client for local blacksmiths. Routine expenses for the company included paying John Francis "his share cutting hammers and anvils," Quinton Pray for "making 3 baskets" used to carry coals, Thomas Foster for "making 2 pickaxes, two half moons, two chaldrons for the bellows," Nicholas Potter for "a crooke for a furnace wheel," and Richard Greene for "2 floating shovels" used to extricate bog iron.[36] These jobs were more often than not completed by residents employed on a part-time basis, but the company did use the Scotsmen to make shoe nails at the slitting mill connected to the furnace. One entry notes a payment of 10s. "to Scots" for "2 thousand of shoe nails." Repairing tools also remained a common task. Nicholas Pinnion earned £2 for "cutting hammers and anvils and mending of tools," and Henry Tucker made it into the books for "mending of hurdles."[37]

Routine errands also fell to local residents eager for more work. The company paid "expenses to John Blaine, on[e] week going from Hammersmith to Braintree, Waymouth and elsewhere in the woods to account with men employed about the Iron workes." On other occasions it paid Quinton

Building the Bay Colony

Pray for "4 dayes going to Boston to for bellow leathers, and nayles," John Parker for "expenses at Boston at sundry times seeking provisions and supplies for the workers and servants," and John Vinton for "his expense going to Boston for grease and nails." Theopolis Bayley and John Lambert earned credits for "several voyages with the company's boat to Boston, Braintree, Waymouth, and Hingham."[38]

Finally, a range of farm chores and miscellaneous tasks further pulled common colonists into the ironworks' active orbit. The company paid residents for chores such as "fencing the company's land at Braintree," "5 days making hay," "3 days fencing a lott," "cleaving of 900 rayles," "mowing, thatching," and "firewood cutting." Additionally, settlers provided the company with an assortment of miscellaneous items, including grease, tallow, powder, and even medical treatment.[39]

TO AN IMMEASURABLE BUT NONETHELESS SIGNIFICANT EXTENT, THE Lynn Ironworks had a comprehensive impact on the Bay Colony's evolving local economy. The internal networks that settlers had spent nearly twenty years establishing, networks rooted in the production and provision of basic goods and services within a manageable geographical scope, proved essential to the ironworks' short but productive life. The relationship between the company and the local economy, however, was mutually beneficial. In providing food, clothing, transportation services, tools, and sporadic farm labor for the ironworks, local residents simultaneously drew upon and buttressed the provincial networks of exchange that they had been nurturing for a generation. These networks, moreover, strengthened society as a whole. Not only did foreigners work in the local economy without undermining Puritanical values but they helped Puritan pioneers to continue their traditional communal habits while interacting with one another on a more routine basis. The internal economy's symbiotic relationship with the ironworks thus raised local production, trade, travel, consumption, and even a sense of community to levels unseen before the establishment of the company. These developments would prove crucial to budding merchants eager to move the economy to a new level of sophistication.

SIX

The Provincialism of Young George Corwin

1653–1656

NO MERCHANT WAS MORE EAGER TO MOVE THE ECONOMY TO A NEW level of sophistication than George Corwin. As one of an emerging group of young merchants endowed with ample capital and transatlantic connections, Corwin hoped to capitalize on the developing local economy with impressive results.[1] His timing was good. By 1653 Massachusetts had effectively developed an economic infrastructure. Its roads, fences, ships, cattle policies, timber regulations, and patterns of local exchange were established enough to foster a substantial level of local production and stability. Five years of constant demand for regionally produced goods by the Lynn Ironworks had served to strengthen the region's production capabilities. A depression had hit, and the depression had hurt. But the colonists, driven in part by Puritan patience and hard work, recovered by pursuing local economic strategies that had already proven their effectiveness. Massachusetts Bay settlers had not seen their standard of living rise significantly since their founding in 1630, but because of men like George Corwin that stagnancy was about to change. For years Corwin had been hearing assertions like the one made by Richard Vines in 1647 that "[the Barbadians] are so intent on planting sugar that they had rather buy foode at very deare rates than produce it by labour."[2] By the early 1650s he and many men like him were, at long last, prepared to act on this assessment.

Corwin teamed up with merchants such as Samuel Maverick, Adam Winthrop, Robert Sedgwick, Valentine Hill, Philip English, and Robert Shrimpton to export a wide range of goods—including timber, shipping goods, and fish—throughout the Caribbean and Iberian markets. These incipient "citizens of the world" traded highly valued commodities for specie, products that they could sell in England, and credits, all of which they used to buy the English manufactured goods that they sold to the colonies. Massachusetts, as a result, gradually saw its wealth increase and its standard of living improve. Not only were angry investors who had once clamored for returns appeased but, later in the century, their counterparts actually feared that New England was becoming an economic competitor. Some called it "the most prejudicial Plantation to this kingdom" because "all sorts of merchandise of the produce of Europe are imported directly into New England, and thence carried to all of the other of the King's dominions in America, and sold at far cheaper rates than any that can be sent from hence." This perceived threat was in fact a real one, and it did little to endear New England to the crown. It does, however, explain why the region became, according to John McCusker and Russell Menard, "a diverse and tightly integrated commercial economy" defined by stability, a modest but comparatively luxurious indulgence in consumer goods, and continued economic growth and development.[3]

A less apparent side of this familiar story, however, has to do with the means by which these entrepreneurial merchants initially stepped into transatlantic channels. One might characterize the New England merchants as the bêtes noires of the Puritan establishment, collectively undermining the pietistic quest for covenanted communities with their acquisitive attitudes and peripatetic ways. Given the overtly materialistic intent of their objectives, they very well might have "represented the spirit of a new age" whose "guiding principles were not social stability, order, and the discipline of the senses, but mobility, growth, and the enjoyment of life." There would have been every reason to see them as experiencing a "growing sense of distinctiveness" as they "shifted from the parochialism of rural and Puritan New England to the cosmopolitanism of commercial Britain." All of these assessments seem reasonable enough. All of them, however, fail to find support in the experience of a young George Corwin, a merchant whose experience suggests a more interesting trajectory, one of continuity with the local economy rather than conflict with it.[4] An examination of his early years reminds us that the local economy proved crucial to the transatlantic transition that changed economic life in Massachusetts.

Through extensive economic transactions, Corwin, rather than heading out after transatlantic wealth and fame, remained embedded in the commercial and social rhythms of provincial Massachusetts. He insinuated himself into the growing networks that dominated the local economy by nurturing bonds with local producers and consumers, namely, his neighbors. Maintaining these bonds made forays into export markets that much more feasible. In the years 1653–56 Corwin established local trade

TABLE 6.1 Overview of George Corwin account sample, 1653–1656

Town	Average account debt	Average account length (months)	Number	Percent of total
Ipswich/Gloucester	£6 8s. 4d.	16.7	17	20
Wenham/Beverly	£4 7s. 4d.	25.3	11	13
Salem	£5 9s. 8d.	13.0	45	51
Lynn/Marblehead	£2 11s. 6d.	17.0	9	10
Rowley/Newbury	£3 3s. 9d.	20.0	5	6

Sources: Verifications relied on George F. Dow, ed., *The Records and Files of the Quarterly Courts of Essex County, Massachusetts,* 9 vols. (Salem, MA, 1911–75), vols. 2–8; *New England Historical and Genealogical Register,* index; and several "marginal secondary sources," particularly town histories. The remaining data are based on the George Corwin Account Book, 1651–1656, in George Corwin's Letters, Bills, Ledgers and Day Books, 1651–1684, The Phillips Library, Peabody Essex Museum, Salem, MA.

Note: The information in this table is based on the 87 out of 132 people who could be positively linked to specific towns.

accounts with 132 residents. Two-thirds of these men and women lived in Essex County, more than half in Corwin's hometown of Salem. Corwin's local trades connected (and endeared) him to farmers and small manufacturers in towns ranging from Newbury down to Lynn, but again, more than half of his local transactions during these years took place in Salem. We tend to imagine New England's merchants working well beyond the intricate networks of local exchange. Corwin, however, was in the thick of it; his work directly depended on it.

Several aspects of Corwin's accounts confirm his intimate involvement in the provincial economy. His accounts deal with small and frequent exchanges. An average balance account comes to a mere £4.5, a figure that stands in sharp contrast to the thousands of pounds in which he would later trade (table 6.1). Accounts with individual clients also extended over surprisingly long periods of time, and with so little cash circulating throughout the economy, Corwin more often than not accepted payments for imports in the form of farm produce. The nature of these payments demanded that Corwin show unusual patience. For one, he had to keep his accounts open for many months straight—on average, about a year and half—without a remittance. None of these qualities suggest the stereotypical image of the powerful New England merchant, but they remained central to Corwin's work nonetheless.

Corwin's account with Benjamin Balch reflects the general tenor of his trading behavior. Balch became a loyal client of Corwin's, purchasing a range of coveted imports, such as powder, soap, wine, cloth, and matches. He bought these goods and others on four occasions in 1652–53 (February 25, 1652, and April 13, May 2, and June 8, 1653) but did not balance his account with Corwin until January 14, 1655, which he did through payments in "work," Indian corn, and wheat. Clients like William Langley were more punctual. Langley bought lace, buttons, and silk from Corwin on November 15, 1656, and paid him back a month later in a 73-pound and a 114-pound parcel of processed pork. Langley, though, was the exception that proved the rule: repayment was a leisurely process at best. A "Mr. Norrice" was more typical. Corwin sold him a variety of imports on fourteen separate occasions from June 1653 to September 1654. Norrice made his first return in October 1653 and paid nothing more until the following December, when he paid Corwin a small portion of his debt in wheat. His final purchase from Corwin came in September 1654, a debt he did not settle until March 1655.[5] Corwin certainly wanted residents to purchase more goods at one time and to settle their accounts with greater diligence. He had no choice, however, but to respect the limits inherent in a local economy that was only a couple of decades old. He had to accept that it would proceed at its own pace, according to its own rules, hidebound by traditional habits.

As a nascent merchant tapping into networks of neighborly production and exchange, Corwin might very well have wished to consolidate trades into a few well-organized transactions. Instead, he adhered to the preestablished pattern of buying and selling on a regular basis. John Leach bought tobacco from Corwin on six separate occasions over seven months, while his brother Richard made thirteen purchases in less than a year. Thomas Gordon bought goods, including pots, vinegar, lace, and cotton, nine times in 1653. John Beckett and Corwin undertook no less than twenty-four trades in 1655, with Beckett buying everything from butter to pipes.[6] Corwin would later become a merchant with enough clout in other markets to execute a few discrete trades involving much larger sums of goods. For the time being, however, with the local economic culture steering the region toward transatlantic involvement, he wisely calibrated his trading habits to fit traditional modes of transaction. Puritan farmers and artisans, ever careful not to overextend themselves or to overindulge, found it more useful to import conservatively and often rather than liber-

The Provincialism of Young George Corwin

TABLE 6.2 Types of returns among and within accounts, 1653–1656

Product	Percent of accounts	Average percent within accounts
Dairy	28	49
Brewing	19	50
Grain	47	50
Livestock	42	50
Fish	1	15
Wood	3	42

Source: Data are based on the George Corwin Account Book, 1651–1656, in George Corwin's Letters, Bills, Ledgers and Day Books, 1651–1684, The Phillips Library, Peabody Essex Museum, Salem, MA.

ally and all at once. Corwin, eager as he might have been to do otherwise, was in no position to ignore these customs.

Perhaps the most revealing aspect of Corwin's early accounts is the nature of the returns he accepted as payment for English imports. Rather than collecting large quantities of fish, timber, and fur to sell in overseas venues, as he would later do, Corwin began his merchant career by trading imports in exchange for the very goods that the Puritans were already producing for themselves and one another, for regional markets, and for the ironworks. His accounts confirm what had become the defining trends of the local economy. From 1653 to 1656, 42 percent of Corwin's clients paid for goods in some form of livestock, be it beef, pork, bacon, or live cows and hogs. Another 47 percent did so in grain, including Indian corn, wheat, oats, and rye. Corwin found a ready market for all of these goods in Barbados, which was now deeper into the process of transforming its economy into a model of monocultural production. Dairy and brewing products also offered acceptable returns, capable as they were of finding a market in another town or a nearby region. Twenty-eight percent of Corwin's 132 clients, in fact, at some point made returns in dairy products, while 19 percent paid in barley, malt, or fresh beer. Within accounts, these homegrown goods accounted for a substantial percentage of returns. In accounts in which they appeared, dairy products constituted 45 percent of returns; beer, 50 percent; and livestock, 48 percent. Interestingly, the products that would later become central to the colony's economic growth were largely absent in Corwin's accounts. Only 1 percent of his returns were in fish, and 3 percent were in timber (table 6.2).

TABLE 6.3 Selected purchases in the George Corwin account sample, 1652–1657

Patron	Total items	Textiles	Manufactures	Groceries
Tho Cromwell	29	16	9	4
John Herbert	8	4	3	1
Ezekial Rogers	4	3	1	0
Mr. Hubert	3	2	1	0
Francis Lawes	8	2	6	0
John White	14	2	8	4
John Barton	5	3	1	1
Daniel Epps	6	2	3	1
Henry Cook	5	1	2	2
Mr. Earos	4	3	0	1
Rich. Johnson	4	3	0	1
Joseph Jencks	26	8	13	5
Joseph Rowell	3	1	0	2
John Barton	3	1	1	1
Zack. Harrick	3	1	2	0
Tho Putnam	39	18	11	10
Isaa Cummings	2	1	1	0
Neal Jewells	11	3	6	2
Sam Shattock	3	0	3	0
Nath. Pickman	31	8	11	12
Will Langley	3	1	2	0
John Beckett	34	12	10	12
Bray Williams	26	9	11	6
John Proctor	32	17	11	4
Mr. Perkins	12	1	9	2

Source: Data are based on the George Corwin Account Book, 1651–1656, in George Corwin's Letters, Bills, Ledgers and Day Books, 1651–1684, The Phillips Library, Peabody Essex Museum, Salem, MA.

Not only did Corwin rely heavily on goods central to the functioning of the Bay Colony but he routinely recycled these goods back into its economy. Corwin's clients relied on him for imported textiles and manufactured goods, but occasionally (18.8 percent of the time) they called on him for provisions produced by neighbors. Nathanial Putnam appears in

TABLE 6.4 Prices and interest charged by George Corwin on selected goods, 1653–1656

Commodity	Price/date in account	Price/date in probate	Percent markup
Indian corn	3s./bu. (Dec. 1655)	2.2s./bu. (Nov. 1654)	27
Wheat	5s. 6d./bu. (Dec. 1655)	4s./bu. (Nov. 1654)	27
Malt	5s. 2d./bu. (Apr. 1656)	4.5s./bu. (July 1656)	10
Brandy	2s. 6d./qt. (Nov. 1655)	2s./qt. (July 1661)	20
Cotton	3s. 9d./yd. (June 1654)	2s. 6d./yd. (Oct. 1654)	33
Stockings	2s. 6d./pair (Feb. 1654)	2s. 1d./pair (June 1654)	17
Lockrum	2s. 3d./yd. (Mar. 1654)	1s. 6d./yd. (June 1655)	33
Canvas	2s. 3d./yd. (Sept. 1655)	1s. 10d./yd. (Mar. 1655)	19
Gloves	2s. 4d./pair (May 1654)	1.3s./pair (Oct. 1654)	43
Serge	5s. 8d./yd. (Mar. 1654)	3s. 8d./yd. (Mar. 1654)	35
Holland	4s. 4d./yd. (Nov. 1653	4s./yd. (Oct. 1651)	8
Linsey-woolsey	4s./yd. (Feb. 1653)	3s. 5d./yd. (Oct. 1654)	15
Kersey	5s. 6d./yd. (Jan. 1653)	3s. 8d./yd. (Mar. 1654)	37

Sources: George Corwin Account Book, 1651–1656, in George Corwin's Letters, Bills, Ledgers and Day Books, 1651–1684, The Phillips Library, Peabody Essex Museum, Salem, MA; George F. Dow, ed., *The Probate Records of Essex County,* vol. 1, *1635–1674* (Salem, MA, 1916).

Corwin's accounts buying not just soap, buckram, and hooks but also malt and pork, goods he paid for with "work at Rittings," "carting of peas from Jeggles," and "work at house." Joseph Jencks, a blacksmith with little time to grow his own grain, relied on Corwin for "corn at Goodman Potter's" as well as shot, canvas, and tobacco. He balanced his account with the production of twenty-four hoes. Elias Stileman took from Corwin nails, liquor, silk, canvas, and a saw, as well as local goods such as corn and pork.[7] The conventional job description of the transatlantic merchant would soon exclude the role of redistributing goods locally, but in the 1650s such a task kept budding merchants such as Corwin attuned to the less sophisticated but equally important homegrown habits.

Corwin's personal relationships with his clients are difficult to decipher from his accounts (table 6.4). The profitability of those relationships, however, is more accessible. A rough price list indicates that Corwin's reliance on a wide scope of clients as his primary producers and consumers was a smart way to generate the capital necessary to ease his way into the export market. Corwin charged anywhere from 8 percent to 43 percent interest on his imports. His plans were to make money, expand, and focus on fish and timber exports. Using these tactics, it seems, he was well on his way.

CORWIN WOUND UP RICH, POWERFUL, AND DEEPLY INTEGRATED INTO the patterns of transatlantic trade. His future can be glimpsed thirty years later in the activity of his counterpart, a merchant named Philip English. Relentlessly, this wealthy Jersey immigrant exploited West Indian and English markets by selling New England commodities as the highest possible prices while buying West Indian and British goods at the lowest possible prices.[8] He enhanced his economic leverage through ownership of several large ships, shrewd management of a well-capitalized fishing operation, and ready access to wood suppliers, who perpetually remained in his debt.[9] English's shipping ledgers reveal his thorough incorporation into the Atlantic trade, providing insight into the sort of economic world that merchants were constructing at the time.

A representative transaction with Josiah Wilcott captures the flavor of an established merchant's work. In the mid-1680s, in preparation for a West Indies voyage, English bought from Wilcott "a barrell of porke," "a quarter of beefe," "31 quintals of merchantable cod," "37 lbs. of bolte rope," "20 quintals of merchantable cod," "10 dozen of mackrill hooks," "3 barrells of tare," "329 foot of board," and, along with a few shipping provisions, "2 bundells of shingells." In return for these exportable goods, he sold Wilcott a few spools of twine, "6 gallons of frate wine," a range of textiles, "coat buttons," "brest buttons," "rum," and "money paid." Although he does not mention it in this particular account, English frequently paid for exportable commodities with tobacco and molasses.[10] English, in short, tied Wilcott into a world of goods well beyond what the region had to offer.

As a powerful merchant, English was participating directly in the crux of the transatlantic economy, trucking consumer goods across cultural and geographical divides. In many ways he was the embodiment of late-seventeenth-century economic growth in colonial New England. Without a doubt, English and the few other merchants of his stature pried open and successfully exploited foreign markets and, in so doing, played pivotal roles in helping to incorporate Massachusetts into the growing transatlantic community. Export trading had been occurring sporadically since the first decade of settlement, but it was not until the last quarter of the century that it became systematized through the efforts of this merchant elite. Expanding trading contacts throughout the Atlantic world, negotiating English mercantile policy, grappling with the region's money-supply problems, and gradually securing political power, New England merchants achieved a veneer of occupational coherence that enabled them to assert collective dominance through the exportation of the region's rich natural resources. Through their efforts, Massachusetts Bay shifted, according to Bernard Bailyn, "from the parochialism of rural and Puritan New England to the cosmopolitanism of commercial Britain."[11]

But in the 1650s Corwin was a man still rooted in parochialism. If we are to understand Massachusetts's economic development, these roots matter. They remind us that the earliest moves into the Atlantic economy took place from the basis of a local economy that Massachusetts settlers had worked twenty-odd years to build and strengthen. The construction of this economy had been a massive undertaking, one that provided Puritans with a competent standard of living and the means to weather a severe depression. And now it was providing an entrepreneur like Corwin a starting point from which to do business. His roots in this world did more than keep Massachusetts tethered to its foundation in mixed agriculture. They also foreshadowed future growth. While men like English charged into foreign venues, the economic realm that once supported George Corwin so sturdily had no intention of fading into obscurity. Indeed, the established work of mixed farming and infrastructure building would continue to thrive as a major source of economic growth and social cohesion as the merchant elite consolidated its considerable power. These developments, moreover, would continue to be strongly interdependent.

This snapshot of Corwin's entrée into the export market reveals not so much a stark transition to a new kind of trade but rather a gradual movement into it. The fact that Corwin had to base so much of his transatlantic work on the local economy suggests that the presence of an established, economically viable, and socially cohesive community was an essential precondition for Massachusetts merchants who hoped to expand their work overseas. It is in light of this connection, moreover, that the supposed transition from "parochialism to cosmopolitanism" comes into question. Such a transition, after all, assumes that the local economy stagnated as export markets came to life. As we will see through a continued examination of the local economy during the second half of the century, nothing of the sort happened. English, Corwin, and their cohorts eventually disappeared into a new world, but the old world they left behind sustained them in their absence.

SEVEN

Economic Continuity and Its Contents

1660–1700

I N THE EARLY 1660S THE PURITAN EXPERIMENT WAS SHOWING SIGNS
of stress. Perhaps inevitably, the original communal covenant with God
weakened as successive generations born into a stable society replaced
a founding generation that had shaped that society in God's image. This
evolutionary change achieved revolutionary pitch with the Halfway Covenant, an expedient policy enacted by Congregational churches permit-
ting the children of baptized parents who were not members of the church
to be baptized. The press of population growth, increasing land scarcity,
and changing economic opportunities further threatened the opportunity
to pursue traditional mixed farming, thus opening fissures for the kind
of local diversification that allowed a merchant like Corwin to thrive. It
would seem appropriate, given these overt challenges to the founding
goals and given the role that merchants were coming the play in the local
economy, to describe this moment in time as the start of the region's declension from communalism to protocapitalism, provincialism to sophistication, and Puritanism to the ways of the secularized Yankee.[1]

The jeremiads of the day provide shrill evidence that such a decline
was underway. John Higginson ranted about "that woful neglect of the
Rising Generation which hath bin among us," noting that they represented
"a sad sign that we have in great part forgotten our *Errand* into this wilderness." Increase Mather leveled his ire against the consuming habits
enervating this "rising generation" when he harangued his congregation,
"What shall we say when men are seen in the Streets with monstrous and
horrid *Perriwigs,* and Women with their *Borders* and *False Locks* and such
like whorish Fashion, whereby the anger of the Lord is kindled against this
sinful Land!" The once covenanted pattern of life, as Higginson saw it, was
"*backsliding indeed.*" Eleazer Wheeler summed it up best when he nostalgically evoked the founding generation as a people who had built a soci-

ety in which there was "Less Trading, Buying, Selling, but more Praying, more watching over our own hearts, more close walking." The ministers, for their part, seemed perfectly assured of declension's cause, and they minced few words in making their thoughts widely known.[2]

But while men such as George Corwin were ushering Massachusetts merchants headlong into the transatlantic world, persistent Puritans were hardly fading into obscurity or undergoing a deleterious transition to capitalism. To the contrary, they evolved in their own way, becoming modestly more commercial while preserving as best they could their traditional social stability. The account books of three commercial farmers and two manufacturers collectively show how the Massachusetts Bay region's development followed an internal logic of its own during the second half of the century. It was a logic, moreover, entirely consistent with the motivations that enabled Puritan pioneers to build an infrastructure, establish networks of local exchange, supply the ironworks, and help a man such as George Corwin achieve prominence in the external market. With the fundamental infrastructure of the local economy now set, these men could trade more systematically and more aggressively than ever before. Their decisions, forged in the nooks and crannies of local exchange, both perpetuated and refined an economic culture that continued to accomplish what Massachusetts's Puritans had been accomplishing for decades—namely, providing for themselves, their communities, and their region's economic health. Seeking profits in the provincial context of the local market, these men also helped forge an economic mentality that was neither purely capitalistic nor purely subsistence in orientation. Instead, it was one that reflected the kind of modest drive for wealth appropriate for a community that continued to remain remarkably cohesive even as merchants pulled it in a new direction. Localism, in essence, not only reinforced the merchants' ties to the provincial economy but reinforced the traditional habits that had tempered that economy from the outset.

For commercial farmers, occupational flexibility and regular access to a wide range of products were the essential prerequisites for participation in local economic affairs. Throughout the seventeenth century and well into the eighteenth, the Massachusetts Bay region's economy demanded that participants maintain the ability to acquire several commodities and perform several services on command. While most Puritans continued to see themselves as pursuing a special calling, the increasingly complex task of doing local business in Massachusetts required proficiency in a range of seasonal employments that stressed occupational fluidity as much as com-

TABLE 7.1   Overview of the transactions of Pickering, Burnham, and Barnard, 1684–1700

Trader	Transactions	Local trades	Overseas trades	Cash exchanges	Clients
John Pickering, Salem	367	296 (81%)	38 (10%)	33 (9%)	17
John Burnham, Ipswich	909	720 (79%)	145 (16%)	44 (5%)	61
John Barnard, Andover	804	600 (74%)	125 (16%)	79 (10%)	89

Sources: John Pickering Account Book, 1684–1716, Bartholomew Browne Account Book (sample included August 1698–July 1699), John Burnham Account Book, 1698–1700, John Barnard Account Book, John Flint Account Book, 1679–1684, and Richard Hobart Account Book, 1699–1701, all in The Phillips Library, Peabody Essex Museum, Salem, MA; Jacob Adams Account Book, 1673–1693, and John Pearson Account Book, 1674–1799, Pearson Family Papers, both in Baker Library, Harvard Business School, Boston, MA.

mitment to a single trade. Thus, while this emerging economy was rewarding narrow specialization on the part of a few powerful merchants, it was also encouraging broad diversification on the part of commercial farmers and local manufacturers. Residents remained intent on developing trading relationships with neighbors whose particular set of supplies and demands complemented their own. This less accessible (and thus less explored) aspect of the local economy must be confirmed in abstruse, torn, and water-damaged account books. But the search is well worth it, because in the end a sustained investigation of these accounts underscores the critical role played by men and women who were doing much more than stagnating on the colonial periphery or reorienting their economic lives around the growing export economy. Puritan pioneers, in other words, were continuing to shape economic development from the tried-and-true perspective of their local venues.

Thousands of accounts reveal the economic diversification practiced by individuals engaged in internal exchange (table 7.2). John Pickering, a Salem farmer, offers an excellent example of this diversity. He possessed a substantial amount of land adorned with several barns, an extensive garden, an orchard with a cider mill, a pasture in the "South Field," advanced husbandry instruments, and extra land bordering a sawmill.[3] His farm in many ways embodied the Puritan quest for self-sufficiency, local trade, and the ability to reach foreign markets whenever the opportunity arose.

TABLE 7.2 Diversity and proportion of goods (in percentages) exchanged by Pickering, Burnham, and Barnard, 1684–1700

Trader	Meat	Grain	Wood	Textiles	Manufactures	Service/labor	Money	Dairy	Miscellaneous
John Pickering, Salem	18	14	8	8	6	25	8	3	10
John Burnham, Ipswich	5	38	7	7	2	18	4	1	18
John Barnard, Andover	5	20	0.6	12	6	39	9	0.2	8.2

Sources: John Pickering Account Book, 1684–1716 (miscellaneous items include oil, lime, molasses, tobacco, land, powder, bricks, hay, and salt), John Burnham Account Book, 1698–1700 (miscellaneous items include molasses, sugar, rum, tobacco, fish, turnips, apples, rosin, a dog, lime, oil, mustard seed, salt, beans, flax seed, and vinegar), and John Barnard Account Book, 1688–1700 (miscellaneous items include salt, turnips, cider, apples, tallow, tobacco, butter, powder bricks, wine, onions, peas, sugar, oil, and hay), all in The Philips Library, Peabody Essex Museum, Salem, MA.

Although it never made him rich, his work was ceaseless and moderately profitable.

The range of Pickering's productive operations is on vivid display in the list of goods he sold to John Hovey in the years 1686–89: lamb, mutton, pork, timber, corn, money, butter, cheese, sweet oil, and a 150-pound hog.[4] His access to a variety of domestically produced goods and natural resources enabled him to acquire products locally that he would otherwise have had to import. It also permitted him to hire skilled labor for tasks that he had neither the time nor equipment to perform on his own. He sold Eleazer Keafer, a Salem neighbor, cow hides, beef, corn, and lime in return for shoes that Keafer made and several pieces of leather that he tanned.[5] Pickering provided John Harvey, a carpenter, with wood, beef, and money in exchange for Harvey's work on framing his house, building a barn, and hauling the timber required for these projects. Over a four-year period, Pickering sold Manassah Marsten bricks, hay, lamb, wood, and mutton in exchange for Marsten's making "shoes for my horse," "mending a hook and putting a link into a chaine," and "mending one plow halter" and for "one plowshare and bolter for horse plow." John Neale cobbled eight pairs of shoes for Pickering in the years 1686–88, for which Pickering returned money, pork, mutton, and cheese. Pickering's far-reaching domestic resources also provided him regular access to unskilled labor. Between 1687 and 1692, Ephriam Kempton and his sons worked twenty-seven days on Pickering's farm, for which Pickering compensated them with the use of his oxen to haul hay, corn, and wood off their own Salem farm.[6] Such exchanges were standard in this relatively small but highly commercialized local economy.

Pickering's relationships with his clients typically extended over the course of several years. They could, however, be fleeting and comparatively isolated in nature, executed only to fulfill a short-term need. On May 4, 1690, he sold Samual Ingersoll 3s. worth of wood, a peck of salt, and seven pounds of pork. A few days later, Ingersoll paid Pickering in five full days of work. It appeared to be the start of a fruitful relationship, but for reasons unknown their account abruptly and permanently closed. During the same year, George Ingersoll bought wood, money, and veal from Pickering in exchange for eight and a half days of work. During the summer of 1684 Pickering purchased five days of labor and about £2 in money from Salem's John Marsten. In January and February 1684 he paid Marsten with ten shipments of Indian corn. These accounts did not drag on for years, as many did, but served an immediate need and ended. Such relatively quick and discrete exchanges, while not typical, were critical in keeping the internal economy humming at full tilt.[7]

Access to a diversity of locally demanded commodities systematized John Barnard's trading habits as well. His account with the couple Frances and Alice Faulkner, his Andover neighbors, lasted more than five years and comprised several hundred transactions, almost all of them involving goods and services that were locally produced and consumed. Barnard provided the Faulkners with Indian corn, wheat, rye, malt, "wool from Ipswich," hay, sheepskins, apples, dung, and a variety of farming and transportation services. Alice Faulkner, in turn, met the bulk of Barnard's textile needs by "making John's coat," "by my Jackit and britches," "by making three kersey jackits," "by making John's waist coat," and by producing many other textiles.[8] The Faulkner account highlights just how tight reciprocal exchanges could be. Barnard hired Frances Faulkner to clear and sow fields and then turned around to sell him milled corn and rye harvested from those same fields. Faulkner, who owned a press, sold Barnard cider for the apples that Barnard had grown in his orchard. Barnard would regularly sell Faulkner wool that he had either sheared from his own sheep or bought in Ipswich. In return, Barnard would buy from Faulkner shirts, pants, and jackets. Faulkner would also do the dirty work of slaughtering Barnard's livestock, then purchase cuts of veal, mutton, pork, lamb, and beef after the slaughter. This tight reciprocity appears in other accounts as well. Barnard, for example, sent several bushels of barley to a trading partner who lived in Bradford, who paid him with a few bushels of malt.

Barnard's other transactions were less directly reciprocal, but they still revolved around the effort to merge local supply and demand. For five bushels of corn, Job Tyler sold Barnard seventy-five pounds of beef, wove thirty yards of cloth, and paid 12s. in money. This exchange was their only recorded transaction. Internal trade depended not only on the presence of internal demand but also on the timing of that demand. Barnard credited Joseph Lovejoy for "mending one day and making hay, by carting 2 loads of hay, by one day of his man," and "by fencing at meadow."[9] Later that year, Barnard paid Lovejoy by "mowing" and "by fencing at the meadow." One might wonder why these men did not just fence their own fields or why Barnard both sold and bought beef. The answer involves timing. When the demand arose—when the fence crumbled or the beef supply diminished—Barnard had already invested his labor, goods, and time in other endeavors. He needed the help of a neighbor then and there. In an economic environment lacking extensive slave or servant labor, indepen-

31

Thomas Abbott Dr

By 1 day of himself & 2 oxen
drawing Rails & Railes
Cr. 4 = 6 pay — 0 = 4 = 6

Dr to pt of his Rate 701. — 0 = 1 = 0
To a pitch of malt land
By Corn — — — 0 = 1 = 0
I allow'd ye malt for damage
done in — her ford by my cattle
June '03

1700 Ephraim Harnum Cr

By Carting 2 Load of Hay . 0 = 5 = 0.
By Carting 1 Load — 0 = 3 = 0
By 1 day in ybr mowing bushes 0 = 1 = 6
rainy pt of ye day
Cr . 2 . 4 . of an old account . 2 = 9
7 ! 2

100 700. Reck'd wth the Epthr. Harnut and due
to me — 2 = 2

Cr By 7 Rod ½ 2 Rail fence — 7 = 6
By 12 Rod of 4 Rail fence 1 = 1 = 0.
To his Corn Rate 7 at — 0 = 6 = 4.
To 1 Bushll corn 3 preston 0 = 3 = 0
To 2 Bushll Corn per Thomas 0 = 6 = 0
Harnum p ye order —
To his Rate 702 — 0 = 7 = 0
To James Ingalls Rate p 0 = 6 = 0
Order
Reckoned wth Epthr. Harnut 15 10th 702
due to him — in pay — 0 = 8 = 0
1704 By Carting 2 Load Hay — 0 = 8 = 0

Page from personal account book of John Barnard. (Photograph courtesy Peabody Essex Museum) dent farmers frequently found themselves fixing one another's fences and selling one another beef in the same month or even the same week. This cooperation was, of course, both neighborly and self-interested, although few would have thought to parse the distinction.

Barnard's economic activity covered a broad gamut of goods, services, and markets. The bulk of his activity, however, involved trading grain. He specialized in selling small amounts of grain locally in exchange for services that both improved his Andover farm and processed its diverse products for sale in regional markets. He cultivated wheat, Indian corn, rye, hops, and barley, selling these goods for services that included carting posts for fences, making plow yokes, carting loads of hay, having hundreds of bricks made, repairing barns, drawing timber, dressing flax, malting barley, carting apples, and even "making the tobacco garden." He often relied on informal business partnerships in order to improve his access to requisite farm improvements. He paid "for quarter part of an ox," which he and three of his clients shared for plowing usage. When the ox ran out of steam, they killed it and divvied up the hide. "Due to me a quarter of the hide," Barnard dutifully noted in the margin of his small, worn leather book.[10]

John Burnham, a third commercial farmer who left detailed records, undertook transactions that further reveal the inner logistics of the local economy. Burnham, like his contemporaries, wore many hats. Surviving records refer to him as a carpenter and a husbandman; deeds confirm his ownership of a gristmill on the Chebacco River; his uncle had an interest in a sawmill; and his will lists marsh and meadow ground, several houses and barns, carpentry items, utensils, husbandry tools, extensive livestock holdings, and horses.[11] Burnham regularly tapped his diverse resources to acquire necessary household goods and to improve the productive capability of his farm. Selling primarily grain, timber, and processed wood, he obtained shoes, cotton, wool, fish, cider, clothes, hides, iron, and all sorts of farm labor. Burnham was no budding merchant. He operated within his provincial economic loop and thrived, however humbly.

Burnham's transactions responded to neighbors whose economic arrangements generated their own specific needs. In the years 1700–1704 Burnham sold Nathanial Perkins, an Ipswich weaver with little time to keep up with farming duties, 15.5 bushels and 3 pecks of corn, 6.5 bushels of barley, 10 sheep, 9 lambs, a pair of oxen, hay, a pound of wood, and a pound of tobacco. He also provided several services, including "tending the cows two days at Ipswich," "a horse for two days," and "shoes mended."

Burnham sold the Ipswich yeoman John Smith hay, corn, wood, and a cow, in addition to providing services such as "fetching hay" and "cutting and drawing wood." To another local farmer he sold turnips and barley.[12]

Burnham had a knack for finding local markets for raw timber and processed wood. Exploiting his access to a sawmill, he sold hundreds of boards, shingles, and raw wood to several small farmers and artisans throughout Ipswich and neighboring towns. To John Whipple, an Ipswich joiner, he provided 198 feet of "sawen boards" in November 1697 and 398 feet more the following June. Nathanial Rust, also of Ipswich, purchased small parcels of wood from Burnham on twenty-two occasions from April 1703 to October 1705. Burnham's accounts mention Thomas Perrin, a Rowley farmer, for owing him "logs sawn at my mill," as well as "1000 foot pine boards, 1438 hemlock boards, 608 pine boards sawen," and "1319 pine boards sawen." Ipswich's blacksmith, Isaac Littlehale, made three visits to Burnham in the years 1692–94 for "407 foot boards, 304 boards and 9 slabs, and 308 foot boards."[13] These transactions hardly made up the bulk of Burnham's exchanges; rather, they were just one critical element in his diverse cache of economic resources.

While wood processing remained vital to Burnham's economic activity, the majority of his trades involved grain. In this endeavor, as in others, Burnham consciously oriented his transactions according to patterns of local demand. Growing his own grain and acquiring it from other commercial farmers, he maintained inventories throughout the year and unloaded them during times of heightened demand. He sold timber, labor, domestic goods, transportation services, and processed wood in order to obtain not only household necessities but also hundreds of bushels of recently reaped grain. He would then wait until the spring and early summer, when most farmers had run low, to unload his inventory. Forty-five percent of his corn transactions occurred in March through June, a time when internal demand would have peaked. On the other end of the agricultural year, 36 percent of his grain transactions occurred from November to February, when he purchased corn from local farmers. The summer months, however, accounted for only 13 percent of his corn transactions. A similar trend occurred with Indian corn. Forty-seven percent of his Indian corn transactions took place in March through June, when he sold scores of bushels locally. Another 36 percent of his Indian corn trades transpired from November to February, when Burnham bought the corn off a relatively well supplied market. Only 14 percent of his Indian corn transactions occurred in July through October (table 7.3). These patterns were not

TABLE 7.3 Monthly breakdown of John Burnham's grain transactions, March 1698–February 1699

Date	Corn/wheat	Indian corn/meal	Barley/malt
1698			
March	21 (10%)	9 (10%)	3 (6%)
April	17 (8%)	18 (19%)	7 (13%)
May	35 (17%)	7 (8%)	6 (11%)
June	32 (15%)	10 (11%)	8 (15%)
July	7 (3%)	8 (9%)	4 (8%)
August	7 (3%)	2 (2%)	1 (2%)
September	6 (3%)	1 (1%)	12 (23%)
October	8 (4%)	2 (2%)	6 (11%)
November	19 (9%)	3 (3%)	3 (6%)
December	17 (8%)	11 (12%)	2 (4%)
1699			
January	20 (10%)	12 (13%)	1 (2%)
February	20 (10%)	8 (9%)	0 (0%)

Source: John Burnham Account Book, 1698–1700.

random; profit obviously remained a driving goal. It was profit, however, that was kept in check by the fact that he depended on neighbors as much as they did on him.

Burnham, finally, did not record prices with enough consistency to construct a comprehensive price list, but a scattering of corn prices supports the economic motivation underlying his grain transactions. From December 1704 to May 1705 (with March being the start of a new calendar year) Burnham recorded enough prices to reveal his strategy for buying and selling corn. In December 1704 and February 1705 he bought corn for 2s. 6d. a bushel. The next month, March 1705, he turned around and sold corn at 2s. 8d. a bushel. The rate rose until the fall harvest, when Burnham started to buy again. In May 1705 Burnham was selling at 3s. a bushel; in June sales dropped slightly to 2s. 9d. a bushel; but by September 1705 the price had returned to 3s. a bushel.[14] This evidence indicates that Burnham traded corn as a local commodity while paying very close attention to levels of local supply and demand. Again, he sought a modest profit in a local setting, and as far as we can tell, he attained it.

This selection of 2,080 transactions executed by Pickering, Barnard, and Burnham during the last quarter of the seventeenth century confirms the ongoing importance of internal demand in shaping the course of economic development. More than three-quarters of their transactions involved the internal trade of goods that were produced and consumed in a local economic context. Historians have traditionally explained the evolution of family farms in terms of either their orientation to overseas markets or their immediate subsistence needs. However, these farmers show that daily economic decisions were profit oriented (to a degree), while adhering to the continuing demand of local residents.

EARLY MANUFACTURING EFFORTS IN COLONIAL MASSACHUSETTS HAVE unfortunately been associated with the region's earliest industrial failure. One major problem with the Lynn Ironworks, as we have seen, was the disconnection between the modest size of the market it served and its investors' bloated expectations for returns. In the simplest terms, the labor, capital, and transportation capabilities were not adequate to serve extralocal markets on a regular basis. Future ironworks, however, avoided this mistake. Exploiting the extensive bogs throughout the Massachusetts Bay, resident entrepreneurs established successful, relatively small ironworks operations in Taunton, Raynham, North Saugus, Rowley, and Braintree in the period 1653–70. These furnaces quickly became fixtures of the landscape and, unlike the initial endeavor, served local markets exclusively, some well into the nineteenth century.[15]

Salisbury's Richard Hobart built a blacksmithing business around these industries. According to a surviving two-year account of his operation, he spent the bulk of his time acquiring iron locally, transforming it into much-needed cooking, farming, and building implements, and selling these items within Salisbury and to neighboring towns. The patterns of his work—which are in accord with the agricultural work of Pickering, Burnham, and Barnard—can be reconstructed from his books (table 7.4).

Hobart's initial concern was raw material. From January 1699 to May 1701, Hobart made sixteen purchases totaling more than 6,128 pounds of iron for £78 3s. 9d. He acquired iron from men whose lucrative transatlantic operations financed their investments in local furnaces. His primary supplier, for example, was Ipswich's Isaac Appleton. Appleton's father had inherited from Boston's John Paine a large share in the Lynn Ironworks. After the ironworks collapsed, Appleton found himself in possession of the furnace's liquidated assets, including extensive operating equipment

1700

Ralph Harnum cr 32.

By Reaping one day)
To his Corn Rate (700) — ; — 0 = 6 = 4
To his mony Rate — — 0 = 3 — 2
By a fence at ye meadow 12 a Rod 0 — 12 — 0
To a Bushell of Rye — — — 0 = 4 — 0.

1701 Ralph Harnum Dr
To his Corn Rate 1701 — — 0 = 6 = 6.
By Dressing 7¼ of flax — 0 = 2 = 5
By Swingling 6 ¾ of flax)
which was broke before — ; — 0 — 1 = 7½
by dressing ¼ of flax r¼ — 0 — 2 = 4
By swingling ¼ of flax 15¾ — 0 = 3 — 9
By dressing ¼ r¾ of flax — — 0 — 3 — 7
By dressing ¼ — — — 0 — 6 — 6
by 4 swinglings — — — 0 — 1 — 0
J = 1 = 2

John Lovejoy cr

1700. By Reaping one day — 0 = 3 = 4
Dr To his Corn Rate 700 — 0 = 1 — 0
To his mony Rate — —
By 1 days work in March —
his he pay his mony Rate to
him Alcott
and I pay Hooker ofgood 2 u pay for J. Lovjoy

William Lovjoy cr

1700. By mowing & making 5 Load ½ of Hay
Aug. By 1 days work mowing Bushes
0 = 16 — 6.
To his Corn Rate — — 0 = 16 — 6

701 By 1 day in Aprill — —
By mowing & making 5 Load & ½ of hay.
By mowing & Making 4 Load —
a part of a Load he by pay
By they day or Load. first J = 12. = 0
To his Rate 701 — — J = J = J
vera

TABLE 7.4   Richard Hobart's iron and coal purchases, January 1699–May 1701

Date	Amount	Cost	Rate
1699			
5 January	n.a.[a] (iron)	£4 3s. 4d.	n.a.
29 January	1,100 lb. (iron)	£12 13s. 0d.	£1 3s. 0d./100 lb.
10 February	n.a. (iron)	£12 0s. 3d.	n.a.
May	n.a. (coals)	£4	—
15 June	100 lb. (iron)	£2 7s. 0d.	£2 7s. 0d./100 lb.[b]
July	72 lb.	£1 0s. 0d.	£1 8s. 0d./100 lb.
25 July	511 lb. (iron)	£5 11s. 3d.	£1 3s. 0d./100 lb.
15 August	611 lb. (iron)	£7 3s. 6d.	£1 3s. 0d./100 lb.
15 August	1,020 lb. (iron)	£5 5s. 0d.[c]	£24/ton
15 August	3 chaldons (coal)	£1 15s. 0d.	—
September	52 lb. (iron)	n.a.	n.a.
4 November	n.a. (iron)	£9 2s. 3d.	£24/ton
1700			
23 March	1,016 lb. (iron)	£3 13s. 4d.[c]	£1 3s. 0d./100 lb.
25 June	116 lb. (iron)	£1 12s. 0d.	£1 8s. 0d./100 lb.
1 July	1,010 lb. (iron)	£11 0s. 10d.	£1 2s. 0d./100 lb.
1701			
29 May	520 lb. (iron)	£6 17s. 0d.	£1 6s. 0d./100 lb.

Source: Richard Hobart Account Book, 1699–1701.
[a]The abbreviation "n.a." indicates not listed at all or illegible.
[b]"To be paid in one month."
[c]Partial payment.

and thirty cords of wood. In 1676 he gave these "appertenances" to his son Isaac, who, in turn, used this material to begin a successful ironworks of his own in Rowley. While the records for this operation do not survive, it seems likely that Appleton financed the ironworks operation with assets generated from his extensive agricultural exports. However he did it, his relationship with Hobart remained strong enough for him to allow Hobart, who was a regular customer, to delay payments for several months without penalty.[16]

Hobart kept other operational costs comparatively low. Labor outlays remained minimal, as he generally worked alone. Throughout the course of two years he recorded only seven instances of hiring day labor, which he did for random jobs such as "boards and fetchin," "fetchin the ironwork," and the generic "for work." This cost him a total of £4 16s. 6d.[17] He valued his own labor at a relatively high 3s. per day.[18] On three occasions he paid rent for his blacksmith shop, but unfortunately he did not specify the rate.[19] Nevertheless, with ample raw material, a small investment in day labor, and a rented shop, Hobart was ready for business. He hammered out thousands of nails and at least 417 separate utensils, including plates, hoes, axes, spades, hinges, anchors, bellows, and pans. His position in the internal economy depended on the consistent production of these commodities for local consumption.[20] Over the course of three years he received more than £50 0s. 6d. in direct payment for these items, collecting payments in the form of money, book credits, and farm produce. When he listed the costs of manufactured goods, Hobart never recorded the specific form of payment he expected to receive. On several occasions, however, he noted payments as credits separate from the particular debited manufactured good. These recordings offer some insight into how his clients paid him for the goods he produced. In addition to cash and book credits, he received onions, shoes, salt, wheat, beer, glass, oil, lime, tobacco, fish, linen, wine, and bricks. These mostly locally produced items totaled a value exceeding £24 4s. 2d. Finally, and again separately from the costs listed for specific items, he collected payments of £13 6s. in the form of cash (see table 7.4).[21]

A wide range of financial arrangements suspended Hobart and his clients in an intricate web of debts and credits. On four occasions, for a total of £30, he took out loans from local residents in order to cover iron payments.[22] One of these, for £5, he paid back within a month, but the others he let sit on the books, never noting the interest rate. Modified installment plans and delayed payments also mark his accounts. After Hobart purchased £9 3s. 1d. worth of iron from a Mr. Jones in November 1699, he did not make his first payment until June 1700, when he tendered £4. He recorded a second payment, of £3, in July, and left £3 13s. 4d. on the books. By that point he had accumulated a sum of £1 10s. 3d. (14 percent interest) on his debt.[23] Typically, Hobart allowed his debtors to do the same. When Sam Stevens bought a thousand board nails, a hundred small board nails, and three hundred pans for £14 17s. 11d., for example, Hobart accepted payments in four installments.[24] These extensions, of course, meant that he too could collect interest, as emphasized by a "Mr. Willis's" debt increasing by 15 percent, from 13s. to 15s., over an undisclosed amount of time.[25] Finally, Hobart and some of his clients enjoyed discounts when they paid with cash. A 14s. payment to a "Ms. Wonsworth" on a £1 6s. 2d. debt "past due" dropped his balance to 9s. instead of 12s. 2d., a discount of just over 25 percent. These financial tactics served both client and producer well, and while they appear only sporadically within accounts, we can be sure, based on other accounts, that they were pervasive aspects of local economic life.

Although Hobart listed the dates of his transactions only 60 percent of the time, a seasonal pattern to his work schedule seems evident. Of the seventy-one transactions dated in his accounts, only eight took place during the planting months, two in April and three in May. During the November harvest period he recorded only four transactions. Forty percent of his work, in contrast, occurred in June (13 transactions) and July (15). Furthermore, because he specialized in producing farming implements, Hobart saw upswings in the months preceding planting and harvesting: 21 percent of his transactions took place during March and early October. This pattern of manufacturing activity responded to and accommodated the predominantly agricultural nature of Salisbury's economy and, as a result, helped Hobart and his neighbors produce and maintain the grain, cider, and livestock necessary for their livelihood.[26]

Hobart structured his business around his shop, his skill, local raw materials, a variety of financial arrangements, and the persistent local demand for manufactured items. Newbury's Jacob Adams similarly worked in a predominantly local venue and employed comparable financial strategies. A shoemaker, Adams quickly learned how to negotiate the circuitous contours of a local economy. For one, he recognized the supreme importance of tact when dealing with neighbors. Debts certainly could not go unanswered, but with neighbors being clients, cordial relations had to be maintained at all costs. Thus, when his neighbor fell behind on a debt for several pairs of shoes, Adams struggled to combine firmness and affection in a single missive, firing off this request to a man with whom he commonly traded: "Friend John Wither, my love to you[.] Wishing you much joy . . . but withall would have you to be honest and send money now by the carrier hereof, or else I shall put you to further trouble."[27] Awkward as the segue might have been, Adams at least tried to soften his demand in order to keep Wither as a future client and avoid a court battle. Clearly, though, he wanted his cash.

Such a concern mattered a great deal to Adams because, according to his sporadically kept account book, which he maintained from 1673

TABLE 7.5   A sample of Jacob Adams's raw-material purchases, February 1675–December 1676

Date	Goods purchased	Cost	Wholesaler
1675			
25 February	Leather	£2 14s. 0d.	John Sawyer (Rowley)
1676			
11 March	2 hides	£1 11s. 0d.	John Sawyer (Rowley)
21 April	2 hides	£1 2s. 0d.	John Sawyer (Rowley)
28 June	1 hide	16s.	John Sawyer (Rowley)
8 July	Leather	1s.	Jo. Robinson (Andover)
14 September	Leather	1s. 4d.	Jo. Robinson (Andover)
16 September	1 hide	10s.	John Sawyer (Rowley)
10 November	1 hide	19s.	John Sawyer (Rowley)
3 December	1 hide	17s.	John Sawyer (Rowley)

Source: Jacob Adams Account Book, 1673–1693.

to 1693, the vast majority of his clients were, like Wither, locals. Adams bought all of his raw materials, mainly leather and hides, from local suppliers and then sold the shoes that he manufactured from them back to clients who lived within a few miles of his shop. Of his ninety-eight clients, all but eight resided in Newbury or in a bordering town.[28] To the extent that his accounts allow us to capture them, his daily interactions with these men and women, his work patterns, and his financial arrangements lend further credence to the claim that economic development followed the pull of local demand rather than adjusting to meet the needs of merchants and the markets they hoped to reach.

Based on transactions recorded in 1675–76, a time for which his books appear to be the most complete, Adams made about nine purchases of hides or leather a year, spending a total of about £10 for these goods (table 7.5). In this particular year he bought most of his raw material from John Sawyer, a farmer who raised cattle in nearby Rowley. Over the years, however, he came to deal with other leather and hide wholesalers. In 1694, for example, he bought material from seven different men.[29] Leather and hides have a long shelf life, and ideally Adams would have bought in bulk. His purchasing schedule, however, suggests that he only acquired enough material to last a month or two. It is difficult to tell whether these limited, frequent purchases reflect a constricted supply or if Adams had limited credit with his wholesalers. Furthermore, like Hobart, Adams avoided dealing with wholesalers during the main planting and harvesting months, another indication of adherence to the regional economy's agricultural routines. Finally, Adams processed most of the raw materials himself; of his nine purchases in 1675–76, six were hides, while the others were leather, and his records mention nothing about working with a tanner.

The leather and hide purchases that Adams made in 1675–76 went directly into the sustained production of footwear. In the period from February 1675 to February 1676 he manufactured sixty pairs of shoes or boots, in addition to repairing dozens of others. Adams cobbled shoes into a diversity of styles and sizes. Customers enjoyed the option of purchasing shoes for children and adults, in sizes 1 through 13, and in styles such as "plain," "English heels," "French soled," or "rounded." Adams produced most of his shoes in April, December, and January. According to a 1675–76 production schedule that lists shop time and shoes produced, he made eight pairs of shoes in the "1st week of December," thirteen pairs during the second week, and eleven during the third week. In January he made eight pairs during week one, twelve in week two, six in week three ("4 days work"), and five during the fourth week ("3 days work"). Finally, in April of the same year he produced six pairs during the first week and another seven pairs during the third week.[30] Given that he sold a total of sixty pairs of shoes from February 1675 to February 1676, the production of seventy-six pairs of shoes in three months during 1675–76 suggests that Adams did indeed concentrate his production schedule into a few months rather than producing continuously throughout the year (table 7.6).

Unlike in Hobart's accounts, cash is rarely noted in Adams's records. We have already seen that he accepted returns in hides and leather, but the majority of payments were in the form of farm produce. Accounts capture clients paying for their shoes in turnips, cows, heifers, pigs, corn, oats, malt, and hemp. Occasionally, Adams's clients would work off their debts by performing farm labor and spinning or through trade in bolts of cloth, fishing equipment, or even a hat.[31] Somewhat curiously, though, throughout these scattered transactions neither "money" nor "cash" is ever mentioned. In many cases, however, Adams fails to indicate the precise form of payment offered. Conceivably, these unspecified transactions may have been in cash.

Adams did not limit his economic activity to shoemaking. He was the youngest of nine children, and by the time that he set up shop in 1673 he

Economic Continuity and Its Contents

TABLE 7.6 Jacob Adams's footwear production schedule, 1675–1676

Time period	Days worked	Items produced
1675		
1st week of December	—	1 pair of size 2, 1 pair of size 10, 1 pair of size 4, 1 pair of size 9, 1 pair of size 10 "English heels," 1 pair of French-heeled, 1 pair of size 11, 1 pair of size 8
2nd week of December	5	2 pairs of size 10, 1 pair of size 6, 4 pairs of size 8, 3 pairs of size 5 (1 rounded), 3 pairs of size 2 (1 with English heels)
3rd week of December	5	1 pair of size 6, 2 pairs of size 5, 1 pair of size 3, 1 pair of size 4, 1 pair of size 1, 1 pair of size 11, 4 pairs of size 10
1676		
1st week of January	4	2 pairs of size 2, 1 pair of size 12 with English heels, 1 pair of size 4, 2 pairs of pumps, 1 pair of size 8 with English heels, 1 pair of size 7
2nd week of January	7	2 pairs of size 2, 2 pairs of size 10 with English heels, 3 pairs of size 12 (1 with English heels), 3 pairs of size 6, 1 pair of size 8, 1 pair of size 7
3rd week of January	4	2 pairs of size 10 with English heels, 3 pairs of size 8 (1 with English heels), 1 pair of size 3 with English heels
4th week of January	3	1 pair of size 4, 1 pair of size 10, 1 pair of child's size 7, 1 pair of size 7 with English heels, 1 pair of size 3 with English heels
1st week of April	5	1 pair of size 11 [with rounded heels?], 1 pair of size 7 with English heels, 3 pairs of size 12, 1 pair of size 8 with English heels
3rd week of April	—	1 pair of size 10 with rounded heels, 2 pairs of size 12 (1 with English heels), 1 pair of size 8, 2 pairs of size 11 (1 with English heels, 1 pair of size 3
Total	>38	76 pairs

Source: Jacob Adams Account Book, 1673–1693.

was nineteen years old. His father had no land left to provide. Nevertheless, Adams managed to save enough to marry in 1677, acquire a small
piece of land, and start a family. From that land he and his wife harvested
and nurtured a variety of goods that he traded in the local market, including lamb, veal, barley, and turnips. Furthermore, like many of the traders
profiled above, Adams was never above leaving the shop and working off a
debt as a day laborer grubbing weeds in a neighbor's field. He even earned
credits for making and mending plows.[32]

But shoemaking dominated Adams's working life. Limited bits of evidence suggest the profitability of his highly demanded product. The price
of shoes varied widely according to size and style, but the average pair cost
about 5s. to 6s. For a brief period during unspecified years Adams recorded
the production cost—labor and raw materials—for the shoes he made.
The numbers reveal, however roughly, the difference between the market
and cost values of his product. Adams listed the cost of "cutting and making" a pair of size 11 shoes at 2s. A pair of size 6 shoes cost 1s. 9d. to produce; a pair of size 4 shoes, 1s. 6d.; and a pair of children's size 6 shoes, 1s.[33]
An overview of his sales in 1676 indicates that he occasionally sold shoes at
cost, as he did to John Kent, Simon Thurlow, and Samual Morse. The vast
majority of the time, though, Adams sold his shoes at a market value that
ensured him a gross profit of 4s. to 5s. per sale.

Adams's financial arrangements, finally, appear to have been fairly
basic. The most frequently employed strategy was the use of third-party
transactions. To cite a few examples, when Adams sold Rowley's Nathanial Brown meat, barley, and a pair of shoes, he accepted from Brown,
"in leu of corn," four bushels of malt "by Steven Michael." On May 13,
1676, he accepted Thomas Woodbridge's payment "for John Jones"; several
months later he recorded "Goodman Morris for Matthew Steward"; and
back when he worked as an apprentice, Adams had noted that he owed his
master 13s. that the master had paid to John Hale in Adams's name.[34] In a
provincial economy, such arrangements made the utmost sense.

These modest profits appear to have added up for Adams and his family. Existing records say nothing about Hobart's social and economic mobility. The course of Adams's career, however, showed modest progress.
Adams sold shoes regularly in Newbury until 1686, when, after inherit-
ing his father's house, he decided to liquidate his assets and relocate to
the frontier town of Suffield, in western Massachusetts. He continued his
trade there while also becoming a large landholder and setting his four
sons to farming patches of that land. By 1693 his situation had improved to

the extent that he was one of Suffield's two representatives to the General Court and "one of the most prominent and influential of the early settlers of Suffield."[35]

THE SECOND HALF OF THE SEVENTEENTH CENTURY WAS A TIME WHEN New England merchants like George Corwin and Philip English made authoritative moves into the transatlantic realm of trade. Consolidating economic and political power, these men were well on their way to mastering a diversified commerce in fish, timber, livestock, grain, whale products, and rum that would generate hundreds of thousands of pounds in profit every year. As the cases of Pickering, Barnard, Burnham, Hobart, and Adams show, however, not everyone gravitated toward the merchants' magnetic allure. These provincial farmers and manufacturers remained intricately tied to their communities while, at the same time, becoming increasingly interested in sophisticated commercial behavior. Lacking the transatlantic political and economic clout that helped merchants consolidate their authority, local traders worked to concentrate their own power locally, and the economic world they sustained and worked within on a daily basis was simply a more intense version of the one that Puritan pioneers had known from the earliest days of the colony's creation.

EIGHT

The Hidden Benefits of Local Trade

1675–1700

THE MOST BASIC ECONOMIC DECISIONS MADE BY MEN LIKE JOHN Burnham, John Pickering, John Barnard, Richard Hobart, and Jacob Adams might seem to be comparatively irrelevant in the grand scheme of the Bay Colony's economic growth. In reality, though, they decisively shaped the contours of the economy. The ongoing effort among commercial farmers and local manufacturers to produce and sell a wide range of goods and services fostered specific economic habits that had precedents in the Old World but were substantially altered in the New World. A pragmatic blend of tradition and modernity, these emerging habits helped accomplish the ongoing goal of establishing a stable colony and, in turn, a sound basis for the merchants' takeoff into foreign markets.

This accomplishment depended on the concrete economic strategies employed by local traders in the specific areas of transportation, financial arrangements, and familial cooperation. While merchants may have been gravitating toward foreign economic venues, which had less explicit use for the habits of Puritan life, the ongoing work undertaken by Puritan pioneers on their farms, in their shops, and in their communities supported the merchants' transition to the transatlantic culture that ministers feared would undermine local stability. Local trade, in short, fostered the economic and infrastructural stability that launched the region into international markets. For this reason alone the accounts of local farmers need to be further explored. Only then can the hidden benefits of local economic exchange, benefits that formed the basis of market activity, become clear.

WHEN A RUDIMENTARY INFRASTRUCTURE FINALLY CAME TOGETHER, access to transportation resources remained a critical element of local economic life. At the very least, every commercial farmer's ability to trade diverse goods and services in diverse settings remained directly dependent on his mobility. By the last quarter of the seventeenth century the once treacherous task of transporting commodities and labor throughout the Bay Colony had eased considerably. Previous generations of settlers had established a solid infrastructure based in part on roads, carts, oxen, ferries, and horses. With this fundamental blueprint in place, and with a settlement society gradually yielding to a more commercially active local environment, enterprising farmers engaged in the routines of local trade further improved the region's transportation capabilities. Pickering, Barnard, and Burnham offer clear cases in point, as they were especially eager to apply substantial resources toward moving goods and services throughout the region. For each trader, a large minority of service transactions involved transportation-related spending. For Pickering, 30 percent of his service transactions involved transportation-related spending; for Burnham, 34 percent; and for Barnard, 23 percent. A close look at these transportation transactions highlights the more precise nature of their exchanges, revealing the economic connections that existed among farmers and traders trying to move goods and services from one farm to another.[1]

Mobility may have been a commercial farmer's most pressing preoccupation. Pickering's business relied heavily on providing and obtaining the ability to move small loads of goods over short distances. In the mid-1680s Pickering charged John Hovey for "dredging 30 foot of timber out of the woods" and Eleazer Keafer for "dragging one load of hay to the south field" in Salem.[2] Later in that decade he billed Ephriam Kempton for "fetching 2 loads of corn out of south field," "draying one load of salt and hay out of south field," and "draying a load of hay and sticks out of south field."[3] We find him delivering "one bu barley . . . to William Harris" on shoemaker John Neale's account, "drawing one load of rye" for his brother William, and delivering "2 cheeses" to Charles Macarter.[4] Consistent with the reciprocal nature of local trade, Pickering purchased transportation services as often as he provided them. In typical exchanges, he credited John Trenchman for bringing him a servant from Rowley and charged John Harvey for "hauling my timber."[5] Such transactions occurred daily, if not hourly, and necessarily demanded a high level of social interaction among farmers, who desperately needed one another's goods and services in order to stay in business.

Burnham and Barnard similarly invested time and resources in acquiring and distributing transportation services. Burnham paid residents for "going and fetch[ing] iron work," "fetching rails at waterside up to his house," and "fetching hay at Mr. Coswell's for Cousin Smith," for "flakes fetched by water from William Batters," and for "10 cords of wood carted."[6] He tapped his own transportation resources when he "delivered to Mr. Bills a bushel of corn on Joseph's account" and sent "2 bu corn on Wm. Haskells account."[7] John Barnard, in an effort to keep his livestock fed and penned, paid local residents on a number of occasions for jobs such as "to cart posts and hay" and "moving poles for a fence."[8] While these choices were small ones, they added up to big results as the accumulation of neighbors' individual decisions made basic movement easier to achieve.

In addition to shuffling goods and services between farms, commercial farmers greased the wheels of regional transportation through the frequent leasing and trading of transportation equipment. Maintaining a spare team of oxen proved to be a boon in a local economy where ownership of such animals was hardly universal. John Burnham regularly capitalized on the local demand for his oxen teams. He charged Robert Annable, his Ipswich neighbor, for "a pair of oxen a day and a half" and, during May planting, "a pair of oxen a day." While employing his son to build a sloop, Burnham provided him with ten days "work with a team" in order to haul the requisite materials to the shipyard.[9] Salem's Samuel and William Giddings frequently contacted Burnham for oxen rentals. Burnham consistently listed his prices for this service; he usually charged 6s. a day, but he sometimes adjusted his price to reflect market conditions. For example, in February 1699 he charged Samuel Giddings 6s. a day for his team. In March, however, when demand for a team to pull a plow would have been considerably higher, he raised his rate to 8s. a day.[10] By November it was back to 6s. Prices rebounded when Burnham leased out human labor along with the oxen, as he did when he charged William Giddings "1 day work with a team and David" and another client for "clay carted by my team and sons."[11] Although the local infrastructure was in place, the logistics of taking advantage of that infrastructure were anything but. The impulse to gouge neighbors in need of transportation services would have been severely tempered, however, by the fact that these men were highly dependant on one another on a daily basis for a variety of goods and services. Economically speaking, what went around was sure to come around. Residents needing a horse or cart to move their goods locally behaved with this interdependency in mind.

John Barnard also capitalized on his oxen supply but, like his colleagues, found it necessary to supplement it during particularly demanding periods of the year. For Frances Faulkner, whose household sewed all of Barnard's clothes, he provided "my oxen one day to cart dung." On another occasion, however, he turned to Faulkner for "his oxen to sled 8 load," thus confirming the common habit among farmers to both buy and sell goods and services they might already possess but were otherwise using. Such reciprocity appeared again in a later Faulkner account, with Barnard recording "by my oxen one day" followed in close succession by "to his oxen one day."[12] This situation prevailed with other clients too. Barnard debited William Blunt for "one day of John and the team to draw loggs I finding one yoke of oxen" but had paid Henry Chandler for "one day of himself, team, and boys to draw stones" just a year earlier.[13] Hooker Osgood further served Barnard "by one day of himself and team to cart bricks" and "1 day of himself, oxen to cart dung."[14] These exchanges kept people, goods, and services in close proximity as they went about the process of making the environment yield a decent standard of living without unduly exploiting each other in the process.

Horses were equally integral to local transportation capabilities, and commercial farmers leased and traded them frequently. John Burnham recorded credits for "Nathanial, horse for one day" and, to an Ipswich weaver, "a horse for two days." Barnard, as he did with oxen, both leased out horses and rented them from others for his own use. Thus, he paid his most active trading partner, Frances Faulkner, 2s. for "2 journeys of his horse to Salem," and shortly after this transaction he recorded "by a journey of himself to Salem village [with] my horse," "to my horse for Alice [Faulkner] to go to Salem village and another journey to bring her home," and "my horse for Thom[as] [Faulkner] to go to Salem." John Flint frequently leased his horses in order to supplement his provisioning service. Accounts reveal him leasing to a Mr. Taley "my horse to Marblehead" and, a week later, "my horse to Nimisemet."[15]

Obtaining carts and maintaining transportation equipment required constant attention. Burnham often leased out his cart when he arranged for others to move his goods, which on one particular occasion forced him to hire Abraham Martin for "5 days work on cart." Barnard continued to tighten his reciprocal trading arrangement with Faulkner when he credited him for "making John's cart—2 days" and then rented one from Faulkner "to cart hay from the meadow and his [Barnard's] cart to cart hay out of the swamp." He frequently dealt in the accessories that linked cart and horse, such as when he bought "a yoke and wooden bolt" from Ezekial Osgood, sold Salem's "Mr. West" a "saddle and a bridle" and Newbury's Benjamin Coker "a bridle without bits." Robert Hobart, the Salisbury blacksmith, sold a neighbor "a guilded saddle" and a bridle in 1700. In the years

1684–86 Manassah Marsten fit Pickering's horses with 17 shoes, in addition to "straitening horse shoes," "mending a plow halter," and making a "bolter for [a] horse plow."[16] Pickering's trade both inspired and depended on Marsten's work, bringing them into the kind of codependent economic relationship that such trades made commonplace in a local commercial environment.

While most recorded transactions among these commercial farmers involved moving goods and services between farms or obtaining and repairing the equipment with which to do so, several exchanges demonstrate the regularity with which traders moved goods to processing centers and markets. Barnard's records, perhaps because of his relative isolation in Andover, are especially useful in this regard, confirming the connections between transportation access, participation in the local market, and personal interaction. Barnard placed an order with Alice Faulkner for a waistcoat and britches, while lending her a horse on two occasions to "bring wool from Ipswich." The immediate demand for fish and pork remained constant in Essex County, and Barnard arranged on two occasions for residents to bring him salt from Salem, one a bushel and the other a barrel. Barnard paid his brother Stephen for "corn sold at Salem" on five occasions during a single year, noting "2 1/2 bu corn for the carrier." He also credited Henry Chandler 8s. for "carrying in 4 load of corn and 1 load apples to the mill" and allowed Thomas Johnson to pay off a debt by "carrying apples for a barill of cider." Nat Lovejoy earned 1s. for "taking my horse to market and selling the load," as did John Johnson for "taking my load to Salem." Brewing beer further integrated Barnard into the region's transportation networks because, like most residents, he did not possess his own malt house. He therefore recorded in John Barker's account his service in hauling nineteen bushels of barley "to the malthouse" and returning nineteen bushels of malt in three trips.[17] When the range of local exchange expanded by even a short distance, the press on transportation remained substantial.

Every internal trade required commercial farmers to move goods over relatively short distances. The collective, daily process of hauling commodities between farms, from farms to processing centers and back, and from farms to local markets had a powerful impact on transportation capabilities in the Massachusetts Bay region. Participants in the local economy fostered the exchange of transportation equipment, used the region's roads and cartways with greater regularity, and dedicated significant resources toward maintaining their equipment. These concerns relied heavily on

Page from personal account book of John Pickering. (Photograph courtesy Peabody Essex Museum) neighborly exchange and adhered closely to the workaday needs inherent in a developing local economy. Without a doubt, big merchant warehouses motivated hundreds of colonists to improve transportation facilities from the hinterlands to the coast. However, so did the less obvious but far more common exchanges that commercial farmers executed with one another hundreds of times a day and with the interest of economic betterment in mind. As the type of work that Puritan pioneers had been doing from the start intensified, so did their mobility. In responding accordingly, these hardworking men and women played a critical role in defining the local economy according to the dictates initiated by the founding generation.

IN ADDITION TO TRANSPORTATION IMPROVEMENTS, PURITANS pioneered local economic habits that preserved traditional economic strategies through the establishment of financial arrangements complementing their trading activity. What little we know about the strategies practiced by commercial farmers shows workers either linked through credit relations with prominent Boston or Salem merchants or engaged in what seems to have been a primitive system of bartered exchange. The records kept by Pickering, Burnham, and Barnard, however, reveal the gears of a more nuanced engine, allowing us to see precisely how commercial farmers established financial arrangements commensurate with the demands of daily economic life.

Many local transactions were simply bartered exchanges. In 1684 Eleazer Keafer sold Pickering shoe leather and calfskins, in addition to shoes "for my negro man," for £3 4s. From 1684 to 1686 Pickering paid Keafer with Indian corn and by hauling hay, and his debit came to a matching £3 4s. Similarly, in late 1689 Pickering sold George Ingersoll a parcel of goods totaling 19s. 6d., and in early 1690 Ingersoll worked for Pickering long enough—eight and a half days—to ring up a credit of 19s. 6d. In March 1701 John Barnard charged Alice Faulkner 7s. 6d. for a half-bushel of rye and a half-bushel of corn, for which Faulkner made three kersey jackets, "2 pr of britches for the boys," and "Thomas Southerd's jackits" for an equal 7s. 6d. This kind of transaction, a simple swap of goods and services that had equal market value, was a fairly common method of local exchange central to the operation of the economy.[18]

Most transactions, however, were not nearly so neat. Commercial farmers relied heavily on more advanced strategies, such as cash discounts and interest charges, in order to maintain leverage locally. Pickering's accounts highlight these arrangements especially well. In 1684 John Marsten, who regularly bought his Indian corn from Pickering, paid for two months' worth of corn in five days' work and in money. His ability to pay with cash earned him a small discount, as Pickering provided £2 1s. 2d. worth of corn for Marsten's payment of £2 1s. Samual Brown similarly benefited from paying in cash. Pickering sold Brown a range of imported goods, including linen cloth, damask, buttons, and silk, charging him £3 13s. 1d. Aside from 10s. in wood delivered to Pickering's mother, Brown paid the rest in cash. As a result, he enjoyed a 6s. discount. When John Johnson paid cash for John Barnard's rye in 1699, Barnard lowered his rate from 4s. per bushel to 3s. per bushel.[19]

Interest worked alongside discounts to complicate the local economy. Like all commercial farmers, Pickering both charged and was charged interest. From 1690 to 1692 he and Joseph Boyce exchanged goods of equal value, canceling out each other's debts on the spot. However, from 1692 to 1695 Pickering provided Boyce with corn, land, molasses, and malt, recording the cost as £3 7s. 8d. Boyce made a payment in 1694 by mending shoes, but a debt of 3s. 1d. remained on the books for another eighteen months. When Pickering recorded Boyce's final charge in January 1695, he tacked on 11d. as interest, or about 20 percent a year. Borrowing cash also incurred a charge, as it did when Pickering charged his carpenter £5 2s. for "five pounds in money borrowed of you by my brother Pickering." Pickering, of course, frequently found himself paying interest to the same clients from whom he often collected such payments. In a 1694 transaction Deliverance Parkman charged Pickering £4 19s. 4d. for several thousand clapboard nails. Pickering paid back most of this sum in 1694 and 1695 in the form of straw, apples, and timber. The remainder, which came to about a pound, remained on Parkman's books for more than two years. When Pickering did pay this debt, he had to pay 4s. 1d., about 10 percent, over the original charge even though he paid part of the remaining balance in cash.[20]

Another common financial arrangement that traders employed locally involved payment through a third party. Trading between neighbors became so systematic that commercial farmers quickly embraced the benefits of triangular transactions as a way to broaden their range of clients, quicken returns, and gain access to more goods and services. John Burnham regularly paid debts to third parties or accepted payments from third parties in lieu of clients' direct payments. Instead of paying William Cogswell the 3s. he owed him, Burnham "pd to Mr. Hadlock on Mr. Wm. Cogswell's account." In so doing, he simultaneously satisfied Cogswell's debt to

Hadlock and his own debt to Cogswell. He paid Jonathan Low, an Ipswich housewright, "1/2 bu of corn on Adam Cogswell's account," and, similarly, he "paid to Mr. Abraham Perkins on Nathanial Perkins the weavers account . . . a bu of corn." In an even more intricate arrangement, as Burnham recorded, "William Haskell received a brindle heffer three years old upon John Drinkers account of John Burnhams sons."[21] While it is often a challenge to untangle these arrangements, they seem to have made perfect sense to the traders intimately tied into one another's economic interests.

Pickering also relied heavily on triangular transactions. He recorded in John Neale's account a debt to him as "one bu barley delivered to Wm Harris." In 1694, rather than relying on his own labor, Pickering accumulated a few more debts when it came time to settle with his brother, paying "Joseph Boyce for mowing yours and mother," "Joseph Pease 1 day mowing your grass," and "Joseph Majory for keeping and binding rye." When Pickering found himself in debt to both his mother and Benjamin Ashby, he arranged for Samual Brown, who owed Pickering for imported cloth, to pay these debts. Brown thus sent "5 feet of wood to Benjamin Ashby" and "5 feet of wood to my mother." In the process of building a farmhouse for Pickering, John Harvey accumulated several debts that he could not pay immediately. Instead of accumulating more interest on his debts to John MacMaily, Samual Pickworth, and the Salem constable, Henry had Pickering pay these debts as partial advance payments on the barn that Henry was in the process of building.[22] The pressure of added interest commonly pulled neighbors into third-party transactions, enhancing their interdependence while making the economy more efficient and balanced.

Although John Barnard, who lived farther away from the coastal commercial nexus in Andover, less often relied on triangular transactions, his accounts nevertheless confirm the tactic's popularity in a remote town. Barnard charged Alice Faulkner for his paying her debts to John Gutter, Ephriam Harnu, and a Mr. Tyler. John Ingalls asked Barnard to pay a debt he owed him to Robert Russell instead, and Barnard accordingly recorded "to 1s 6d on Robert Russell's acct." He received credit for "corn paid to Baxter" on Richard Barker's account, and on Goodman Bointon's account he paid "to Mr. Day the weaver in money 14s 6d."[23] The extension of this technique so far inland speaks powerfully to its overall popularity.

A final financial tactic frequently exploited by commercial farmers trading internally was the use of a technique called a "reckoning." As the term implies, a reckoning was a rough balance assessment that occurred when a commercial farmer decided that a particular account had extended

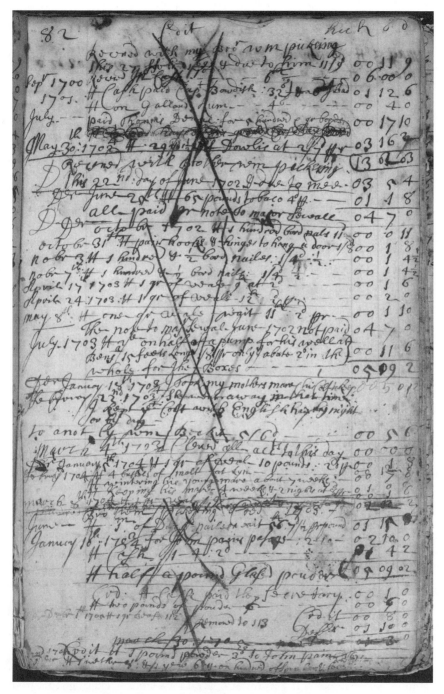

Page from personal account book of John Pickering. (Photograph courtesy Peabody Essex Museum)

too far without being checked. Payment did not necessarily occur at a reckoning, but the sum that one trader owed another was dutifully calculated and confirmed. Disagreements at reckonings sometimes landed traders in court or led to a reluctant out-of-court settlement, as it did when John Barnard wrote that "upon reconing with Mr. Price in the year 1701 his account differed from mine in the price of corn upon which account, sent him a bushel of wheat which he said would be to his full satisfaction," or when he discovered that he had "overpaid Goodman Bainton."[24] Most of the time, however, the parties parted amicably, leaving the transactions in question to resume. No single pattern of reckonings dominated. Pickering, Barnard, and Burnham each approached the matter idiosyncratically and even within a single account book varied their reckoning strategies according to the client. As unofficial mechanisms, reckonings were a vivid manifestation of an economy that was balancing the needs of neighborliness and market-oriented behavior in the interests of stability and progress.

Pickering's approach reflects his relative power in the local economy. He made frequent reckonings on relatively small amounts when the balance weighed in his favor, but he waited for others to call for a balance assessment when he was on the debtor side of the ledger. With Manassah Marsten he recorded eight credits from June 1684 to November 1685. During this time, however, Marsten received only two credits, albeit larger ones, from Pickering. Nevertheless, in January 1685 Pickering called for a reckoning and noted "due to me on balance 2s." As we have seen, Pickering's carpenter, John Harvey, called on Pickering to pay off some pressing cash debts to a third party while he was building a house and a barn for him. Pickering had also lent Harvey £5. There is every reason to think that these gestures forestalled Harvey's calling for a reckoning until Pickering's debt had reached an unusually large £6 15s.

Some of Pickering's clients, however, were equally eager to make sure that both parties saw eye to eye on standing balances. Pickering, for example, had to assess his account with Joseph Boyce after sending Boyce eight shipments of grain because Boyce wanted to ensure that his eleven days of work in return for this grain exceeded Pickering's shipments by 5s. "Reconed with Joseph Boyce," Pickering dutifully entered, "and due to him on balance 5s." Less than a year later, when Pickering had contributed corn and powder toward this balance, Boyce again called for a reckoning to remind Pickering that as a result of Boyce's son's labor, Pickering still owed

3s. 6d. on balance.[25] In such ways did neighbors keep each other honest as the economy became more commercialized and impersonal.

Compared with Pickering, John Barnard and John Burnham recorded reckonings more systematically. Barnard typically assessed his largest accounts on a yearly basis. For his account with Frances and Alice Faulkner, he recorded assessments in March 1702, April 1703, March and December 1704, June 1706, and March 1707. These reckonings occurred without regard to the amount in balance, which ranged from 2s. to 17s. He likewise checked accounts with his brother Stephen in March 1705 and again in March 1706. He and George Abbott met for six reckonings in the years 1699–1706. Burnham varied a little more, but he generally assessed his accounts with major clients either every few months or every couple of years. For example, he recorded reckonings with Jeremiah Buckman in February and December 1698 and June 1699 and with Robert Annable in March 1698, January 1701, March 1704, and March 1707. With many clients, and for reasons that remain unclear, Barnard and Burnham never used reckonings at all, not even when accounts stretched over two or three years.[26]

On the rare occasions when these commercial farmers kept accounts with merchants selling imported goods, reckonings disappeared from the transactions altogether. When John Burnham bought rum, molasses, sugar, and cotton wool from the commissioned Captain Jonathan Cogswell, he recorded no assessments from June 1703 to August 1705. Likewise, when Barnard purchased calico, serge, crepe, buttons, and silk from "Mr. Deering of Boston," he noted no assessments from 1692 to 1695. And when Pickering sold Samual Brown imported linen and damask between from 1699 to June 1702, yet again the traders did not call for a customary reckoning. This absence suggests how reckonings reflected the vagaries of maintaining accounts in a local economic setting, where transactions occurred more often, were more reciprocal, involved more goods, and included commodities whose prices were not determined by an external market. It also highlights the role of reckonings as a highly personal means of ordering the economy. As transactions unmediated by established institutions, local trades had to be negotiated through social relationships rather than law, a form of mediation to be trusted—but not completely so.

While these financial methods had pale reflections in England, they were largely homegrown strategies. Residents living in the Massachusetts Bay certainly became more financially astute as they participated in the emerging export market. Carting timber, wheat, or beef to Salem for export would certainly have required that commercial farmers quickly learn a thing or two about interest, credit, third-party accounts, and market prices. Export trade relations, however, were not solely responsible for this education in commercial relations. While these operations, as Margaret Newell has observed, "fueled the dissemination of commercial values," they also reflected a series of financial strategies that emerged from the ground up. Designed to foster the routines of local trade, they tightened Puritan pioneers' dependence on one another rather than on an unknown foreign entity. As such, they fostered an ethic of exchange that, for all its provincialism, strengthened the economy.[27]

Familial connections helped further define local economic habits.[28] The father-son working arrangement was, of course, central to working life. Without the luxury of imported labor, fathers in New England "exploited with doubled intensity the only labor source available to them—their sons."[29] Young men withstood the exploitation because future land ownership awaited, as fathers often turned land over to them when they reached their mid-twenties. At about the age of five, boys did jobs such as guard fence gaps against wandering cattle, fetch tools, and guide livestock into stables, all under close supervision. By the age of ten, "having acquired the skills and physical strength to produce as much as they consumed," boys began to hold their own on their father's farm. They could be trusted to work independently while caring for cattle and plowing fields. By their late teens, sons had intensified their work on the family farm and often ran it alongside their father. At twenty-one, young men "finally crossed something of a watershed" and began to think seriously about starting their own farms.[30] This trajectory was typical for New England boys.

While the father-son relationship on the family farm was integral to economic stability, a son's working experience often extended well beyond the farm. Within the nexus of local trade, fathers frequently used their sons' labor as a tradable asset, meeting debt payments on a regular basis with the skilled and unskilled services boys could readily perform. Pickering, Burnham, and Barnard—and the many clients with whom they traded—routinely dispatched their sons to work off debts in the local economy. Twenty-five percent of Pickering's service spending involved the labor of his own or his clients' sons. When he and Ephriam Kempton traded from 1687 to 1692, Kempton paid 75 percent of his debt with his sons' labor, leasing them to Pickering for twenty-eight days to haul hay and plow fields. In exchange for Pickering's Indian corn, John Marsten lent to Pickering his son James for five days' work in March 1684. And in the years 1690–94 Joseph Boyce paid Pickering in ten days' work by his sons Jonathan and Joseph, whom Pickering called on to execute such tasks as "mowing stumps."[31] However sons felt about the work, leasing them was an important strategy farmers used to maintain economic leverage in the local economy.

Burnham's sons were especially integral to broadening the range of his economic activity. Thirty percent of his service transactions involved the leasing of labor performed by sons—his and those of his clients. Occasionally he leased out his son to satisfy small debts, as he did in 1698 when he paid Joseph Marshall "for a day's work by my son Joseph" or for "my son Joseph with the oxen." But as Joseph matured, Burnham arranged for him to spearhead a small fishing venture to complement the family farming business. This venture initially involved building a sloop, which Joseph did with the help of his younger brother Jacob in 1700. Over the course of the year, Joseph and Jacob worked seventy-nine days building the vessel. Their father joined them on thirty-eight of those days. Once they had finished the sloop, Burnham's oldest son John took it on "summer voyages" along the Atlantic coast, once sailing as far as Barbados. While Joseph and Jacob were building the ship, the elder Burnham arranged for his son John to literally learn the ropes from Humphry Woodbury, with whom John "went to sea" in 1698 and 1699.[32]

John Barnard's sons are mysteriously absent from his accounts. Nevertheless, like Pickering, Barnard frequently accepted returns from his clients' sons. While he regularly employed Alice Faulkner to make and mend his clothes, he also drew on her sons' labor for killing and dressing hogs, carting dung, and cutting wood. When Barnard's servant fell ill during the May planting, he hired "2 of John Marbles sons to help me when he was sick." Their work must have proven satisfactory because he later hired them for five days in 1701 to "cut bushes" and for "weeding." He credited John Parker for "one day of his boy to plant," Henry Chandler "one day of himself and boys to draw stones" and "to break flax," Moses Tyler "by his boys 1 day to weed," and John Granger "by his boy 1 day to gather corn." These accounts demonstrate that sons supported a father's quest not only for more efficient family farms but also for greater flexibility in the local markets that those farms served.[33]

Labor prices reflected the market value of a boy's age as farmers traded their daily labor. When Pickering hired Boyce's son Joseph in May 1691, he paid a daily wage of 2s. 6d. By 1694, however, Joseph was demanding 3s. a day. When Burnham's sons worked on his sloop, he paid the elder son, Joseph, 2s. 6d. a day and Jacob 2s. a day. But when Burnham lent his son to Joseph Marshall for a day's work, Burnham pegged the rate at 3s. a day in 1698; by 1701 he had raised this figure to 3s. 3d. a day.[34] This graduated price scale reflects the regularity with which fathers treated their sons as a salable commodity among neighbors within the nexus of local trade.

As popular as the father-son connection was, local economic transactions relied just as heavily on sibling relations. In an economic context that lacked anything as organized as authorized credit ratings, a judicious way to protect oneself against unpaid debt was to deal with the brothers or cousins of those whose reputations for financial reliability were already firmly established. Sixty-two percent of John Barnard's eighty-nine clients were related to other clients of his. In small communities these connections were highly advantageous. When Steven Branard owed Barnard work in his fields but fell ill before he could perform it, he paid the debt "by his two brothers James and Robert." In 1699 Barnard accepted payments on Samual Fry's debt for hauling services from both Samual and John Fry. Barnard's transactions with the Parker brothers often involved third-party payments, as when Joseph Parker paid a debt to Barnard by crediting 2s. to his brother John's account. He did the same thing with the Chandler brothers, allowing Thomas to fulfill a small debt by paying his brother Will what Barnard owed him from a previous transaction.[35]

John Burnham, 28 percent of whose clients were related to other clients, organized his account books around families, including brothers and cousins, under the rubric of a single written account. Between June 1703 and August 1705 he shifted the transactions of Jonathan, Adam, and William Cogswell into one account, consistently allowing the credits of one brother to replace those of another. Further increasing Burnham's rate of return was the fact that the Cogswells were simultaneously engaged in several other accounts, an arrangement that expanded the number of potential third-party creditors and debtors with whom Burnham could subsequently transact. Thomas Pritchart paid Burnham "a bu of corn on Wm. Cogswells acct," while Barnard "pd to Mr. Hadlock 3s on Mr. Wm Cogswells account." A similar arrangement prevailed with the Fosters—all four of them. When the timing was convenient, Burnham continued to allow the brothers to substitute debt payments for one another. As with the Cogswells, he enjoyed broadened access to debtors and creditors. Accordingly, we find entries such as "pr shoes mended for Wm Rodgers" and "ordered by Goodman Foster at Deacon Lowes for me 4s in malt." His account with Joseph and John Dennis brought the accounts of two families together when, in January 1699, Burnham recorded, "payed by Jonathan Cogswell to John Dennis for me 0-11-9 in money." Burnham also regularly collapsed the accounts of Job and Samuel Giddings into one, as he did, for example, when he "pd to Job Giddings on Samuels account two pounds of cotton wool."[36]

Husbands and wives, finally, always worked together to support a household.[37] Widows appear with some regularity, but wives generally only stood in when their husbands were unavailable, as husbands were the ones who generally purchased the goods necessary for household production and consumption. Wives most commonly appear in entries such as "to one pr shoes for my wife."[38] On rare occasions, though, wives appear in the forefront of economic transactions as "deputy husbands." In Pickering's accounts, for example, he lists under John Downing's debts, "received of your wife in money." Burnham, when he worked with deputy husbands, referred to them by their own names. Under John Russell's transactions, for example, he noted in April 1703, "Mary Russell, 2 quarts of wheat." John Barnard did the same. "Borrowed from Mrs. Coker in money at Newbury Court," he entered, followed by "sent to Mary Coker 20 money by Samual Osgood." In a long account with Captain John Price, Barnard conducted his reckonings with "Mrs. Sarah Price" and noted that his debt was "due to her" even though he listed it under the captain's account.[39]

There is one interesting exception to the deputy-husband arrangement worth noting. John Barnard maintained long-standing accounts with both Frances and Alice Faulkner. Each partner's account involved the domestic domain that he or she controlled. Through the Barnard–Alice Faulkner account, for example, the otherwise hidden world of laboring daughters comes to light. Barnard made returns for "2 days Abigail and 3 day's Bethia in making Theos coat and Stephens jackit" and "2 days Abigail to make Johns and Theos jackits." Barnard paid Alice for, among other tasks, "making linen britches," "cutting out linsey woolsey," and, on many occasions, "making clothes." On Frances's side we find the familiar labor arrangements: "to Henry to cart posts," "by Paul helping to kill a hog," and "Edmond and Paul a day to cart dung." Most accounts were headed by men, but for whatever reason, Alice and Frances controlled their own domains and, with Barnard at least, their own accounts.[40]

ALTHOUGH ALMOST CERTAINLY UNAWARE THAT THEY WERE DOING SO, commercial farmers like Burnham, Barnard, and Pickering were defining the ground rules of local economic life. As men who were both deeply involved in their local communities and clearly intent on making the most of economic opportunity, they relied heavily on discounts, conventional interest payments, third-party transactions, reckonings, bartered transportation services, and familial connections to secure and improve their place in the local economy. Local mobility, trade strategies, reckonings, and intergenerational exchange fostered the economic interdependence necessary for economic progress. This combination became, through the daily efforts of common farmers and artisans, a standard aspect of the Massachusetts economy at the very time when merchants were undergoing the transition into larger, more impersonal venues.

To what extent they tried to improve their status in life is hard to discern, but very few commercial farmers broke the provincial barrier to become sophisticated merchants in the George Corwin mold. Most of them, in fact, stayed close to home, traded locally, and drew on conventional local tactics to meet basic needs and enjoy the modest but manifest benefits of land ownership in Massachusetts. The economic strategies they so heavily relied upon to shape their economic lives reflected a trend that Puritan pioneers had been pursuing since they first began to organize the local economy back in the 1630s: they practiced local economic habits characterized by personal ambition, community cohesion, and tradition.

NINE

Back to Business as Usual in the Bay Colony

1660–1700

W HILE PURITAN PIONEERS CONTINUED TO DEVELOP ECONOMIC habits relevant to both the local economy and their unique social norms, merchants moved to exploit overseas markets. Their move has long been associated with the "declension" that the region supposedly underwent from its founding covenanted mission into an acquisitive, profit-driven enterprise. The merchants' aggressive embrace of the very factors that Puritans had long avoided—ethnic diversity, conspicuous consumption, worldliness, a sense of individualism, and overt desire for cash—threatened to transform the "New Zion" from a "peaceable kingdom" into an underworld of self-centered ambition. The economic bonds that had effectively kept the young George Corwin rooted in local habits of exchange were facing the possibility of becoming frayed as merchants tried to transform local communities into little more than impersonal markets to absorb luxury imports.[1]

Philip English embodied this transition to a modernity of sorts. As a Frenchman who cavorted with mariners and fishermen who were more concerned with the bottle than the Bible, English did not invest his considerable profits in churches; rather he used them to build a tavern, a warehouse, wharves, and a mansion of conspicuous proportions on the east side of Salem. The unwavering focus of his contemplation was the secular rather than the spiritual world. His "calling," as it were, grated against the Puritanical cohesion that the colony had so long valued. English represented a class of men—relatively new and substantially empowered—who fundamentally violated the Puritanical dictum that "God will rather have his people poor and humble than rich and proud." He had no time for such pithy quaintness. As a result, the advocates of tradition often confronted him and his cohort with overwrought expressions of impending doom.

121

This declension story has traditionally shaped the popular understand-ing of New England's early economic history. It has done so, however, while relying on a couple of questionable assumptions. First, it purports a stark dislocation between the internal and external economies, taking it as established fact that the export market determined the internal one. Second, it suggests that economic endeavors that remained insulated from the transatlantic world withered into insignificance as an antiquated, barter-based moral economy yielded to a transatlantic one. In other words, one sector of the economy remained subsistence oriented, while the other embraced capitalism and forged into the future. This dichotomy continues to characterize discussions of the colonial New England economy.[2]

As the following profiles of two men active in the local economy sug-gest, the assumption that merchants inspired a complete ideological tran-sition to a new set of values is highly questionable. In fact, as the examples of John Flint and John Pearson show, men who remained distant from the transatlantic economy that merchants like English embraced not only sus-tained the local economic habits that Puritan pioneers had been honing for decades but created new opportunities within the internal economy for both themselves and the merchants they served. Their work was hardly subsistence oriented; to the contrary, they wanted to improve their lot in life, and they generally did. They were, however, bound by the limits and opportunities inherent in the local economy, and as such, they were similarly bound to the social values that kept the economy strongly tied to community concerns. At the same time, though, these men were also businessmen carving out niches in the local economy with the purpose of bettering themselves and their families. Instead of men and women cling-ing nostalgically to a "moral economy," they were a more aggressive breed of Puritan pioneers whose work supported the merchants' turn to overseas markets. Their economic activity, often hidden in plain sight, was crucial to the region's integration into the Atlantic economy. These men, in short, took economic competency to a new level without compromising the sta-bility of the economic and social system their ancestors had worked so hard to achieve. A close consideration of their business activities indicates that the traditional Massachusetts economy did not decline, but endured as Puritan pioneers practiced business as usual.

LOCAL SUPPLY AND DEMAND OF BASIC GOODS REMAINED THE PRIMARY economic focus of most residents' working lives. As in the founding de-cade, the internal need for wood remained ubiquitous. John Flint's account book (which unfortunately lists only his debtors) offers substantial insight into the effort to meet that demand. A supplier of agricultural goods, Flint had many local orders to fulfill, but wood topped his list. Local demand for timber became especially intense as the overseas trade in boards, staves, and hoops increased after 1660. Concerns over internal supplies became especially evident when investors moved to establish a sawmill. Merchants and mill owners directed the flow of timber toward the coast for export. Towns, however, strove to keep timber local. Thus they countered with regulations intended to ensure that local demand did not suffer as a result of overexporting one of the region's most sought-after resources. In 1650, for example, Salisbury granted William Osgood and his team of investors the exclusive right to construct a sawmill, but with the stipulation that "he will pay unto the town of Salisbury one half hundred of board and plank Marchantable for every thousand that the mill shall saw." Additionally, town residents maintained "libertie at all times to make use of any pine trees either for canoes or to saw with the whip saw, or any other necessary use"—except, of course, the construction of another sawmill.

In their rush to export processed timber, however, mill owners repeatedly violated residents' private timber demands. Even worse, they often failed to honor their own promise to pay a portion of their boards to the town in return for monopolistic rights to the mill. Salisbury thus sued Osgood and, in 1667, reclaimed the land that Osgood and Company had been exploiting for timber supplies, dividing it among "all the townsmen inhabiting the old towne of Salisbury." Osgood and his partners neglected the mill for the next eleven years, during which time the townsmen, on their own initiative, "laid out and improved both land and timber" and went about repairing the sawmill and using it for local projects. At this point, in 1682, Osgood suddenly reasserted his claim to the mill, dismissing the improvements as the handiwork of squatters. The outcome, unfortunately, went unrecorded. Nevertheless, what matters for our purposes is the intense interest that the town and townsmen expressed in assuring that their internal timber needs would not be sacrificed to Osgood's rapacious quest for transatlantic profits. As in the founding decades, colonists continued to protect their ample local supply of wood with dogged vigilance.[3]

Other towns controlled timber access by designating more land as common ground, while limiting timber rights to their inhabitants. At a 1664 Topsfield town meeting, selectmen declared that "all the commoners in the Towne shall have share in the Common on the other side of the River with the Timber which is to be divided according to the rule as is expressed." This rule held that those men who paid the highest ministers' rate "shall have one of the greatest shares" in the common timber supply, while those who paid the lowest rates "shall have the least share." The measure both adjusted the extent of timber access to a household's need and, in diluting control of five hundred acres of land, ensured that mill owners could not monopolize timber rights and endanger the local supply of wood.[4]

As these policies suggest, private arguments over timber access were commonplace. Settlers from hinterland towns frequently petitioned the court to prevent merchants from stripping timber on land that bordered more commercial inland towns. When Salem's John Putnum began felling trees pell-mell on the Topsfield border, five Topsfield residents approached him in a panic and showed him "an order from Topsfield to demand of any of Salem men that claimed land within Topsfield bounds to show them their bounds and grants." Putnum, convinced of his ownership, was unable to prove it with a deed. The deponents, in response, wasted no time in claiming the land's timber and, in a less than subtle gesture, "before his face felled one timber tree within Topsfield line." An incensed Putnum protested, but the "deponents told him he had more than his due there [in Salem] and he had no reason to claim theirs."[5]

These kinds of conflict intensified as merchants worked to direct supplies overseas. Nathanial Putnam and James Allen, in another recorded dispute, fought bitterly over a spread of timber-rich land situated near "ye old saw mill," bordering a highway connecting Salem and Ipswich, and enjoying a bridge over a small waterway. Allen argued that the land in question belonged to his three-hundred-acre Salem farm. Putnam, who drew regularly on the plot's timber, continued to do so. Allen recalled for the jury Putnam's reaction to his accusation: "I forwarned him for cootting the wood downe any mor: boott he sayd he had coott and carried of[f] that land wood and woold still coott and carry away as he caes." Allen responded with an idle threat to dismantle Putnam's bridge and destroy his corn. Putnam won the case, however, and continued to take his wood at will. Allen evidently never followed up on his promise.

Traditional demands persisted. Fence upkeep now required even more extensive supplies of timber than in the early years. An economy so thoroughly based on livestock required the frequent oversight of fence viewers, who called for improvements on the slightest defect. In a typical Lynn fence viewer's report, Robert Burgess, who only oversaw a small portion of Lynn's fences, noted in his jurisdiction "46 rods of the general fence . . .

insufficient, from Daniel Gott's fence to Gillo's house 10 poles . . . little or no fence; from Randall's corner by Richard Whod's lot to the dwelling house of Gillo, 22 poles . . . no fence; from Gillo's house by the country road until the fence joins with John Ramsdell's, the outside of the orchard, 24 rods, with fencing stuff on it, but out of repair. . . . In all there were 55 poles with fence but it needed many new posts and rails and needed to be reset, which was worth 30s. There were 110 rods insufficient and to make a good 5 rail fence would cost 2s per pole." In Rowley, townsmen who owned land in the north field maintained 444 rail lengths of fence, owners in the ox pasture kept up with 212 rail lengths, landowners between the ox pasture and "mill ward" oversaw 225 lengths, and proprietors in the east pasture tended to 168 rods and 68 feet of fence. Indicative of this need we find, in 1680, John Pudney carrying away wood from Thomas Flint's saw-mill, with the boards "being used for fence around his tobacco."[6]

Home upkeep, additions, and repairs intensified local demand for timber as well. The rate at which the colonists constructed new homes had diminished since the 1630s, but the process of maintaining existing structures and adding barns, stables, and houses intensified throughout the century. Leases often ensured that a tenant "was to have what timber he needed for finishing the house, building a barn and other housing for cattle, also for firing and fencing." John Sockman sued his employer "for not satisfying him for work done for him in . . . felling timber, hewing, and framing, and setting up a house for him, 24 feet long and 20 in breadth, now standing to the northward of the former dwelling house." Settlers in Topsfield made a yearly effort "to put into good and sufficient repair the ministry house . . . where their minister Mr. Hobart now lives, together with the outhouses and fences about the land." When Newbury's Henry Jacques built a house for a client, he required wood for making "a gable end in the front and cover[ing] all the outside of the house with clapboards and shingles." He also "laid all the floors, made two flights of stairs, a closet in the chamber, with partitions to the rooms and doors to the same." When testifying about the quality of a sawmill, Nathan Gold approvingly recalled "the heap of boards" that he had processed at the Salisbury mill "to build his shop." Michael Bowden contracted with several Marblehead residents to cut timber on their property and haul it away for local sale. After cutting eleven trees on Nicholas Merrit's lot, for example, he sold much of it to John Codner, who arranged to have Salem's George Darling build a house frame with it. These kinds of activities and transactions occurred daily and sparked ongoing demand for local timber.[7]

The constant need for fuel further sustained the local quest for timber. Not only did local ironworks require thousands of cords of wood but every home needed its own supply for cooking and heating. The process of obtaining this supply provoked numerous lawsuits, as boundaries in wooded areas often blurred, thus fueling frequent debates over timber rights. Joseph Wolcott testified in court about being "in the woods with a cord of wood on a sled going towards home." When asked by John Webster "if he came honestly by that wood," Wolcott responded that "they cut it last Spring." Webster countered that a man named Atkinson "said it was their wood and they left it near a walnut tree on the hill," to which Wolcott responded, "Atkinsons knew no more than a dog where their wood lay." Less contentiously, we find John Blaney, "hired to cart firewood" for Capt. James Smith, Goodman Buckley, and Mr. Maverick, in addition to Ipswich's Samual Pippin securing from Sam Cogswell "the right to cut timber for finishing the house and building a barne and other housing for cattle, also for firewood and fencing."[8]

Settlers, despite the export transition under way, thus gathered wood for more reasons than simply fulfilling demand in export markets. John Flint's business operated squarely within the broad context of this pervasive local demand. Timber did not walk itself to projects, and many colonists simply lacked the time and resources to gather it themselves. Flint acquired and sold a variety of agricultural products, but the bulk of his recorded accounts had to do with timber. His sales almost exclusively responded to daily, workaday needs. A look at his accounts with three of his biggest clients offers telling glimpses into the impact of internal demand on the sale and movement of timber to meet these local needs. Little evidence in these accounts suggests that the merchant-driven transition to export markets either isolated Flint in a subsistence-oriented netherworld or dominated the direction of his local work routines. He worked to seek profit in a local economic context by serving current needs and following rules dating back to the colony's foundation.

John Newman was Flint's biggest client. Flint's account with Newman shows him carrying timber away from Salem, a vibrant shipping center, into Wenham, a less commercialized agricultural town. In the years 1680–82 Newman purchased thirty-eight loads of timber from Flint, never receiving more than one load at a time. About 60 percent of his purchases occurred during the summer, when wood was cheaper to transport. It was also a time when Newman would have undertaken more involved domestic improvements. Flint sold him another 10 percent in November, when the summer supply began to diminish and fuel demand rose. The limitation to one load per sale reflected the humble transportation capacity of an old cart, a limitation that led Newman to deliver wood several days in close succession (e.g., June 2, 8, 12, 13, 21, 26, and 30 and November 4, 7, 8, and 9). Flint's accounts generally reveal little about the process of acquiring the timber that he sold. In one instance, though, he does note that he took timber from "Howard's," "Endicott's," "Felton's," and "Frol.—all neighbors."[9] About the specific financial arrangements sealing their connection we know almost nothing. Nevertheless, the Newman connection shows how a local supplier moved goods in the opposite direction of the export market in order to ease the considerable pressure of internal demand for a basic commodity.

Batholomew Gedney, a Salem attorney, was Flint's second most active client. Their transactions took place in 1682, a year during which Gedney purchased fourteen loads of timber from Flint on thirteen separate occasions. While the fairly concentrated sale of a relatively large supply of timber might suggest that Gedney, a man who cultivated extensive overseas commercial connections, aimed to export these deliveries, the fact that he purchased five loads as payments on debts to third parties strongly indicates a local commercial intention. Furthermore, when Gedney bought timber for himself, he had it delivered straight to his home rather than to a mill, where it normally would have gone before export.[10] When commercial leaders such as Gedney did intend to export wood products, they acquired their goods in very large quantities and in processed form. For example, when George Deane prepared for an overseas shipment, he bought from John Griffen in Bradford 1,050 pipe staves, 1,250 boards, 1,850 hogshead staves, and 2,400 barrel staves.[11] By contrast, Gedney's purchase of relatively small parcels of unprocessed timber from his neighbor suggests that his motivation in this case was to meet internal debts and acquire wood for use at home. Local demand, once again, was the primary motivating force driving Flint's activity.

Flint's account with Thomas Newell, of Lynn, offers a third insight into the effort to meet local timber demand. Newell owned a shop, which he occasionally shared with Flint in order to retail timber and other goods.[12] According to court records, Newell also nurtured extensive connections with fence viewers and sawmill owners, as the town often called on him to appraise mills and oversee fence repairs.[13] Newell thus seems to have maneuvered himself into the self-interested position of providing timber for the very repairs he ordered, buying thirteen loads of timber from Flint, as well as the use of a team of oxen to haul the timber to the specified locations. George Booth's inventory offers some confirmation of this arrangement since it mentions a debt to Newell for providing "two pieces of timber to lay from Arch to Arch over the water course," a repair authorized by none other than John Flint.[14]

Flint arranged his business to capitalize on local demand. Although he would never become rich by selling wood and other products in local markets, he would generate enough profit to purchase the occasional batch of imports from one of the region's prominent merchants. He would do so while remaining deeply integrated into his local community of trade. This integration served to reinforce not only the patterns of exchange that Puritan pioneers had been practicing for a couple of generations but also the habits that framed those patterns—cooperation, community, and hard work. Neither nostalgic for a mythical lost age nor an unabashed advocate of capitalism, a man like Flint prospered in the context of the traditional economy.

WHILE HIS WORK COULD NOT HAVE BEEN MORE DIFFERENT FROM Flint's, John Pearson played a similar role in the local economy. We do not know the extent to which it was done, but we do know that many settlers spun wool into yarn and then loomed yarn into cloth. In Rowley, enough homes participated in these tasks to motivate Pearson to build a fulling mill sometime in the 1660s. The details of his project's inception have gone unrecorded, but its construction must have been a notable project. An Ipswich town meeting later granting Richard Satchwell the right to build his own fulling mill "provided he finish it within three years."[15] The demand for such services was obviously ripe. When Satchwell applied for the Ipswich grant, the town noted its need for a mill, "it being above four years since & the Towne not haveing had any profit by it as yet."[16] Colonists certainly continued to purchase substantial quantities of imported textiles, but this did not keep them from trying to produce a portion of their woolen cloth on their own. Import substitution was not an all-or-nothing venture. This local production, therefore, had an economic impact that was evident in the daily operation of Pearson's mill.

Fulling was a process that cleansed woven wool of animal grease and thickened the fabric by shrinking and felting it. It distinguished woolen cloth from worsted wool, as the cloth became more compact once the knitted woolen fibers tightened. A complex mill was required for this task. Situated on a river, Pearson's mill had a large waterwheel exactly like the

TABLE 9.1   A one-year analysis of John Pearson's fulling mill, March 1675–February 1676

Date	Transactions	Percent	Income	Yards/ client	Yards fulled	Price/yard (in pence)
1675						
March	34	18	£5 14s. 3d.	22.12	752	1.8
April	39	21	£7 11s. 5d.	21.56	841	2.1
May	27	14	£5 18s. 10d.	25.44	687	2.1
June	7	4	£1 0s. 5d.	17.57	123	1.9
September	1	0.5	£0 3s. 1d.	18	18	2.1
October	34	18	£6 5s. 8d.	20.91	711	2.1
November	29	16	£5 10s. 8d.	20.79	603	2.2
December	19	10	£2 15s. 11d.	16.95	322	2.1
1676						
January	3	1	£0 6s. 8d.	13.6	41	2.0
February	2	1	£0 2s. 7d.	7	14	2.2

Source: John Pearson Account Book sample, 1675–76, based on John Pearson Account Book, 1674–1799, Pearson Family Papers, Baker Library, Harvard Business School, Boston, MA.

Note: July and August of 1675 had no transactions.

ironworks' multiple wheels. This wheel rotated huge wooden hammers, or stocks. The stocks plunged into a vat of soapy water holding the wool. Hammers, which the fuller could adjust at different angles depending on the size of his load, pounded away at the cloth in the sudsy water. At the end, the fuller fished the cloth from the vat, tented it to dry, and waited for his patrons to return for their transformed woolen textiles.[17]

Traditionally, English fullers worked when farming tasks were the least rigorous. However, Pearson's Rowley operation, according to a one-year analysis of his working schedule, launched into full tilt when farmers would have been especially busy in the fields (table 9.1). The seasonal emphasis of his work is thus, on the surface, a bit strange. One possibility for this difference from English seasonal patterns could be its reflection of the more fluid gendered work assumptions that many scholars believe prevailed in the seventeenth century throughout colonial British America. In England, weavers were all men, so they did their work during the agricultural off-season, saving the other time for farming tasks. On the colonial periphery, however, the workaday demands of a frontier economy and the

129

accompanying labor shortages not only necessitated common participation in many employments but blurred traditional gendered expectations about work. Women's domain normally included the home and its immediate environs, but women may have played a more direct role in weaving since men spent so many of their days in the fields. Hence the emphasis on fulling from March to May (53 percent) and from October to December (44 percent).[18]

Pearson's position in Rowley as the town's lone fuller ensured a hectic working pace. His business during these months was, by any standard, brisk. He conducted more than 195 transactions with more than 206 local clients from March 1675 to February 1676. He accepted anywhere from 5 to 45 yards of woolen cloth at a time, with clients bringing him an average of 18.2 yards each. Pearson frequently dealt with several clients within the course of a single day. In fact, the regularity of high-volume days suggests that he may have worked to achieve the sensible strategy of running the mill only when demand reached full capacity. For example, on March 27 he accepted deliveries of 28, 16, 20, 22, and 17 yards of wool, and on March 20 he fulled for four clients. On these two days he met with 26 percent of his clients for the month and fulled 25 percent of the month's wool. April 2 was also a busy day, as Pearson took in separate parcels of 4, 10, 24, 10, 23, 22, and 18 yards for fulling. On April 24 he accepted another five orders, thus again doing 26 percent of his business for the month in just two days. In November he followed a similar strategy. On November 7 he accepted five parcels totaling 102 yards of cloth, which was 17 percent of the cloth he fulled for the month. All of his very few January and February transactions occurred in a single day.[19]

As for returns, Pearson followed patterns similar to those of the commercial farmers (table 9.2). He accepted the majority of his payments in the form of farm produce and light manufactured goods such as shoes or hats. Cash, however, was hardly absent from his credits, and in order to encourage such payments, he offered discounts for those who paid hard money for his services. Sometimes this discount was small (about 5 percent), as it was for two clients in May, who paid 2d. per yard, when the average price that month was 2.1d. per yard.[20] On most other occasions, however, the difference was more pronounced. In December, for example, he sold twelve yards of fulled cloth to a client who paid cash. The client paid only 18d. for Pearson's service, a rate of 1.5d. per yard, compared with the average price that month of 2.1d. per yard.[21] In March a client brought in forty-six yards of wool and offered to pay cash. Pearson agreed

TABLE 9.2 A one-year analysis of John Pearson's returns, March 1675–February 1676

Date	Number of returns	Value	Items tendered
1675			
March	6	£2 4s. 6d.	Shoes, wheat, fowl, money, work, soap
April	10	£4 3s. 9d.	Salt, money, hops, wheat, malt, beef, corn
May	12	£3 9s. 9d.	Cheese, barley, work, money
June	1	£0 5s. 0d.	Money
August	2	£2 10s. 0d.	Money, shoes
September	1	£0 1s. 6d.	—
October	13	£4 8s. 6d.	Malt, money, corn, hops
November	6	£2 14s. 7d.	Corn, shoes, money
December	3	£0 15s. 11d.	Corn, money, wheat
1676			
January	1	£0 10s. 0d.	Money
February	6	£3 17s. 2d.	Corn, hats, money, peas

Source: John Pearson Account Book sample, 1675–76, based on John Pearson Account Book, 1674–1799, Pearson Family Papers, Baker Library, Harvard Business School, Boston, MA.

Note: July of 1675 had no transactions.

and quoted him a rate of 1.5d. per yard, when the rate that month was 1.8d. per yard. To cite another example among many, he granted a cash discount on April 5, when a client paid for thirty yards of fulling at, again, 1.5d. per yard, compared with the average rate for that month of 2.1d. per yard (see table 9.1).[22]

Like his colleagues, Pearson relied heavily on third-party transactions with other local residents to settle payments in a timely fashion. One client earned a credit with Pearson by paying Pearson's brother, Samual, 3s. in cash. Pearson accepted several payments of third-party labor, as he did when he credited Joseph Pike for "2 days work with Joseph G.'s boy." Collections took place regularly, but an evaluation of Pearson's long-term progress can only be tentative. Based on this single year, 1685, Pearson seems to have done well in comparison with at least one private English fuller. Surviving records for a Slaithewaite, England, fulling mill's operation in 1684, for example, reveals that it brought in £34 14s. 11d. Pearson grossed £35 9s. 5d. He managed to accomplish this impressive return for the year while losing only 35 yards of cloth out of the 4,112 yards that he fulled.[23]

CONSIDERED TOGETHER, THE CASES OF FLINT AND PEARSON FURTHER uncover the hidden complexity of Massachusetts's local economy during the second half of the seventeenth century. Their experiences, even based on details gleaned from incomplete and sporadically kept account books, reveal men providing services to local clients at the very moment when merchants were becoming deeply engaged in the business of meeting foreign demand. Responding to internal demand, Flint and Pearson did what residents had been doing ever since the first days of settlement. They just did so more efficiently, with a more sophisticated infrastructure, and alongside men who were venturing into more capitalistic venues. Pearson and Flint were in no way hostile to the changes that the merchants were initiating. In fact, embedded as they were in the process of buying, selling, and transporting goods locally, they seem to have paid those changes little mind. They therefore quietly perpetuated the economic and social attitudes and behaviors that the ministers, with their overwrought condemnations of "a rising generation," were certain were in decline. The cases of Flint and Pearson remind us that the emerging quest for profit in a local venue intensified even as merchants moved into the transatlantic market. As a result, their activity shaped the region's economic development from within.

Flint and Pearson joined Burnham, Barnard, Hobart, Pickering, and Adams in keeping the Massachusetts economy revolving around local demand and wedded to customary economic habits. They did so, moreover, as scores of merchants were pulling the region in a transatlantic direction. Examinations of the precise nature of the work performed by men who limited their business to the local economy demonstrate that, in one sense, local economic habits continued in the same general vein established by the first generation of settlers, who were intent on building a viable economic infrastructure. In another sense, though, Flint and Pearson were more explicitly interested in personal economic improvement. Only nominally farmers, they worked as businessmen seeking profit within the limits of the local economy. They worked in the space between subsistence agriculture and merchant capitalism, and the evidence suggests that they managed this niche rather well.

The nature of work in the local economy continued to be entirely consistent with the general culture that Puritans had valued so strongly from the outset. The economy in which these men did the vast majority of their business was one that most Puritans would have known quite well, and it was one that, by its nature, encouraged but also limited the acquisitive impulse; reinforced the importance of community as a social and economic entity valued for its conservative qualities; nurtured the need for constant, peaceful interaction; and, again, never forgot the spiritually affirming benefits of old-fashioned, physically demanding work. Rather than resisting modernization or hewing to its irresistible pull, Puritan pioneers worked in a way that both sparked entrepreneurial ambition and stabilized the Massachusetts economy. Their efforts enabled the region to accommodate the transition that merchants were in the process of undertaking without sacrificing the cohesion they had long enjoyed. Their efforts also proved to be, as the following chapters show, a necessary catalyst for that critical economic transition.

TEN

Merchant Anxiety and the Local Economy

1670–1710

THE ECONOMIC EXPERIENCES OF MEN WORKING IN THE LOCAL ECON-
omy have been obscured by the story of the New England merchants'
steady rise to power. It is a familiar story that has changed little since Bernard Bailyn's 1955 landmark publication, *The New England Merchants in the
Seventeenth Century*. Bailyn's pioneering treatment of this once elusive group
of colonial prime movers centered upon their gradual acquisition of political power, their reciprocal ties to the London merchant class (and subse-
quent credit arrangements with them), their incorporation into transatlantic patterns of trade, their solidification and propagation of power through
familial links and intermarriage, their creation of financial arrangements
commensurate with a growing economy, and their structuring of trade arrangements around fish and timber. Later examinations of seventeenth-
century merchant activity in England and other British American regions
have reinforced the transatlantic thrust of Bailyn's analysis, following merchant activity into the intricate economic milieu of an emerging international marketplace and uncovering the variety of commercial strategies that
merchants perfected in the quest to become figures in the transatlantic market. These examinations collectively promote an image of merchant activity
as a phenomenon existing exclusively within an emerging capitalistic system that was flush with staple commodities, credit, and hard cash.[1]

The account books of Massachusetts merchants overwhelmingly support this perspective. Those of Robert Gibbs provide another example.
In the years 1661–66 Gibbs made twenty-nine purchases of timber products—mostly pipe staves and boards—worth a total of £449 6s. 2d. from a
supplier named Theodore Atkinson. After making these purchases, Gibbs
recorded entries that highlight the extensive effort required to transport
these goods throughout the Atlantic world. His accounts record entries

made in Boston while he was preparing for a West Indian voyage that included "hire of the ketch Beaver to Barbados," "the hire of a seller," "the dockage of the boat," and "the hire of the ketch to sayall." Once the shipments arrived in Barbados, Gibbs debited his brother William for "4 hh and two and thirty barrells of molasses, three barrells of rum, and one barrell sugar." Next, from Captain Thomas Breedon he purchased "8 hh rum (when gauged—507 gallons)," and from Thomas Darnell, "10 barrells of molasses." And he took more than £103 worth of sugar, rum, and molasses from several other Barbadian traders.[2] Much of this rum, sugar, and molasses found its way into Bay Colony homes, distilleries, and taverns, but a majority of it went toward the purchase of English textiles and manufactures, including wool, cotton, buttons, lace, serge, pins, shoes, and other consumer goods that Massachusetts residents were not producing in measurable quantities.[3] This decisively transatlantic trajectory further illuminates the conventional version of the New England merchant, with Gibbs's accounts revealing strong familial ties, an emphasis on staple goods, connections with English merchants, and a basic fluency in the new language of transatlantic trade. In so many respects, Gibbs seems a world away from the likes of John Barnard, John Burnham, or John Pearson.

Several other merchant accounts mirror Gibbs's activity. The accounts of Salem's John Higginson and Ipswich's Samual Ingersoll, two of the region's more notable merchants, demonstrate not only New England merchants' emerging overseas focus but also their impressive consolidation of regional economic power. Higginson, for his part, had his hands in several independent fishing companies. In 1680, for example, he purchased £218 worth of merchantable fish and "refuse cod" from Isaac Woodbury and Company and another £214 worth of mostly refuse cod from Joseph Phippany and Company.[4] Higginson then consigned the fish to several merchants who were preparing overseas journeys. Ingersoll, who had substantial interests in several ships and West Indian ventures, became one of Higginson's regular outlets. On February 29, 1694, according to one particularly well documented case, Ingersoll recorded, "shipt by John Higginson Jr. three hog[sheads] of fish and goods consigned to Samual Ingersoll."[5] Like Gibbs, Ingersoll arranged for his agent to trade his staples for rum, sugar, and molasses, some of which he kept and sold and the rest of which he traded for English textiles and manufactures. Both Higginson's and Ingersoll's accounts show them selling these goods to Bay Colony residents. Tobias Carter purchased laces, thread, tape, paper, and hooks;

Samual Wakefield bought gloves, tobacco, buttons, horse whips, silk, and stockings; and Richard Friend took lines, hooks, and nails from Higginson's cache of imports.[6] Ingersoll sold to his father "7 cask of sope" and "2 bar. tar.," and to a Mr. Trunchard he sold "20 bar. of tar."[7] These prominent merchants, in short, reiterate the standard image of the merchant class as an interconnected group of elite New England traders who were exploring novel economic opportunities in the late seventeenth century.

Even this cursory overview of these merchant accounts establishes the familiar story of a rising merchant class forming extensive interconnections, moving into the transatlantic economy, and centering their trade on high quantities of staple goods. But given what we know about the continuity of the local economy, this picture, while valid in outline, remains one-dimensional. A more sustained examination of merchant account books from the perspective of the internal economy reveals that merchants relied heavily on a local economy that had become an essential precondition for their expansion into foreign markets.

Indeed, a look beneath the surface of these accounts finds these merchants involved in the Bay Colony's economy on an entirely different level, negotiating a different world of goods, interacting with a different group of people, and handling a different network of economic connections. This less obvious economic activity evokes the early experience of George Corwin and brings into sharp focus the previous half-century of internal economic development. When he was not organizing a West Indian trading mission, Robert Gibbs retreated to his general store in order to barter small amounts of imported and local produce with neighbors. When Goody Seavers visited him on March 6, 1675, he sold her linen, sugar, pins, and serge in exchange for a roasting pig, fowl, milk, eggs, apples, peas, and butter. Similarly, Margaret Tomkins swapped him eggs, fowls, "homespun," and butter for coat buttons, tobacco, thread, linen, and sugar. With Goodman Langdon, Gibbs traded boards and pork for "mowing, cutting."[8] Gibbs's social and economic roots extended not only outwards into the emerging transatlantic world but also inwards into the established local economy. Many of his accounts, in fact, are hard to distinguish from those of Pickering, Barnard, and Burnham. Trading eggs and butter with local housewives is not an activity that we commonly associate with prominent merchants. Nevertheless, it gives us a more complete picture of how elite Massachusetts merchants operated. It also directly confirms the critical role that internal economic development played in both driving Massachusetts into the Atlantic world and, at the same time, preserving the traditional economic habits that defined the local economy.

Gibbs was not alone in his negotiation of these seemingly disparate worlds. Thomas Maule can also be found participating in the basic routines of traditional local exchange. When he was not traveling back and forth between Salem and Boston in order to settle overseas accounts, Maule could be found in the Salem marketplace, fulfilling his duties as the town clerk. He may have garnered the loyal respect of his West Indian agents in Boston, but on one particular occasion at least, Salem's Elizabeth Darby did not share the admiration. When she fell into a dispute with Maule over some "baking bread" that she supposedly had purchased, Maule recalled, "as soon as I was weighing it [the bread], Elizabeth Darby came into my shop and in a violent manner took me by the throat and with her fist punched me in my breast so that I was feint for want of breath and beat my fingers from my bagg of bread, so it is questionable whether I shall have the use of my finger again." Darby, "with the help of the Negro," ended up walking home with the "said bagg bisket." While an interesting scene in a number of respects, the fact that it was not at all unusual for a merchant of Maule's stature to participate in such an economic transaction as trading bread, however violently, says a great deal.[9] Maule may have lost his grip on the "biskett," but he never let go of the established, smaller realm of local economic exchange. To a large extent, his survival as a merchant depended upon it.

The same held true for John Higginson and Samual Ingersoll. At the same time that these powerful merchants were working together to send vast amounts of cod to the West Indies, they enmeshed themselves in local networks of exchange. After purchasing nails, buttons, and cloth from Higginson, for example, John Raymond made returns in five parcels of butter and two payments in malt. For pipes, glass, pins, pork, and wood, Joseph Reed promised "work in cording wood and sope boiling." John Simpson took serge, silk, and tobacco for carting goods for Higginson.[10] Ingersoll, for his part, can be found, even in the midst of provisioning ships, making deals like the one in which he paid a "Mr. Edwards" for essential ship supplies with goods including "a quarter mutton," "a quarter lam," "a leg of mutton," and beer.[11] Throughout these accounts, the necessity of the local market in larger ventures becomes increasingly evident.

The examples of Gibbs, Higginson, Maule, and Ingersoll participating in the local economy offers a telling glimpse into a less obvious side of elite merchant activity. Like a vine crawling up a wall, the Bay Colony merchant nurtured economic connections that grew upwards and outwards into larger and newer economic markets while shooting roots deep into the soil of the more familiar local environment. On the surface the internal and external economies appeared to be distinct entities operating in relative isolation from one another, but the Bay Colony merchant relied heavily on their intimate connection. Three trends evident in the accounts of elite merchants help establish this critical relationship. One of the most important of these trends was fear.

As already suggested, merchants showed an intimate familiarity with the intricacies of local economic exchange. In part this familiarity was borne of a subtle anxiety. While merchants' efforts to integrate themselves into the transatlantic economy met with dramatic success during the last quarter of the seventeenth century, this progress came at a cost. As merchants embraced overseas trade, they forfeited personal control over economic transactions. Market conditions, exchange rates, credit outlets, and terms of exchange were no longer local issues. They were now removed from immediate economic experience. As economic activity moved into the Atlantic world, it lost its familiarity. Thus, one reason that merchants stayed locked into the familiarity of the local economy was to compensate for a feeling of helplessness. Staying close to home helped ensure some level of economic competence and control as they sacrificed security by moving into potentially devastating overseas ventures. In short, their conscious efforts to keep one foot in what had now become a traditional realm of local economic exchange partially reflected a need to stay rooted in a safer, more stable social environment and system of exchange. The impulse to stay local played a partial but nonetheless significant role in tying internal and external economic developments into a solid knot.

In a typical missive to his Barbadian agent, Phillip English instructed, "Knowing not what is best I leave it to your descretion to make returns in what you think best for my advantage." These were words not likely written in a spirit of optimism. Allowing someone else to determine what was "best for my advantage" hardly put merchants at ease. Having to admit "knowing not what is best" went against the merchant's traditional instinct for control. Leaving economic affairs to the discretion of others, however, remained an unavoidable fact of life for Bay Colony merchants. The language of English's letter hints at a pervasive anxiety over the contingencies of having to entrust a valuable investment to a stranger. It includes references such as "in case the ketch should not return," "return the produce . . . in Barbados goods if to be had (if not) in dry goods," "send the effects by the first that is bound for Salem if Barbados goods[,] if English goods by [buy] any bound for Salem or Boston." These contingencies—these ifs—were indications that English ultimately had no clue what would happen.[12] As the examples of commercial farmers, traders, and artisans have shown, residents were accustomed to conducting their business with a relatively clear notion of their interests. They made economic decisions in a context of fairly fluid information and expectations. As the scope of business expanded, however, the steps between production and consumption lengthened. When this happened, familiarity diminished and anxiety, in turn, increased.

Not that actually being on location helped. "I wish I had stayed at home," an exasperated Dan King whined to English from his temporary base in St. Christopher. Trading on English's behalf in 1688, King noted that "a bad markett, constrains me to stay here while Spring, although much to my charge and disadvantage." As for the fish, it was "rotten or almost . . . what I have sold . . . I have sold low, by reason of its being decayed."[13] Writing from London several years later, John Seale complained of inadequate communication with English during Queen Anne's War. "I have not been forwarded any answer," he wrote. "I conclude that either they miscarried or that your answer might be on some of those ships that had the misfortune of being taken . . . in this wartime." He admonished English always to "take care to send copy of your letters by severall ships, by reason of the many of them that are taken into france."[14] Such precautions were foreign measures to those mired in local economic ways.

The inability to interpret or predict market conditions, as well as the relative difficulty in attaining quick credit, also placed merchants in a relatively helpless position. Reckonings, a way to organize trade in a local setting, were not possible in an international context. Despite the assurances of agents that "you may depend I will always study your interest," merchants found themselves awash in uncertainty.[15] "I have now the opportunity to supply myself with sugar," Sampson Sheafe wrote to Jonathan Corwin in 1688, "but then I shall incapacitate myself to pay my engagement for fish." He suggested to Corwin that perhaps "you speake with your bro or Mr. Benjamin Brown that they will accommodate me."[16] In 1689 William Hollingsworth wrote to his mother from the West Indies asking her to "pray let my brother see this letter" and confessing that "I cannot tell what to advise him to send as yet." As was so often the case in the unpredictable realm of export trade, a merchant had to await unforeseeable circumstances, keep his fingers crossed, and find out where his brother was through his elderly mother. Hollingsworth continued: "[W]ee shall see what these Newfoundland men will do[,] what quantity of fish they bring in[,] and then I will advise further."[17] In the late seventeenth century, just as the Bay Colony economy was starting to become deeply integrated into the Atlantic marketplace, the export economy, for all its potential, hindered comfortable access to a wide range of clients, credit sources, market information, and lines of communication—all factors that were taken for granted in the local economy. These uncertainties would diminish throughout the eighteenth century, but for the time being, merchants' letters seethed with frustration over the instability of commercial life.

Merchant accounts demonstrate one reaction to this anxiety. Massachusetts's internal economy reveals the continuity of local economic habits forged during the first decades after settlement and perpetuated throughout the seventeenth century. While merchants branched out into export markets, they simultaneously strengthened their hold within the internal economy. Indeed, when merchants loaded timber products and cod onto their ships, they pulled their region into an emerging world economy. In making this transition, however, Bay Colony merchants did not abandon those traditional habits forged within the local economy. Throughout the middle decades of the century, as we have seen, local traders defined the domestic economy through several specific economic characteristics. A man like George Corwin, who back in the 1650s was just getting into the business, naturally had no choice but to adhere to local custom. Prominent merchants in the middle of their career, however, continued to pursue these strategies locally. In doing so, they anchored their high-profile export activities in the more stable routines of the Bay Colony's local economy. Massachusetts merchants did not undergo a transition from provincialism to modernity; rather they simultaneously became both more provincial and more transatlantic in their economic orientation.[18]

John Higginson's accounts strongly suggest the ongoing significance of local economic activity to the merchants' strategies. Higginson's credits with Bay Colony residents reveal not only typical imported items like textiles and small manufactures but also a substantial amount of commonly exchanged, locally produced goods and services. Selections from a 1680 account sample show that Higginson sold Joseph Roade goods such as salt pork, beef, and butter in exchange for "10 days work at severall times" and "tubs of tallow." In a deal with John Trask, of Beverly, Higginson paid

Indian corn to John Dodge as a third-party payment, and in a similar arrangement he sent some sheep's wool to William Whittredge. John Clifford purchased basic commodities such as peas, Indian corn, and potatoes in exchange for "pasturage of my horses," and "bringing four cord of wood." Other scattered payments include "to Samual Southwick for one load of hay," "to 50 bu of oats," "to John Neale for pasturage," and to "James Poland for iron work." In his dealings with Joseph Phippany, a notable fish exporter, Higginson regularly sold butter, Indian corn, rye, hops, and pork for Phippany's private consumption.[19] If these kinds of transactions seem familiar, they should. They recall the same sort of economic activity that dominated the accounts of men like John Burnham, John Pickering, and John Barnard, whose economic lives revolved primarily around the contingencies of local economic affairs.

Robert Gibbs's transactions with his neighbors, all conducted from his general store, further demonstrate the intimate connection that transatlantic merchants maintained with the local market. As indicated in these especially telling documents, Gibbs sold a mixture of imported and locally produced goods to his neighbors in exchange for farm produce and services. With Goodman Seaver, for example, Gibbs swapped butter, flannel, and cash for "9 1/2 days work" and oakum. David Flint paid Gibbs in beef, suet, veal, and lamb in exchange for sugar, rum, and rye grains. For boards and "pieces of timber" Gibbs accepted "work" from Goodman Landin, and from Goody Hacker he took butter and eggs in a swap for veal. Robert Cole bartered eggs, pork, milk, butter, a roasting pig, cheese, and fowl for butter, sugar, flour, lace, and "to Goody Marchfield received." Goody Weborn offered milk for peas, sugar, butter, and linen. Goody Peale traded her washing services for a bushel of Gibbs' apples.[20] This kind of trading activity, of course, had been occurring in the Bay Colony for generations. Gibbs's participation in it simply provides an important reiteration of the local economy's significance to the rising merchant class.

A large minority of Gibbs's trading partners were women. Gender historians have conventionally portrayed economic opportunity on the colonial periphery as a short-lived phenomenon, momentarily opened by the fluid economic environment of a settlement society. Opportunities to participate in a traditionally male economic world would, according to this interpretation, quickly diminish once a more stable economic system matured.[21] The Gibbs example, however, complicates this line of argument. Gibbs's accounts show him exchanging goods with dozens of women, and the trades he executed with them normally involved swapping their domestically produced items for his imported textiles. Goody Spring took cotton and wool for butter, eggs, and veal; Goody Seavers traded apples, milk, fowl, Indian corn, butter, and eggs for linen, spice, cloth, broadcloth, and packing cloth; and Goody Courser bought string and sugar in exchange for milk.[22] These women and many others traded frequently with Gibbs at his store. Their participation in the local market should not in any way suggest a breakdown of traditional gendered norms. After all, their trades indicate that their foray into the local economy was at the behest of workaday domestic needs—cotton, wool, sugar, and spice—and underwritten by conventional domestic produce—eggs, butter, and milk. Nevertheless, Gibbs's own direct involvement in the internal economy counters the perception that this economic realm was somehow less important to larger economic concerns. As the underlying reasons for merchants' participation in the local economy become clear, the notion that women were relegated to a less significant economic position in the colonial economy seems less convincing. As we grasp the ways in which local economic behavior structured incorporation into export markets, and thus the ways in which it fueled the region's economic growth, the seemingly marginal act of swapping eggs for wool—an act more often than not performed by colonial women—becomes critically important.

The significance of the local economy in the strategies of Bay Colony merchants is further supported by several other merchant accounts. While the vast bulk of Philip English's accounts revolve around importing rum, sugar, and molasses and exporting cod and timber, a less evident aspect of his economic activity centered on distributing locally produced goods throughout the internal economy. His accounts show him purchasing wheat, Indian corn, and peas from Thomas Loball, accepting payments in pork, Indian corn, hides, malt, and wheat from dozens of other residents, and then incorporating these goods into sales made to an altogether new set of clients. In a transaction with John Hornbry on August 3, 1667, for example, English provided, in addition to rum, cloth, tobacco, and sugar, "34th of beefe . . . 2 bu Indian corn . . . 1 bu wheat."[23] Complementing local goods with those destined for exportation was a tactic often employed by John Higginson as well. In a typical transaction with John Pickering, Higginson sold him malt, hay, a hog, two third-party payments in hogs, Indian corn, and twenty quintals of refuse fish. In a trade with John Baylor, Higginson unloaded Indian corn, pins, shoes, lace, and money in exchange for barley, "trimming hogsheads, packing hogsheads."[24]

Like Gibbs, Samual Ingersoll kept a general store, and his store records further confirm the importance of the local economy to a merchant's overall activity. His accounts are especially useful in revealing the strategy of keeping an inventory that mixed local and imported goods. In a 1692 account he recorded the following goods "landed in my store": "1 bar. rum[,] 1 bar pork[,] 3 bar sugar[,] 1 bar tobacco[,] 1 bar pork[,] 1 bar rum and 1 hh rum[,] 1 bar carrotts[,] 6 bar tar[,] 2 bags of hops[,] 1 cake[,] 3 bar sidor[,] 1 bar mackerel[,] 2 bar beefe[,] 1 bar beere[,] 2 . . . [illegible] bread[,] 1 hh peas[,] 1 bar porke[,] 1 bar sidor[,] 5 bar porke[,] 2 bar sidor[,] 3 bar pork[,] 2 bar sidor[,] 1 bar barke[,] 2 hh molasses."[25]

A surviving list of ten accounts reveals how Ingersoll dispersed these goods:

To Mr. May: 1 bar beefe, 1 bar apples, 2 bar tar, 1 bag hops, 2 bar barke

To Mr. Poor: 1 bar apples, 1 bar tar

To Mr. Shane: 2 bar barke, a bar tar, 1 bar sidor

To Mr. ?: 1 hh molasses, 3 bar sidor, 2 bar beere, 2 bar tar

To Mr. Mounds: 1 bar tar, 1 bar porke, 1 bar beefe, 1 bar rum, 1 hh molasses

To Mr. ?: 15 qt refuse [fish], 24 qt fish, a barrell of carrots

To Mr. Dunkard: 1 bar sidor, 1 bar porke, 1 bar tar, 1 bags hops

To Mr. Marten: 1 bar apples

To a man living at ?: bar porke, 1 bag of hops, 60 pound of sugar, 100th tobacco

To Mr. Stone: 1 bar porke, 1 caske sugar (120 lb), 20lb tobacco

To Mr. ?: 1 bar beefe, 40 lb tobacco[26]

Ingersoll, like Gibbs and the rest of his merchant peers, interspersed his imported inventories with domestically produced goods, thereby assuring that if conditions in the overseas marketplace faltered—as they inevitably did on a periodic basis—he would continue to maintain leverage with his neighbors. It was his way of sticking to what he knew he could count on.

MERCHANTS ACTIVELY PARTICIPATING IN THE EBB AND FLOW OF THE traditional internal economy highlighted an essential force driving the rise of the merchant class in colonial New England. While the emergence of easy credit, more systematic shipping, bond markets, and established wholesalers throughout colonial British America helped lure Bay Colony merchants into the transatlantic world, the stability of local exchange simultaneously provided merchants with a familiar foundation upon which they could leap into those growing and dynamic markets. Few merchants made this connection explicit in their correspondences, but a reading of their accounts demonstrates a fear of uncertainty complemented by a concerted effort to keep a foothold in a local economy that had, from New England's perspective, a much better track record in terms of stability and longevity. Merchants were loath to condemn the social and economic values that held the local economy together. In fact, one suspects that there was every reason for them to take those same values with them into the less familiar world of foreign trade

ELEVEN

The Local Basis of International Trade

1670–1710

B Y THE LAST QUARTER OF THE SEVENTEENTH CENTURY MOST MER-
chants had stopped exporting primarily farm provisions and started to
concentrate on cod and timber products. Nevertheless, the significance of
locally produced and traded goods and services in fueling export activity
remained critical. Two tangible connections between the internal and external economies stand out. First, the local economy played a critical role
in provisioning export ships. The pork, beef, beer, and grain that drove
local exchange and fueled the ironworks' growth was, after all, the same
pork, beef, beer, and grain that stocked ships carrying timber and cod to
overseas markets. Second, when traders sent fish and timber from New
England, they depended on an intricate series of transactions that involved
not only provisioning services but also networks of local transportation,
internal trading links, the provisioning of the labor used to extract these
exports, and several other basic aspects of the local infrastructure. These
export-oriented activities, in short, drew directly on economic strategies
that had been pioneered internally, in response to local demands, throughout the century.

THE MOST CONCRETE MEANS BY WHICH LOCAL ECONOMIC ACTIVITY
helped push merchants into the export world was in provisioning ships.[1]
Provisioning required as much effort as did preparing the exported commodity itself. Moreover, it sent merchants deep into the local economy, as
central provisioning warehouses would not appear until well into the eighteenth century. Samual Ingersoll's accounts provide an especially detailed
look at this activity. In 1688, as he prepared the *Secretary* for a Barbados
trip, Ingersoll spent more than £13 on provisions, including "2 bar. beefe,
peas, bread, oyle, barrell of pork and butter, anchor, horse to transport

goods, ballast, canvas."[2] The list largely confirms what Ingersoll believed every man aboard the ship should consume each day, which was, according to his accounts, pork, flour, "2 biskett a man per day," "what peas they will eat," and "what fish they will eat."[3] The *Little General,* which Ingersoll apparently used for shorter, intercoastal trips, demanded frequent provisioning as well, and the records for it show Ingersoll drawing on locally produced goods with systematic regularity throughout the summer shipping season. The following is a partial list of his preparation for the summer fishing season:

> 5 May 1689: 1.5 hundred of bread, 1 bar. pork, 2 bu peas, one gal oyle, 2 bar beere
>
> 22 July 1689: one bar of porke, one bu pease, one gal. oyle, one hund. bread, 2 bar beere, 3.5 gal. mollases.
>
> 26 August 1989: 1/2 bar. porke, one gal. oyle, 1 1/2 bar pease, 3/4 hundred bread, 6 1/2 gal. mollases, 1/4 hundred of bread

The ship went in for repairs during the summer of 1690 but was again demanding local provisions the following summer:

> 22 May 1691: one bar. beere, one pound hops, one pound pepper
>
> 7 June 1691: one bar of beer, one hundred of bread
>
> 26 July 1691: butter, beer
>
> 27 August 1691: 1/2 bar porke, 7 gal. mollases, 1 gal. oyle, 4 lbs. candles, 1 1/2 hundred [of bread], 5 pecks peas, 2 bar beer

The *Little General*'s provisioning needs continued into 1692 and 1693:

> 11 July 1692: 5 pad locks, key for cabin door, beef, a cart, fresh meat, water, 2 h. pumpnails, 1h cask nails
>
> 28 March 1693: 172 lb porke, 159 of bread, 3 bar. beer, one gal. oil, 1 bu and 1/2 peck pease
>
> 4 May 1693: 1 1/2 hundred of bread, . . . [illegible] pounds of porke, 2 bar. of beer, 1 gal oil, 1 bu pease, 3 peck of pease, 4 qt. oil, 70 pounds of porke, one hundred of bread, 2 bar of beere, 1 gal. molasses
>
> [June 1693?]: one bar porke, 90 th of bread, one gal. oil, 3 bar. beer, 1/2 bu peas
>
> 26 July 1693: 2 bar. beer, one gal oil, one bushel of peas, 98th of bread, a sheep
>
> 5 September 1693: 3 bar beer, bread, 1 bu peas, 1/2 quarter of flour, beefe, lam, oil[4]

Other merchant accounts routinely reiterate this kind of provisioning activity. Just scratching the surface of these documents shows Philip English preparing for a Bilbao voyage by provisioning the *Repair* with, among other goods, "sweet oyle for the men," salt, "twine for mending the sail," "75 wt of fresh beef," and a "cask of pitch." On board the *Dragon* he provided his men "parcel of beans, bread . . . 113 gal. rum, 3 barells cider . . . 1 bu beans . . . 1 firkin butter." And on the *Susanna*, water, beef, flour, wine, and a hog.[5] John Higginson's ketch, the *Friendship*, required "2 hundreth of bread, 1 barrel of porke, 1 bu peas, candles . . . beer" for a 1679 Madeira voyage, while the *John and Thomas* took "1 bar. porke, mackerall, candles, 1 bu peas, 2 qts. oil, 1 bu peas, 2 candles, peas, powder . . . 7th of bread . . . 12 barells beer and cask" for a Newfoundland fishing voyage. Another fishing voyage, this time on the *Dolphin*, demanded "pork and tar, peas, net . . . oil, butter, candles . . . barell porke, peas, mackerell, bread . . . 12 barrells of beer and 8 candles." These provisions kept the men at sea long enough to pull in £233 0s. 6d. worth of cod.[6] Other than recording an unusually high number of entries for ship repairs as part of the provisioning account, Jonathan Corwin also adhered to this pattern. For the *James Bonaventure* he recorded provisioning "1 lb. bread," "work on ship by John Andrews," and pork; for the *Salem* he noted "25 lbs. beef, 7 barrells beer" and "for carting"; and the *Speedwell* went to Barbados with "boat nails . . . barrell of beere, bread, 9 bu peas . . . one side of mutton" after being refurbished with a new anchor, "joiner's work," and new rigging.[7]

Acquiring these goods and services demanded an intricate familiarity with patterns of local trade. Much as these provisioning accounts reveal a wide range of goods, they also reveal numerous internal suppliers. Merchants, most of whom had had their start in the local economy, turned to local suppliers for provisions on a regular basis. For example, Ingersoll's records reveal him buying beer from John Tapley, bread from John Bulols, and apples from John Jeffords and "Mr. Nick." He obtained pork from "Mr. Jeffries" and "Mr. Brown." Other entries show him venturing into the local economy to purchase pork, molasses, rum, flour, bread, and peas from "Mr. Lolley"; bread and cider from "Mr. Allen"; and bread, tobacco, apples, and beef from "my own vendor."[8]

Higginson also delved into the local economy to obtain his goods. In preparation for a 1680s voyage, he visited Samual Gardener for bread, John Hill for beer, John Ormes for wheat, and William Dodge for malt and hops (which he then sold to John Hill). John Raymond provided his butter, William Bowditch supplied beer, Benjamin Small sold him linen and tobacco,

Henry Henrick provided Indian corn and cheese, and Timothy Lindall grew his peas.[9] Jonathan Corwin found John Andrews when he needed work done on his ships and Edward Littlefield when he needed bread and Indian corn.[10] English similarly drew on his extensive connections in the local economy to obtain his shipping provisions. English obtained peas, fish, and salt from Thomas Woodbury; peas, beef, and pork from Humphry Woodbury; barrels of beer from Job Holyard; and wheat, corn, and tobacco from William Hombart.[11] These trades for provisions were nothing new. They had been going on since the earliest days of settlement, but now they served a new purpose. The internal economy was adjusting and, through its adjustments, serving the needs of a maturing export economy. When these merchants bought provisions from local suppliers, they were capitalizing on the internal economic contacts that had been evolving for generations, consistently responding and adjusting to local growth and development.

Merchants relied heavily on the local economy not only for food and drink but for routine ironwork repairs as well. Jonathan Corwin paid several ironworkers for the following repairs on the *Swallow* before a 1687 voyage: "two pump bolts, mending anchor, rudder staples, anchor weighing 131 lbs., anchor weighing 130 lbs., anchor weighing 133 lbs." An inventory for the *Speedwell* included purchases for "ironwork of boat nails, pump nails . . . carting of ironwork for ship . . . the ironwork for anchors"; the *Salem* inventory showed "ironwork for the boat."[12] Higginson, once again, tapped the local economy to obtain the requisite ironwork for his fleet of ketches. "To William Coates," he recorded on February 10, 1680, "for all the small ironworks." A week earlier, he had recorded payments to "James Pollard for ironwork, William Curtis for ironwork, Edward Bridges for mending an anchor . . . 1 anchor from Edward Bridges."[13] When English sold a hull to a John Gobe in 1691, he noted that the shipwright William Becket had originally constructed it with iron forged at the Lynn Ironworks back in the 1650s. The iron had since been replaced, he explained, with the help of local ironworkers "and other carpenter works that is accustomed to bring her afloat." English's records show that he paid more than £6 to a Mr. Cornbury for "upkeep of William and Mary" and another several pounds to a Mr. Barton for "carpenter work."[14]

Eleanor Hollingsworth is another example of an individual supplier adjusting to the shipping trade. Although complete documentation for her domestic beer production does not exist, Hollingsworth—who, being very wealthy, was not a typical brewer—produced beer regularly for her family, for neighborly exchange, and for consumption in resident ordinaries.[15] In 1687 and 1688, however, Hollingsworth also embraced the opportunity to fulfill provisioning requirements by regularly producing "ship's beere" for several merchants whom she met through her husband. William Bowditch reminded John Price before an August 1689 journey to "Pray pay Mrs. Hollingsworth for five barrels of ship beare the which I have had of her for the use of the ship Mayflower." Later that year, Benjamin Allen wrote a receipt for "Mrs. Hollingsworth four barrels of beer on the acct of Capt. Price." An unattributed account orders "pay unto Mrs. Ellinor Hollingsworth two pounds four shillings worth . . . this is for beer and barrells." Hollingsworth accepted payment in leftover fish, as she did with a client who agreed to "pay unto Mistres Hollingworth . . . [illegible] pound five shillings and six pence in refuse." This activity seems to have been going on sporadically for years. In 1688 Allen wrote another receipt for "four barrels of Ms. Hollingsworth on the acct. on Capt. Price"; in 1887 Captain John Price agreed to "pay unto mistress Elanor Hollingsworth seven pounds . . . upon account it being for beare and barrells"; and finally, in 1686, a receipt records "Capt. John Price . . . to pay unto Mistress Hollingworth for fourteen barrels of beer . . . for William Balt and company."[16] Hollingsworth did not create her brewing business in response to the demands of Price's merchants. Nevertheless, her brewing activity, which had its roots in the local economy, easily adjusted to this new demand.

One reason that late-seventeenth-century Bay Colony merchants succeeded as well as they did was that shipping provisions were, by the last quarter of the century, easily obtainable. It is critical to stress that the process of supplying ships did not emerge as a response to increasing export activity. Instead, it nurtured its roots in a preexisting network of local economic exchange tied to emerging local demands. Whereas the gap between export ideals and the much more difficult reality of getting goods into export markets had once been enormous, by the 1670s it had been effectively bridged. The evolution of an internal economy played a substantial role in building that bridge. Through the seemingly simple (but actually intricate) task of provisioning ships, merchants thrived because they tapped a local economy already teeming with the goods and products necessary for lengthy voyages. Infrastructural inadequacy had, by the last quarter of the century, become infrastructural strength, and that strength became the platform upon which merchants braced themselves as they eased their well-stocked ships into the Atlantic Ocean.

BECAUSE THE TERMS *INGATE* AND *OUTGATE* OBSESSED SEVENTEENTH-century merchants, conventional approaches to the export trade have asked the following questions, and expected the following answers, about the *Susanna*'s 1688 trip to St. Christopher's. What was the outgate? The answer would surprise no one: cod, barrels, mackerel, oil, boards, staves, and shingles. What was its value? Again, a familiar answer: £18,458. To whom did the commander, John Lamb, sell in St. Christopher? Twenty-five plantation owners. What was the ingate? Molasses and sugar. What was its value? A matching £18,458. How many agents did Lamb deal with? Three. What commission did the merchant earn? £587.[17] Collectively these questions and answers provide precisely the sort of information that economic historians have long sought in order to establish the significance of external trade for local developments.

Nevertheless, as precise as these answers are, the question still remains, What had to occur *before* ships like the *Susanna* ever even left port? If Massachusetts's export trade is conceptualized as a circulatory system, the scene described above—the ingate and outgate—would be the pumping heart at the system's center. That said, how did exporters obtain their products? How did they get them to port? How did they fund and provision the efforts to obtain exportable staples? In other words, where were the arteries and veins and blood vessels? What emerges from an investigation of these questions is the outline of an intricate internal economy. These questions, moreover, lead to answers that reveal the ultimate significance of the internal economy in buttressing the export trade.

THE ACQUISITION OF FISH FOR EXPORT REQUIRED MERCHANTS TO NEGO-tiate an industry that even in the late seventeenth century was sprawling and decentralized.[18] While shipments on vessels bound for the West Indies or the Madeira Islands usually contained thousands of quintals of fish, merchant records reveal a kind of scattershot approach to acquiring cod and mackerel, with merchants buying small amounts from scores of small suppliers and then selling or consigning their parcels to exporters.

Robert Gibbs provides a clear example of the process of getting fish to market. A 1669 account includes the following fish purchases in May and June at Marblehead and Winter Island. On May 28 and 29 Gibbs purchased 114 quintals and 18 quintals from George Alley and Company and another

50 quintals from William Waters and Company. From June 2 to June 4 he bought 23 quintals from William Waters and Company, 68 quintals from William Clater and Company, and 90 quintals from John Roads and Company. Similar purchases occurred on ten other days in June, from seven more companies and dozens of individual suppliers. These purchases, averaging 23 quintals of fish, added up to about 803 quintals.[19] Obtaining this quantity of fish demanded that Gibbs shuffle between Boston, Marblehead, and Winter Island, deal with dozens of fish companies and individuals, and make scores of small purchases—all in a period of about two months. After obtaining these parcels of fish, Gibbs consolidated and sold them to nine merchants in quantities ranging from 11 to 522 quintals.[20]

Gibbs was not alone in obtaining his fish from so many sources and in such relatively small quantities. In order to export fish on his own ships, Philip English similarly negotiated the fishing industry's decentralized structure. Like Higginson, he relied on Woodbury and Company for some portion of his fish. As one surviving receipt notes, "Mr. Isaac Woodbury do please to pay unto Mr. Philip English fower quintals of refuge fish."[21] Scattered accounts show English buying just £2 worth of mackerel from Edward Homan, 5 quintals of refuse from William Leach, £3 worth of refuse fish from Thomas Cromwell, and even 10s. worth of rotten fish.[22] Two accounts for English's ship the *Repair* further confirm the decentralized structure of the industry. In August 1687 English purchased cod from James Ropes, Henry Burrell, Michael Lambert, and Jonathan Bradshaw. In September he bought another parcel from Bradshaw, as well as loads from Elizabeth Wishorett, Mary Farlow, and Job Cox. In October he made a single purchase from Anthony Archer. In February 1688 English made two purchases of cod and two of mackerel. In May, June, and July 1688 he made four more purchases to complete his yearly fish purchases for the *Repair*.[23] As it did for Gibbs, obtaining fish for export required English to cover considerable ground.

Jonathan Corwin's accounts reveal more of the same: small and frequent purchases of fish from wholesalers scattered throughout the region. Most of these purchases were from Higginson, to whom Corwin sent an agent to buy fish. On one occasion, when the terms of sale fell into confusion, Corwin directed his agent to "speake with Mr. Turner, Higginson, and Gardiner and to see that they do deliver good fish . . . if in case they refuse to comply I will go to Marblehead . . . and deal with them as well as I can."[24] To one Salem resident he sold peas, corn, iron, sugar, and tobacco for "155 quintals fish."[25] Jeremiah Taylor wrote a receipt that confirmed "from James Skimmer for the use of Mr. Jonathan Corwin merchant in Salem fourteen quintall of winter cod fish."[26] While Corwin exported a portion of the fish he acquired, he also resold it down the road in Boston. Jeremiah Taylor noted, "received from Mr. Jonathan Corwin . . . thirty nine quintals of fish upon the account of Mr. Peter Seargent merchant in Boston." And James Barton noted, "Mr. Jonathan Corwin be so kind as to pay to Benjamin Marden . . . eighteen quintals of refuse cod fish." The payment was most likely for a third-party debt, since a few months earlier William Knight had recorded, "Jonathan Corwin forty and five quintals of pollack . . . for the use and upon account of James Barton."[27] Much like Gibbs, Corwin regularly participated in the local trade of fish as a crucial step in the long process of preparing large parcels for export.

Some merchants tried to impose order on the chaos. The relationship between John Higginson and Samual Ingersoll demonstrates how merchants were beginning to coordinate their efforts to better concentrate fishing ventures. Higginson spent a great deal of time cultivating a vested interest in two fishing companies, Isaac Woodbury and Company and Joseph Phippany and Company. Preparing for a 1680 fishing voyage, Higginson stocked Woodbury and Company with £22 worth of provisions, including beans, bread, oil, candles, "salt of Capt. Price," pork, "salt at Beverly," and beer that he had bought from John Hill. In July and August 1680 Woodbury and his crew landed three major shipments of fish: 58 quintals, 98 quintals, and £34 worth of refuse cod. The following March, they pulled in two major shipments of merchantable fish (70 and 27 quintals). In the end, Higginson owned just over £218 worth of cod.[28] Also in 1680, Higginson outfitted Joseph Phippany and Company with pork, salt, oil, beans, peas, butter, wood, candles, pork, beer, and bread, totaling £25 17s. 1d. In June through August the company returned five fish loads averaging 32.6 quintals. In November and December it landed four more loads, averaging 39.5 quintals. The total for these shipments came to £214 1s.[29] In order to complete these provisioning requirements, Higginson had to deal with several residents. To supply Phippany, he bought bread and peas from John Collier, a barrel of pork and oil from "Mr. Batter," candles from Joseph Elpay, and "bread of Sam Gardner."[30] By funding and provisioning these ships and securing labor, Higginson began to establish a more centralized process of acquiring fish.

Samual Ingersoll did not nurture such connections with small fishing companies. He was, however, keenly interested in obtaining fish to load on his ample fleet of export ships. His accounts thus reveal him buying small parcels of fish from Mr. Jeffords, Mr. Cole, Mr. Evans, and Mr. Barenton and then loading these quintals onto a ship for export, as indicated by his "goods on bord the sloop" account. Higginson, like Jeffords, Cole, and the others, was one of Ingersoll's regular wholesalers. Ingersoll's books are scattered with references such as "shipt by John Higginson Jr. three hog of fish and goods consind to Samuall Ingersoll," "received of John Higginson," and "3 hh for Mr. Higginson, 2 hh for Mr. Higginson."[31] Unlike English and Corwin, who seem to have assumed the dual role of funding fishing companies and exporting cod in their own ships, Ingersoll and Higginson divided these tasks and worked together.

Despite the best efforts of Higginson and Ingersoll, there was nothing systematized about the fishing trade by the late seventeenth century. Men still found themselves buying and selling fish sporadically, from scores of vendors, and in very small parcels. Higginson's accounts not only confirm his relationship with fairly well established fishing companies but also reveal his reliance on a wide range of individual suppliers. A brief overview of his 1680–81 accounts indicates that in addition to buying fish from the fishing companies, Higginson purchased fish from at least eight resident fishermen. These purchases occurred in the context of routine local economic exchange. For example, Higginson purchased some fish along with malt, hogs, and Indian corn from John Pickering; from Richard Flander he took "refuse cod, boys work" in exchange for a variety of imported goods; and with John Trask he traded Indian corn for a few quintals of merchantable fish.[32] When Ingersoll prepared for a 1692 summer voyage, he purchased fish from nine vendors, with no parcel exceeding 29 quintals.[33] So while these merchants strived for coherence, they worked within the industry's sprawling structure.

The internal anatomy of the fishing industry sheds sharp light on the local economy's role in export endeavors because the decentralized nature of the fishing trade created conditions that placed a significant burden on routine local processes. To appreciate the significance of these factors, it is necessary to conceptualize the fishing industry's internal operation in the widest possible context. We have seen thus far several participants in this industry: the fishing companies, individual suppliers, wholesale merchants, retail merchants, and exporting merchants. These participants, as we have also seen, engaged in numerous interactions before the exporter actually loaded the casked cod and embarked upon the Atlantic. But what held these innumerable interactions together?

Local economic habits, particularly the trade in farm produce and transportation services, were essential to getting exports to port. Perhaps most important, farm produce held internal transactions together at nearly every link in the process. As we have seen, merchants drew heavily on local produce to provision fishing voyages run by established companies, as well as export ventures. But they also relied heavily on local produce when obtaining catches from individual fishermen. When acquiring a parcel of fish from William Henfield, for example, Higginson paid part of his bill in butter and pork. John Trask provided Higginson fish in partial exchange for Indian corn. Higginson sold Ezekial Wallers malt that he obtained from William Dodge so that Wallers could produce the ships' beer for the companies' voyages. Higginson paid John Beckett for "work on John & Thomas, work on Friendship, work on Dolphin" in salt pork and hops.[34] Samual Ingersoll also relied on local produce to acquire fish for export. In 1692 he inventoried "goodes landed in my store." These goods, which he used to acquire fish for an August venture, included apples, pork, tobacco, cider, beef, beer, bread, and peas. He sold these products, mixed in with a few imported goods, to "Mr. Stone, Mr. Cole, Mr. Prouse" in exchange for about sixty quintals of cod and mackerel.[35] In short, a closer inspection of the pivotal transactions supporting the export trade reveals the familiar components of the local economy. It stands to reason that merchants stayed involved in the internal economy. Without its support, the ability to gather fish for export would have been greatly diminished, if not rendered impossible.

Transportation services also proved to be crucial in binding the internal anatomy of the export cod trade. Merchants were men obsessed with their ships, but their accounts reveal them to have been equally concerned with internal modes of transport. Reliance on preexisting modes of local transportation was evident at every stage in the convoluted process of getting goods to shore for export. The accounts of Jacob Pudetor, a local iron worker, recall the prevalent role that transportation played in the Bay Colony's developing internal economy. Merchants continually went to him to have their horses fitted for shoes, for "iron work for the cart," "mending a horse chain," and so on.[36] When Ingersoll prepared the *Secretary* for a 1688 journey to Barbados, he recorded 5s. for "horse to transport goods." When provisioning a ship in 1692, he included a cart as one of his expenses. To truck fish from Marblehead to Boston for export on the *Prudent and Mary*, Ingersoll included "my expenses in going to the bridge," "paid Tom . . . [illegible] for 3 days work [transporting]," and "to the bridge for the business."[37]

The accounts of Jonathan and George Corwin and John Higginson reiterate the importance of an established transportation network in the internal process of getting fish to market. When Jonathan Corwin arranged to have some work done on the *Speedwell*, he included debits for "carting iron work for ship" and the transportation of anchor and pump nails. Provisions loaded onto the *Salem* required a 1s. 6d. expense "for carting." Other records show him paying 8s. 1d. on "fraight of the small bindall to the Isle of Shoales." When imports came off a returning ship, he paid 6s. for "porterage to storidge."[38] Jonathan's brother George included charges such as "to carting 21 bar. pork from the warehouse and severall other goods," "to 2 days work in going to Marblehead about the pump," and "for a journey to Boston."[39] In 1682 Higginson paid more than 16s. for the "freight and cullege" of 149 quintals of fish sent to Boston for consignment. Just before this delivery he recorded an entry for "work done on my cart," and later he included a 17s. charge for "carting salt pork" to provision Benjamin Small's fishing boat.[40]

The intricate tasks of hauling goods to and from ports and the surrounding countryside, provisioning fishing voyages, and obtaining the produce to make these jobs possible are easy to take for granted. Infrastructure, however, was critical to the operation of the export economy. In such a geographically dispersed industry as the fishing trade, it remained essential for merchants to maintain constant access to local produce and transportation equipment and services. Without that access the transition to export trade would have been impossible to achieve.

THE OTHER MAJOR EXPORT INDUSTRY TO EMERGE IN THE LATE-seventeenth-century Massachusetts Bay region, the timber trade, similarly relied on a highly functional local economy. Judging from the accounts of Robert Gibbs and Jonathan Corwin, merchants first secured a grip on the industry by gaining ownership of sawmills in heavily forested areas away from the towns from which they exported. Corwin established a mill in Wells, Maine, on the Cape Porpoise River, while Gibbs formed connections with several mills on the Piscataqua River in Rhode Island. Both locations were a couple of days' journey from Salem and Boston, and this distance required both merchants to draw heavily on the local economy to keep the mills in constant operation and to provide and obtain supplies. Like the internal anatomy of the fishing trade, the local economy played a significant role in provisioning and providing transportation for the timber trade.

Large timber companies had yet to form in order to supply mills, so Gibbs and Corwin found themselves working within a sprawling economy that demanded constant interaction with scores of small suppliers. For example, Gibbs traded thread and needles for wood from Ezekial Giles, and he swapped Holland and calico for timber with "John Kimall's wife."[41] In preparation for one voyage he bought boards and staves from a wide range of suppliers living in between Boston and the Piscataqua River, including John Gill, Richard Mason, George Haskett, a Mr. Chadorne, and Jacob Legay.[42] When it came time to find a way to consign these various wood products to an overseas venture, Gibbs again dealt with the decentralized structure of the export economy. In the early 1660s, over the course of about eighteen months, he supplied small quantities of timber products to several merchants with great regularity. On twenty-eight occasions, for example, he delivered timber products to at least eight merchants, and never at a value exceeding a relatively small £5.[43]

The wide geographical scope of the timber trade placed an even heavier burden on internal transportation resources than did the fish industry. Jonathan Corwin's records reveal a constant preoccupation with travel between Salem and Cape Porpoise, as well as his near-total reliance on local transportation services to truck provisions and timber products between these towns. His mill accounts, for example, include payments for services such as "by two days for his oxen in bringing goods to town," "bringing goods to town by his cart for two days," "2 days work with his cart in bring[ing] goods to the shore," "much carried to loggers" for "rafting boards, by two days work for getting goods to towne."[44] Gibbs also allows some insight into his transportation arrangements. William Deane received "coat, shoes, and linen" for "bringing wood from wharf," while he entered a debit on a delivery of white oak staves for "the freight of the staves by Swayne."[45]

These tasks were invariably fraught with complications. Corwin's Cape Porpoise agent, Joseph Stover, continually despaired over the difficulties he and his workers were having moving logs and timber products. In July 1682 he complained that hired cart men could not "hall up the logs . . . which is a great hindrense" because "the rope that they now have is break so many times that they are forced to use all the loggers chains." In November the problem was ice. Although Stover and a helper "took care to raft the boards down to the plante," they encountered a situation in which "the river is frozen up; it is some charge to raft them down." The biggest frustration of all came when transportation was not available on demand.

"There is more merchantable boards at the mill," Stover noted, "but they was not hauled down to the landing plane which forced me to send 500 foot of refuse board."[46]

Corwin remained similarly dependent on the local economy for food and services for his mill employees and transporters. He delivered a hog from Salem to several Wells residents for "work about the dam," sent "4 bu Indian corn to Francis Blackhorn," a manager of the Cape Porpoise operation, and routinely supplied his workers with beer, rum, wheat, hides, horses, butter, pork, and cheese. One list of mill provisions included 1,169 pounds of pork.[47] The mill's range of demands on the Salem economy was reminiscent of the ironworks' demands on the local economy. The mill was even debited for "a payre of playne shoes for the loggers and 2 or 3 pairs of playne shoes for a child."[48] Then there were the routine rounds of repairs and miscellaneous projects upon which the mill relied heavily on local residents. Corwin's mill accounts include payments for saws, shovels, spades, board nails, locks for the mill dam, and "one house to be built for the sawers," "smith work," "mending dam," and "boards to loggers house."[49] In these small ways, and in so many others, the logging industry's internal anatomy relied directly on a number of routine goods and services that only the local economy could provide.

GIBBS, CORWIN, ENGLISH, AND THEIR COLLEAGUES BECAME HIGHLY successful international merchants. Their efforts to export cod and timber, however, reveal not only extensive transatlantic connections but, more surprisingly, deep connections to the local economy. It is tempting to downplay the significance of such activities as provisioning export ships with locally produced beer, bartering eggs and butter at the merchant shop in order to supply the workers who were catching fish, using well-traveled internal routes to truck supplies to commercial wood mills in Maine, and arranging for local couriers to consolidate small catches of fish into a single large shipment. As merchant accounts books confirm, however, there was nothing incidental about these basic economic tasks. The pivotal points at which the internal and external economies met indicate that merchants relied heavily on an integrated economic environment that smoothed the historically difficult transition from local commercial exchange to international commerce. This integration evolved not only from the export economy down but, relying as it did on the continuity of local economic life in early Massachusetts, from the ground up as well.

Epilogue: The Parsons and the Goulds

THROUGHOUT THE SEVENTEENTH CENTURY, MERCHANTS MADE THE most of the economic opportunities that came their way. As a result, by the end of the century Massachusetts had become a place where it was entirely possible for fortunes to undergo substantial shifts over the course of a lifetime and, if one were fortunate enough, to intensify dramatically in the decades thereafter.

This transformation is precisely what happened to the Parsons family. When Gloucester's John Parsons, the son of a small farmer, died in 1714, his three brothers inherited an impressive diversity of assets, including a "flake room" for drying the fish they caught, a sawmill, extensive farmland, and livestock. Seven years later, when brother Nathaniel died, the brothers had substantially increased their holdings to three ships, a wharf, a warehouse, an entire building for housing fish, and a retail business specializing in fishing provisions. By the time Nathaniel's son William died in 1752, he had turned these holdings into a full-fledged and highly profitable fishing business that systematically traded cod in the Caribbean and on the Iberian peninsula. His net worth was more than £2,000, an astounding amount of money for the time. Indeed, Parsons had come a long way from the hardscrabble life led by his grandfather.

Although William became only a middling merchant, the story of his family's success was no anomaly. The most prominent merchant families in Massachusetts, in fact, came to prominence at the turn of the century, and they often came from humble origins. The Belchers, Wentworths, Bowdoins, Olivers, and Faneuils, for example, all saw their familial stocks rise in the course of a generation and solidify into institutions over the years. For those men seeking prominence and wealth in the transatlantic world, it was a good time to be alive and ambitious.[1]

It was also a time, however, when the vast majority of Massachusetts residents led working lives marked by monotonous continuity. The economic activities that structured their lives were indistinguishable from those of earlier generations. The largely agricultural, local, and inherited habits forged by Puritan pioneers intent on maintaining a competency persisted through the generations, preserving an impressive level of social cohesion and economic competence by virtue of the scale, scope, and personal nature of the settlers' work. It the kind of work that, because of its ubiquity, did not draw the notice of contemporaries and, as a result, has generally not drawn the attention of historians. Nevertheless, when a man like Nathaniel Parsons was taking his business to a transatlantic level, a contemporary of his like John Gould—a common Ipswich farmer—was doing what his father, grandfather, and great-grandfather had done since settlement: exchanging goods and services to the best of his advantage within the confines of the local economy. For too long, historians have missed the connection between the Parsons and the Goulds.

Gould's economic behavior was inherently traditional. It balanced profit and competency by highlighting, among other staples of local economic behavior, the roles of familial connections, local networks of neighborly exchange, third-party transactions, and an ongoing concern with transportation facilities and equipment. His activity was, for all of its simplicity, central to the evolution of Massachusetts's economy and society. A few snapshots of Gould's typical working days capture the essence of what it was like to be a Puritan pioneer. On July 20, 1698, Gould "reckoned with Zachus Gould . . . for flaxseed and hens and other things that we could think of." He noted that "the flaxseed and peas and other money I had of him was eight shillings and four pence." Referring to his brother, his accounts explain that Joseph Gould was a creditor "to 2 bu and one bu of oates and his half bushel of oats paid in the year 97." He mentioned "Goodwife Cary's sheep," explaining that he had from her "2 old ewes and 2 young ewes." On April 15, 1702, John Gould seemed especially concerned with his father, who had become elderly and in need of help. "I began to look after father's work," Gould wrote, "and I let father have one bushel of seed barley to sow and one bushel of oates and a peck of flaxseed." He also noted that "my wife made a coat and westcoat for father." On July 21, 1708, Gould entered, "Brother Courtice Cr[edit] . . . to thre days work about clabording the house, to two rakes, to two days work about shingling the leanto, to one plow, mending the dormer window and the floor, and one day killing my cow." He paid "Brother Courtice" with his son's labor ("to mow for Mr. Coper"), a bushel of malt, a bushel of Indian corn, turnips, and the "making of one barril side."[2] The year was 1708. But as we have seen, it might just as easily have been 1638, 1658, or any day in between.

On the surface, the work habits that structured the days of John Gould and the Parsons brothers would seem to have nothing in common. In fact, they might very well appear to represent a fundamental dichotomy in the way that Massachusetts residents participated in economic life, a dichotomy that has conventionally been described as subsistence and capitalistic modes of production. In this interpretation, Gould and Parsons would live in different worlds, belong to different classes, espouse different values, and have different dreams. As the farmers and merchants profiled have shown, however, the direct and indirect connections that evolved between men like Gould and Parsons became central to the larger patterns of economic development that characterized Massachusetts throughout the entire seventeenth century. When merchants moved into overseas markets, they stood on the shoulders of the men, women, and children who provided the infrastructural preconditions for them to do so—people who, like Gould, were going about their business in a local setting. In providing the basis for a sound local economy capable of supporting a systematic export trade, the largely hidden work of Puritan pioneers allowed the Parsons of the region to flourish conspicuously.

This connection was not limited to the seventeenth century. A continued look at Gould's account book, which was taken over by his son, reveals that the essential (if often numbing) continuity of local economic life persisted well into the eighteenth century. From 1713 to 1718 Gould traded regularly with a Mr. Symonds, weaving ninety-seven yards of cloth. In exchange, Symonds paid Gould with a bedstead, a table, and a bushel of corn. On April 19, 1720, Gould succinctly recorded, "all accounts settled." With Isaac Peabody, in April 1722, he recorded a debt for "sledding 2 loads of timber out of the woods and [the use of] 2 oxen 2 days" and "one day with my team and one man to fetch timber for you so far as my house." In return, Peabody paid "8 shillings in money" and "one hide cord." Gould took "3lb and ½ fish" and "one pr of shoes" for "carting one load of plank from woods," "three oxen steers," "to fetch plank from woods mill," and "1/2 day of Solomon to plow." In December 1717, for a Mr. Farley, he recorded weaving seventeen yards of wool cloth, twenty yards of wool cloth, and "2 geese" for "fulling, dying, and pressing." What is noteworthy about these transactions is that from the perspective of the seventeenth century they seem so routine, so common, and so reflective of the way the local economy had always worked. What is revealing, in other words, is that there is nothing new going on. This continuity continued to be a prerequisite for more conspicuous change.[3]

Even late into the century local economic habits showed no signs of changing. By the 1770s the original Gould's grandson was in charge of the worn-out account book; his refreshingly clean script recorded transactions that could just as easily have occurred a hundred years earlier. He sold to William Booth "2 bu of rye" for flax and "making a suit of clothes" in 1775. In 1783 he traded "making a pair of breeches" for "cutting a coat" with John Balch.[4] He exchanged bushels of corn, rye, and oats and engaged in such services as weaving, hauling hay, and loaning carts and oxen. In undertaking these trades Gould not only met immediate needs but honed the familiar economic strategies that had served local economic development so well: third-party transactions, familial trading arrangements, and reckonings. As he did so, he improved transportation systems, fostered provisioning skills, and made available specific skills and tools that merchants would need in order to get goods from inland locations to the loading docks that now crowded the coast.

When Nathaniel Parsons eased his ship from the port of Salem, headed past Winter Island, and turned right into the Atlantic stream, he would have enjoyed an expansive view of the landscape behind the bustling Massachusetts shoreline. Chances are that he would have known that landscape, and the Goulds who lived there, better than he knew the markets toward which he sailed.

Notes

Introduction

1. John J. McCusker and Russell R. Menard, *The Economy of British America, 1607–1789*, 2nd ed. (Chapel Hill, NC, 1991), 90–95; John Winthrop, "Arguments for the Plantation of New England," in *Winthrop Papers, 1498–1649*, 4 vols. (Boston, 1929–47), 2:138–49; David Grayson Allen, *In English Ways: The Movement of Societies and the Transferal of English Local Law and Custom to Massachusetts Bay in the Seventeenth Century* (Chapel Hill, NC, 1981), 228; Darrett B. Rutman, "Governor Winthrop's Garden Crop: The Significance of Agriculture in the Early Commerce of Massachusetts Bay," *William and Mary Quarterly* 20 (1963): 396–415; Richard L. Bushman, "Markets and Composite Farms in Early America," ibid. 50 (1998): 351–74; Karen Ordahl Kupperman, *Providence Island, 1630–1641: The Other Puritan Colony* (Cambridge, MA, 1993).

2. Edward Johnson, *Johnson's Wonder-Working Providence, 1628 to 1651* (1654), ed. J. Franklin Jameson (New York, 1910); anonymous letter of 1637, in *Letters from New England: The Massachusetts Bay Colony, 1629–1638*, ed. Everett Emerson (Amherst, MA, 1976), 214.

3. The classic study of New England merchants remains Bernard Bailyn, *New England Merchants in the Seventeenth Century* (Cambridge, MA, 1955). See also McCusker and Menard, *Economy of British America*, 91–111; Phyllis Whitman Hunter, *Purchasing Identity in the Atlantic World: Massachusetts Merchants, 1670–1780* (Ithaca, NY, 2001), 72–106; Margaret Ellen Newell, *From Dependency to Independence: Economic Revolution in Colonial New England* (Ithaca, NY, 1998), 55–71; Richard L. Bushman, *From Puritan to Yankee: Character and the Social Order in Connecticut, 1690–1765* (New York, 1967), 107–21; Ralph A. Davis, *The Rise of the English Shipping Industry in the Seventeenth and Eighteenth Centuries* (London, 1962); idem, *The Rise of the Atlantic Economies* (Ithaca, NY, 1973); David Hancock, *Citizens of the World: London Merchants and the Integration of the British Atlantic Community, 1735–1785* (Cambridge, 1995); Paul Langford, *A Polite and Commercial People: England, 1727–1783* (Oxford, 1989), 160–68; and Thomas Barrow, *Trade and Empire: The British Customs Service in Colonial America, 1660–1775* (Cambridge, MA, 1967).

4. Discussions of the "declension" thesis can be found in Jack P. Greene, *Pursuits of Happiness: The Social Development of Early Modern British Colonies and the Formation of American Culture* (Chapel Hill, NC, 1987), 55–56; Perry Miller, "Declension in a Bible Commonwealth," in *Nature's Nation* (Cambridge, MA, 1967), 25–30; Stephen Foster, "New England versus the New England Mind: The Myth of Declension," *Journal of Social History* 3 (January

1970): 95–108; Robert G. Pope, *The Half-Way Covenant: Church Membership in Puritan New England* (Princeton, NJ, 1969), 275–76; Stephen Foster, *Their Solitary Way: The Puritan Social Ethic in the First Century of Settlement in New England* (New Haven, CT, 1971), introduction; and Sacvan Bercovitch, *The American Jeremiad* (Madison, WI, 1978).

5. Hunter, *Purchasing Identity in the Atlantic World*, 71–81; Bailyn, *New England Merchants*, chap. 5. This thesis is especially well developed, albeit for a later period in New England's history, in Robert Gross, *The Minutemen and Their World* (New York, 1976), 80–93.

6. Christine Leigh Heyrman, *Commerce and Culture: The Maritime Communities of Colonial Massachusetts, 1690–1750* (New York, 1984), 13–28; Bailyn, *New England Merchants*, 142–55; Hunter, *Purchasing Identity in the Atlantic World*, 14–32; Mark A. Peterson, *The Price of Redemption: The Spiritual Economy of Puritan New England* (Stanford, CA, 1997), 3.

7. Excellent overviews of mixed farming in New England can be found in Bushman, "Markets and Composite Farms"; Daniel Vickers, *Farmers and Fishermen: Two Centuries of Work in Essex County, Massachusetts, 1630–1850* (Chapel Hill, NC, 1994), 31–83; McCusker and Menard, *Economy of British America*, 91–95; Rutman, "Governor Winthrop's Garden Crop"; Gross, *Minutemen and Their World*, 85–87; William I. Davisson, "Essex County Wealth Trends: Wealth and Economic Growth in 17th Century Massachusetts," *Essex Institute Historical Collections* 103 (1967): 291–342; Terry L. Anderson, "Wealth Estimates for the New England Colonies, 1650–1709," *Explorations in Economic History* 12 (1975): 151–76; and Donald W. Koch, "Income Distribution and Political Structure in Seventeenth-Century Salem, Massachusetts," *Essex Institute Historical Collections* 105 (1969): 50–71.

8. One could write a book on the books and articles that have dealt with this massive historiographical issue. The debate has been nicely summarized in McCusker and Menard, *Economy of British America*, 102–7; Heyrman, *Commerce and Culture*, 52–95; James A. Henretta, *The Origins of American Capitalism* (Boston, 1991), 90–96; Greene, *Pursuits of Happiness*, 93; and Joyce Appleby, "The Vexed Story of Capitalism as Told by American Historians," *Journal of the Early Republic* 21 (Spring 2001): 1–18. Several interesting studies on the probability of self-sufficiency have informed this debate. See Carole Shammas, "How Self-Sufficient Was Early America?" *Journal of Interdisciplinary History* 13 (1982): 247–72; Bettye Hobbs Pruitt, "Self-Sufficiency and the Agricultural Economy of Eighteenth-Century Massachusetts," *William and Mary Quarterly* 41 (1984): 333–64; and Karen J. Friedman, "Victualling Colonial Boston," *Agricultural History* 47 (1973): 189–205.

9. Daniel Vickers, "Competency and Competition: Economic Culture in Early America," *William and Mary Quarterly* 47 (1990): 3–29; Alan McFarland, *The Origins of English Individualism* (New York, 1978), chap. 3; Keith Wrightson, *English Society, 1580 to 1680* (London, 1982); Peterson, *Price of Redemption*, 3; Darren Marcus Staloff, "'Where Religion and Profit Jump Together': Commerce and Piety in Puritan New England," *Reviews in American History* 27 (1999): 8–13. On Puritans and consumption habits, see Hunter, *Purchasing Identity in the Atlantic World*, 72–106. Quotations are from Vickers, *Farmers and Fishermen*, 19–21.

10. Winifred B. Rothenberg, "Farm Account Books: Problems and Possibilities," *Agricultural History* 58 (1984): 106–12.

1. Getting Lost in a New World

1. McCusker and Menard, *Economy of British America*, 93. The authors explain that "plans for settlement had included elaborate arrangements to develop the staples that the organizers of the colonies expected to find there." See also James Sheridan, "The Domestic Econ-

omy," in *Colonial British America: Essays in the New History of the Early Modern Era*, ed. Jack P. Greene and Richard Pole (Baltimore, 1984), 55–59; Bailyn, *New England Merchants*, 1–15; Vickers, *Farmers and Fishermen*, 86–91; Bruce C. Daniels, *The Connecticut Town: Growth and Development, 1635–1790* (Middletown, CT, 1979), 10–44; Charles Carroll, *The Timber Economy of Puritan New England* (Providence, RI, 1975), 57–68; and "Original Proprietors of Sudbury, Mass.," *New England Historical and Genealogical Register* 13 (1859): 261.

2. McCusker and Menard, *Economy of British America*, 17–34; Greene, *Pursuits of Happiness*, 28–54; Jon Butler, *Becoming America: The Revolution before 1776* (Cambridge, MA, 2000), 51–88; David Hackett Fischer, *Albion's Seed: Four British Folkways in America* (New York, 1989), sections on "wealth ways"; Marc Egnal, *New World Economies: The Growth of the Thirteen Colonies and Early Canada* (Oxford, 1998), 37–45.

3. Alice Hanson Jones, *Wealth of a Nation to Be: American Colonies on the Eve of the Revolution* (New York, 1980); Terry L. Anderson, *The Economic Growth of Seventeenth-Century New England: A Measurement of Regional Income* (New York, 1975); idem, "Economic Growth in Colonial New England: 'Statistical Renaissance,'" *Journal of Economic History* 39 (1979): 243–47; Winifred B. Rothenberg, *From Market Places to a Market Economy: The Transformation of Rural Massachusetts, 1750–1850* (Chicago, 1992); Egnal, *New World Economies*, 46–51; Bruce C. Daniels, "Long Range Trends of Wealth Distribution in Eighteenth-Century New England," *Explorations in Economic History* 11 (1973–74): 123–35; Heyrman, *Commerce and Culture*, 207–30. Statistics charting Massachusetts coastal exports in the eighteenth century can be found in James F. Shepherd and Samuel H. Williamson, "The Coastal Trade of the British North American Colonies, 1768–1772," *Journal of Economic History* 32 (December 1972): 397–422; and David C. Klingaman, "The Coastwide Trade of Colonial Massachusetts," *Essex Institute Historical Collections* 108 (1972): 217–34.

4. John Winthrop to Simon D'Ewes, 20 July 1635, in *Winthrop Papers*, 3:200; John Tinker to John Winthrop, 28 May 1640, ibid., 4:113, 251; Matthew Craddock to John Winthrop, 27 February 1639, ibid., 4:207; Edmund S. Morgan, *The Puritan Dilemma: The Story of John Winthrop* (Boston, 1958), 56–58; William Cronon, *Changes in the Land: Indians, Colonists, and the Ecology of New England* (New York, 1983), 36–38; Johnson, *Johnson's Wonder-Working Providence*, 66; Thomas Dudley to Countess of Lincoln, letter of 12 March 1631, in Alexander Young, *Chronicles of the First Planters of the Colony of the Massachusetts Bay, From 1623–1636* (Boston, 1746), 312. For an example of how early observers distorted the early difficulties, see Christopher Levett, "Voyage into New England" (1628), *Massachusetts Historical Society Collections* 3 (1843): 179.

5. Thomas Dudley to Lady Bridgett, Countess of Lincoln, 12, 28 March 1631, in Emerson, *Letters from New England*, 74; William Hubbard, *A General History of New England* (Boston, 1840), in *Proceedings of the Massachusetts Historical Society* 5 (1840): 111; John Pond to William Pond, [ca. 1632], *Winthrop Papers*, 3:18–19; Nathanial Ward to John Winthrop Jr., 24 December 1635, ibid., 3:216.

6. Stephen Innes, *Creating the Commonwealth: The Economic Culture of Puritan New England* (New York, 1995), 7; Virginia DeJohn Anderson, *New England's Generation: The Great Migration and the Formation of Society and Culture in the Seventeenth Century* (Cambridge, 1991), 131–76; Peter N. Carroll, *Puritanism and the Wilderness: The Intellectual Significance of the New England Frontier, 1629–1700* (New York, 1969), 713; Charles Lloyd Cohen, *God's Caress: The Psychology of Puritan Religious Experience* (Oxford, 1986); Alan Heimart, "Puritanism, the Wilderness, and the Frontier," *New England Quarterly* 26 (1953): 361–62, 376–77.

7. Innes, *Creating the Commonwealth*, 61; Virginia DeJohn Anderson, *New England's Generation*, 12–17; David Cressy, *Coming Over: Migration and Communication between England and New England in the Seventeenth Century* (Cambridge, 1987), chap. 3; Fischer, *Albion's Seed*, 13–42; Charles E. Banks, *The Planters of the Commonwealth: A Study of Emigrants and Emigration in Colonial Times* (Boston, 1930); idem, *Topographical Dictionary of 2885 English Emigrants to New England, 1620–1650* (Philadelphia, 1937); G. Andrews Moriarty, "Social and Geographical Origins of the Founders of Massachusetts," in *Commonwealth History of Massachusetts*, ed. A. B. Hart, vol. 1 (New York, 1966), 49–65; Eben Putnam, "Two Early Passenger Lists, 1635–37," *New England Historical and Genealogical Register* 75 (1921): 217–27.

8. Background on the investors' goals comes from Bailyn, *New England Merchants*, 17–18; John Frederick Martin, *Profits in the Wilderness: Entrepreneurship and the Founding of New England Towns in the Seventeenth Century* (Chapel Hill, NC, 1991), 9–37; Innes, *Creating the Commonwealth*, 62; Roger Thompson, *Mobility and Migration: East Anglian Founders of New England, 1629–1640* (Amherst, MA, 1994), 14–110; Albert Matthews, "University Alumni Founders of New England," *Publications of the Colonial Society of Massachusetts* 25 (1924): 14–23; Lucius R. Paige, *History of Cambridge, Massachusetts, 1630–1877*, vol. 1 (Cambridge, MA, 1877), 1–50; and *The Journal of John Winthrop, 1630–1649*, ed. Richard S. Dunn, James Savage, and Laetitia Yeandle (Cambridge, MA, 1996), 160–70.

9. The classic work on the New England cod industry is Harold A. Innis, *The Cod Fisheries: The History of an International Economy*, rev. ed. (Toronto, 1954). See also Vickers, *Farmers and Fishermen*, 86–91; Earl J. Hamilton, "American Treasure and Andalusian Prices," *Journal of Economic and Business History* 1 (1928): 20–25 (on cod prices); Ralph Greenlee Lounsbury, *The British Fishery at Newfoundland, 1634–1763* (New Haven, CT, 1934); and Peter E. Pope, *Fish into Wine: The Newfoundland Plantation in the Seventeenth Century* (Chapel Hill, NC, 2004), 33–65. Quotations come from "The Company's First Letter of Instruction to Endicott and his Council," 17 April 1629, in Young, *Chronicles of the First Planters*, 162–63; John White, *The Planter's Plea* (London, 1630), 26; "The Company's Second Letter of Instruction to Endicott and his Council," 28 May 1629, in Young, *Chronicles of the First Planters*, 185; and Alan Davidson, *The Oxford Companion to Food* (Oxford, 1999), 198.

10. Francis Higginson, *New England's Plantation. Or a Short and True Description of the Commodities and Discommodities of this Country* (London, 1630), reprinted in Young, *Chronicles of the First Planters*, 249–50; Nathanial B. Shurtleff, ed., *Records of the Governor and Company of the Massachusetts Bay in New England*, 5 vols. (Boston, 1853–54), 1:158; John Winthrop, *Winthrop's Journal: 1630–1649*, ed. James K. Hosmer, 4 vols. (New York, 1908), 1:173; Shurtleff, *Records of the Governor and Company*, 1:230, 257–58; Winthrop, *History of New England*, 2:119, 165; Raymond P. Stearns, *The Strenuous Puritan: Hugh Peter, 1598–1660* (Urbana, IL, 1954); Vickers, *Farmers and Fishermen*, 91–100.

11. Charles Carroll, *Timber Economy of Puritan New England*, 33.

12. Ibid.; Governor Craddock to John Endicott, letter of 16 February 1928, in Young, *Chronicles of the First Planters*, 132; "The Company's Second Letter of Instruction," 179; George Cheever, "Some Remarks on the Commerce of Salem, from 1626 to 1741, with a Sketch of Philip English—A Merchant in Salem from About 1670 to about 1733–4," *Essex Institute Historical Collections* 1 (1859): 67–76; George B. Emerson, *A Report on the Trees and Shrubs Growing Naturally in the Forests of Massachusetts*, vol. 2 (Boston, 1887), 576–78; John Smith, *Advertisements for the Unexperienced Planters of New England, or any where* (London, 1631), 25–30.

13. Governor Craddock to John Endicott, 16 February 1628, 132; Shurtleff, *Records of the Governor and Company,* 1:101; Edward Trelawny to Robert Trelawny, 10 October 1635, in Everett Emerson, *Letters from New England,* 175; Ronald Oliver MacFarlane, "The Massachusetts Bay Truck-Houses in Diplomacy with the Indians," *New England Quarterly* 11 (1938): 48–65; Arthur H. Buffington, "New England and the Western Fur Trade, 1629–1675," *Publications of the Colonial Society of Massachusetts* 18 (1917): 160–92; Sylvester Judd, "The Fur Trade on the Connecticut River in the Seventeenth Century," *New England Register* 11 (1857): 217–19.

14. Bailyn, *New England Merchants,* 19; Francis Moloney, *The Fur Trade in New England, 1620–1676* (Cambridge, MA, 1931), 96; Daniel Vickers, "The Northern Colonies: Economy and Society," in *The Cambridge History of the United States: The Colonial Era,* ed. Robert Gallman (Cambridge, 1996), 213–15; *Journal of John Winthrop,* 99; Samuel Eliot Morison, "The Plantation of Nashaway—an Industrial Experiment," *Publications of the Colonial Society of Massachusetts* 27 (1927–30): 207–10; Alden T. Vaughan, *New England Frontier: Puritans and Indians, 1620–1675* (Boston, 1965), 215–17, 250.

15. Moloney, *Fur Trade in New England,* 48; Martin, *Profits in the Wilderness,* 19–20; Stephen Innes, *Labor in a New Land: Economy and Society in Seventeenth-Century Springfield* (Princeton, NJ, 1983), 40; Daniels, *Connecticut Town;* Shurtleff, *Records of the Governor and Company,* 1:140, 322. On Willard, see John Gorham Palfrey, *History of New England during the Stuart Dynasty,* vol. 2 (Boston, 1865), 329–30; William D. Williamson, *The History of the State of Maine: from its first discovery, A.D. 1602, to the separation, A.D. 1820, inclusive,* vol. 1 (Hallowell, ME, 1832), 334–40; and Lemuel Shattuck, *A History of the Town of Concord, Middlesex County, Massachusetts: from its earliest settlement to 1832: and of the adjoining towns, Bedford, Acton, Lincoln, and Carlisle, containing various notices of county and state history not before published* (Boston, 1835), 4–5.

16. "The Company's First Letter of Instruction," 132; "The Company's Second Letter of Instruction," 182.

17. Endicott to Winthrop, April 1631, *Winthrop Papers,* 3:24.

18. Rutman, "Governor Winthrop's Garden Crop," 398. See also idem, *Winthrop's Boston: Portrait of a Puritan Town, 1630–1649* (Chapel Hill, NC, 1965), 177–81; McCusker and Menard, *Economy of British America,* 94; Marion H. Gottfried, "The First Depression in Massachusetts," *New England Quarterly* 9 (1936): 655–78; Virginia DeJohn Anderson, *New England's Generation,* 34; Bailyn, *New England Merchants,* 32–39; Howard S. Russell, *A Long, Deep Furrow: Three Centuries of Farming in New England* (Hanover, NH, 1976), pt. 1; Vickers, "Northern Colonies," 231.

19. Philip J. Greven, *Four Generations: Population, Land, and Family in Colonial Andover, Massachusetts* (Ithaca, NY, 1970); Terry L. Anderson and Robert Paul Thomas, "White Population, Labor Force, and Extensive Growth of the New England Economy in the Seventeenth Century," *Journal of Economic History* 33 (1973): 634–67; Vickers, "Northern Colonies," 224–25. The quotation is from Vickers.

20. England, and especially East Anglia, had a highly developed infrastructure. Background can be found in Joan Thirsk, ed., *The Agrarian History of England and Wales,* vol. 4, *1500–1640* (Cambridge, 1967), 195–96; R. A. Dodgshon and R. A. Butlin, eds., *An Historical Geography of England and Wales* (London, 1990), 188–91; Peter Clark and Paul Slack, *English Towns in Transition, 1500–1700* (London, 1976), 18–28; L. A. Clarkson, *The Pre-Industrial Economy in England, 1500–1750* (London, 1971), 152–57; Wrightson, *English*

Society; Joan Parkes, *Travel in England in the Seventeenth Century* (London, 1925), 96–111; T. S. Willan, *The English Coasting Trade, 1600–1750* (Manchester, 1938), 11–15; J. A. Chartres, "Road Carrying in England in the Seventeenth Century: Myth and Reality," *Economic History Review,* 2nd ser., 30 (1977): 73–94; and C. B. Riding, ed., *Rural Economy in Yorkshire in 1641, Being the Farming and Account Books of Henry Best, of Elmswell, in the East Riding* (Durham, England, 1857), 99–100.

21. William Wood, *New England's Prospect* (1633), in Young, *Chronicles of the First Planters,* 263; John Pond to William Pond, [ca. 1632], *Winthrop Papers,* 3:18.

22. Cronon, *Changes in the Land,* 19–33; Douglas R. McManis, *European Impressions of the New England Coast, 1497–1620* (Chicago, 1972), 116–33; William Wood, *New England's Prospect,* ed. Alden T. Vaughan (Amherst, MA, 1977), 51.

23. *Journal of John Winthrop,* 137, 87, 129–30.

24. George F. Dow, ed., *Records and Files of the Quarterly Courts of Essex County, Massachusetts,* 9 vols. (Salem, MA, 1911–75), 1:50, 39.

25. Hubbard, *General History of New England,* 234; Johnson, *Johnson's Wonder-Working Providence,* in Young, *Chronicles of the First Planters,* 114–15; *Winthrop Papers,* 3:24; George F. Dow, ed., *The Probate Records of Essex County,* vol. 1, *1635–1674* (Salem, MA, 1916); *Wills and Inventories from the Registry at Durham,* 4 vols. (London, 1835–1929).

26. Shurtleff, *Records of the Governor and Company,* 1:141; John Davenport and Theophilus Eaton to the General Court, 12 March 1638, *Winthrop Papers,* 4:19.

27. *Journal of John Winthrop,* 71, 131; John Winthrop to John Winthrop Jr., May 1639, *Winthrop Papers,* 4:118; *Journal of John Winthrop,* 124.

28. Dow, *Records and Files of the Quarterly Courts,* 1:3; Hubbard, *General History of New England,* 138–39, 196; Sir John Clotworthy to John Winthrop Jr., April 1635, *Winthrop Papers,* 3:196.

29. Karen Ordahl Kupperman, "Climate and Mastery of the Wilderness in Seventeenth-Century New England," in *Seventeenth-Century New England,* ed. David D. Hall and David Grayson Allen (Boston, 1984), 3. For a more general comment on the connection between geography and settlement see Vickers, "Northern Colonies," 219. See also W. R. Baron, "Eighteenth-Century Climate Variation and Its Suggested Impact on Society," *Maine Historical Society Quarterly* 21 (1981–83): 201–14; and David C. Smith, "Climate Fluctuations and Agriculture in Southern and Central New England," ibid., 179–200.

30. See McManis, *European Impression of the New England Coast,* 110–33; Smith is quoted on 113.

31. *Journal of John Winthrop,* 162, 42, 56, 136, 156.

32. John Winthrop to John Winthrop Jr., 4 April 1636, *Winthrop Papers,* 3:275.

33. *Journal of John Winthrop,* 141, 105, 137; John Winthrop to John Winthrop Jr., April 1639, *Winthrop Papers,* 3:107–8.

34. Morgan, *Puritan Dilemma,* 37.

35. Ibid.

2. Mapping the Landscape

1. Wood, *New England's Prospect* (1633), in Young, *Chronicles of the First Planters,* 412–14.

2. Richard Saltonsall to Emmanual Downing, n.d., in Everett Emerson, *Letters from New England,* 93; Higginson, *New England's Plantation* (1630), reprinted in Young, *Chronicles of*

the First Planters, 245–48; Thomas Dudley to Countess of Lincoln, letter of 1630, in Young, *Chronicles of the First Planters*, 324.

3. See Sumner Chilton Powell, *Puritan Village: The Formation of a New England Town* (Middletown, CT, 1963), 16–17; James A. Henretta, "Families and Farms," *Mentalité* in Pre-Industrial America," *William and Mary Quarterly* 35 (1978): 3–7; and Kenneth A. Lockridge, *A New England Town: The First Hundred Years* (New York, 1970), 57–63.

4. Morgan, *Puritan Dilemma*, 41.

5. The power inherent in the decision to organize the environment along English lines is explored in Patricia Seed, *Ceremonies of Possession in Europe's Conquest of the New World, 1492–1640* (Cambridge, 1995), 16–40.

6. On inherited ways of ordering the landscape, see Brian Roberts, "Planned Villages from Medieval England," in *Man Made the Land: Essays in English Historical Geography*, comp. Alan R. H. Baker (Devon, 1973), 46–58; Alan R. H. Baker, "Field Systems in Medieval England," in ibid., 60–78; Oliver Rackman, *Trees and Woodland in the British Landscape* (London, 1983), 180–86; and Allen, *In English Ways*, 57–61.

7. See Virginia DeJohn Anderson, "King Philip's Herds: Indians, Colonists, and the Problem of Livestock in Early New England," *William and Mary Quarterly* 51 (1994): 601–24; idem, "Animals into the Wilderness: The Development of Livestock Husbandry in the Seventeenth-Century Chesapeake," ibid. 59 (2002), www.historycooperative.org/journals/wm/59.2/anderson.html; Carl Bridenbaugh, *Fat Mutton and Liberty of Conscience: Society in Rhode Island, 1636–1690* (Providence, RI, 1974), 16–17; Cronon, *Changes in the Land*; Alfred Crosby, *Ecological Imperialism: The Biological Expansion of Europe, 900–1900* (New York, 1986); Darrett B. Rutman, *Husbandmen of Plymouth: Farms and Villages in the Old Colony, 1620–1692* (Boston, 1967), 14–16; Keith Thomas, *Man and the Modern World: A History of the Modern Sensibility* (New York, 1983), 26; and Virginia DeJohn Anderson, *Creatures of Empire: How Domestic Animals Transformed Early America* (Oxford, 2004).

8. Wood, *New England's Prospect* (1633), in Young, *Chronicles of the First Planters*, 405–6; *The records of the town of Cambridge (formerly New-towne) Massachusetts, 1630–1703* (Cambridge, 1901), 6.

9. *Fourth report of the Record Commissioners of the City of Boston, 1880, Dorchester town records* (1883; reprint, Bowie, MD, 1999), 24; *Records of the town of Cambridge (formerly New-towne) Massachusetts, 1630–1703*, 5–6, 18–19; *The early records of the town of Dorchester* (Boston, 1867), 1.

10. *Records of the town of Cambridge (formerly New-towne) Massachusetts, 1630–1703*, 23, 28, 30; *Early records of the town of Dorchester*, 3; William B. Upham, ed., "Town Records of Salem," *Essex Institute Historical Collections* 10 (1869): 85.

11. *Records of the town of Cambridge (formerly New-towne) Massachusetts, 1630–1703*, 22, 25, 39; *Second report of the record commissioners of the city of Boston: containing the Boston records, 1634–1660, and the book of possessions* (Boston, 1877), 5; *Early records of the town of Dorchester*, 23.

12. Shurtleff, *Records of the Governor and Company*, 1:86, 87, 101, 106. For background on swine in England, see Julian Wiseman, *The Pig: A British History* (London, 1986); H. R. Davidson, *The Production and Marketing of Pigs* (London, 1966); and W. Harwood Long, "Regional Farming in Seventeenth Century Yorkshire," *Agricultural History Review* 8 (1960): 103–14.

13. *Town Records of Salem, Massachusetts* (1868; reprint, Salem, 1934), 68, 100; *Records of the town of Cambridge (formerly New-towne) Massachusetts, 1630–1703*, 24, 42; *Early records of the town of Dorchester*, 24; *Boston town records [1631]–1822*, 11 vols. (Boston, 1881–1906), 1:40; *Records of the town of Cambridge (formerly New-towne) Massachusetts, 1630–1703*, 34. It is possible to chart how the Massachusetts General Court began to echo these policies as they took root and proved effective. See, e.g., Shurtleff, *Records of the Governor and Company*, 1:181, 188, 238.

14. Shurtleff, *Records of the Governor and Company*, 1:280.

15. *Records of the town of Cambridge (formerly New-towne) Massachusetts, 1630–1703*, 6, 9; *Town Records of Salem, Massachusetts*, 9; *Early records of the town of Dorchester*, 9.

16. *Early records of the town of Dorchester*, 11, 17, 22; *Boston town records*, 1:12.

17. *Town Records of Salem, Massachusetts*, 67; *Records of the town of Cambridge (formerly New-towne) Massachusetts, 1630–1703*, 10; *Town Records of Salem, Massachusetts*, 14.

18. On the use of fences in England, see Seed, *Ceremonies of Possession*, 19–25; Joan Thirsk, "Enclosing and Engrossing," in *Agrarian History of England and Wales*, 4:200–255; and Thomas Tusser, *Five Hundred Points of Good Husbandrie*, ed. William Maver (London, 1812), 200. Tusser explains that "ill husbandrie loseth for lack of a good fence; Good husbandrie closeth." Quoted in Seed, *Ceremonies of Possession*, 20.

19. *Town Records of Salem, Massachusetts*, 84; *Boston Town Records*, 1:3; *Early records of the town of Dorchester*, 9.

20. *Early records of the town of Dorchester*, 23, 19; *Boston town records*, 1:14, 4; *Records of the town of Cambridge (formerly New-towne) Massachusetts, 1630–1703*, 46; *Early records of the town of Dorchester*, 36; V. R. Ludgate, *Gardens of the Colonists* (Washington, DC, 1941); John R. Stilgoe, *Common Landscapes of America, 1580 to 1845* (New Haven, CT, 1982), 99–105.

21. Information on fence viewers was gleaned from the following cases in Boston and Dorchester records: *Early records of the town of Dorchester*, 6, 10, 20, 31, 33, 37; *Boston town records*, 1:3, 4, 9, 33, 52; *Muddy River and Brookline records* (Boston, 1875), 10 (18 October 1634); John J. Currier, *History of Newbury, Mass, 1635–1902* (Boston, 1902), 53. On a decrease in cases of trespassing, see *Note-Book Kept by Thomas Lechford, Esq. Lawyer, in Boston, Massachusetts Bay from June 27, 1638 to July 9, 1641*, ed. Edward Everett Hale and Hammond J. Trumbull (Cambridge, MA, 1885); and Dow, *Records and Files of the Quarterly Courts of Essex County*, 1:1–60.

22. Shurtleff, *Records of the Governor and Company*, 1:74, 76, 77, 79, 84, 91, 127. Historians have conventionally understood the General Court's economic regulatory policies as a clear indication of a precapitalist mind-set. These pious settlers, they have argued, embraced a moral economy over a market economy. In so doing, Puritans legislated a "just price" for a variety of goods and services. More recently, other historians have refined this interpretation to argue that Puritans were not pursuing a moral economy with their regulatory regime so much as they were preparing themselves against what Stephen Innes has called a "capitalist shock." *Creating the Commonwealth*, 275. Insofar as settlers lacked even the most basic, functioning marketplace, however, they could also be seen as experiencing a "settlement shock." The following interpretation places the Puritans' regulatory plans in the context of this assumption.

23. Shurtleff, *Records of the Governor and Company*, 1:111. Beer was legislated at 1d. per quart in 1634 and at 2d. per quart two year later; beaver fur at 10s. per pound; and corn at

anywhere from 6s. to 3s. per bushel. On the impact of usury threats, see Bernard Bailyn, "The *Apologia* of Robert Keayne," *William and Mary Quarterly* 7 (1950): 568–87.

24. "The Company's Second Letter of Instruction," 188; "The Company's First Letter of Instruction"; Governor Craddock to John Endicott, 16 February 1628, 136; Upham, "Town Records of Salem," 30–31; "The Company's First Letter of Instruction," 148; Shurtleff, *Records of the Governor and Company,* 1:65; *Journal of John Winthrop,* 184.

25. Johnson, *Johnson's Wonder-Working Providence,* 92; "Robert Clap's Memoirs," in Young, *Chronicles of the First Planters,* 353.

26. "Robert Clap's Memoirs," in Young, *Chronicles of the First Planters,* 353n1; The Planters of New England to King Charles I, 1634, in Everett Emerson, *Letters from New England,* 122.

27. "The Company's First Letter of Instruction," 152–53; Shurtleff, *Records of the Governor and Company,* 1:32; "The Company's Second Letter of Instruction," 187–88, 176–77; Shurtleff, *Records of the Governor and Company,* 1:35.

28. Morgan, *Puritan Dilemma,* 39; Shurtleff, *Records of the Governor and Company,* 1:35; "The Company's Second Letter of Instruction," 176–77.

3. Founding Industries

1. *Journal of John Winthrop,* 200; Wood, *New England's Prospect* (1633), in Young, *Chronicles of the First Planters,* 410n4; William Hilton to John Winthrop Jr., 1 May 1633, *Winthrop Papers,* 3:121; James Cudworth to Dr. Stroughton, December 1634, in "Early New England Papers from the British Archives," *Essex Institute Historical Collections* 30 (1889): 83; *Journal of John Winthrop,* 28–29; Wood, *New England's Prospect* (1633), in Young, *Chronicles of the First Planters,* 410n1; Thomas Welde to his former parishioners at Tarling, June 1632, in Everett Emerson, *Letters from New England,* 96; Johnson, *Johnson's Wonder-Working Providence,* 85, 91.

2. A consideration of these industries in the context of the early local economy differs from traditional perspectives on the New England economy in a couple of ways. First, it stresses the region's staple products rather than focusing exclusively on conventional ideas of mixed farming. James Sheridan writes, "Perhaps at least in part because they produced so few staples, the New England colonies, more than any other region of America, have suffered from a neglect of their internal economic development in favor of their extensive involvement in Atlantic commercial enterprise." "Domestic Economy," 55–56. Second, fish and timber, insofar as they are studied, are immediately placed in a transatlantic rather than a provincial perspective. Extremely valuable in their own way, the following sources reflect this bias, one that fails to see fish and timber as initially local products. Richard Pares, *Yankees and Creoles: The Trade between North America and the West Indies before the American Revolution* (Cambridge, MA, 1956); H. E. S. Fisher, *Portugal Trade: A Study of Anglo-Portuguese Commerce, 1700–1770* (London, 1971); T. Bentley Duncan, *Atlantic Islands: Madeira, the Azores, and the Cape Verdes in Seventeenth Century Commerce and Navigation* (Chicago, 1972); Stanley D. Dodge, "The Geography of the Codfishing Industry in Colonial New England," *Geographical Society of Philadelphia Bulletin* 25 (1927): 43–50; Innis, *Cod Fisheries,* 30–50.

3. The best descriptions of mixed farming detail the tasks that typified life on a family farm without including the possibility that the idea of mixed farming might also have in-

cluded work in fishing and timber production. The flexibility that was inherent in mixed faming, however, would have easily allowed settlers to incorporate these tasks into conventional notions of agriculture. See Bushman, "Markets and Composite Farms"; Christopher Grasso, "The Experimental Philosophy of Farming: Jared Eliot and the Cultivation of Connecticut," *William and Mary Quarterly* 50 (1993): 53–55; Henretta, "Families and Farms," 3–32; Pruitt, "Self-Sufficiency in the Agriculture Economy"; Allan Kulikoff, "Households and Markets: Toward a New Synthesis of American Agrarian History," *William and Mary Quarterly* 50 (1993): 342–55; and Christopher Clark, *The Roots of Rural Capitalism: Western Massachusetts, 1780–1860* (Ithaca, NY, 1990), chap. 3. The quotations are from William S. Hudson, "Puritanism and the Spirit of Capitalism," *Church History* 18 (1949): 14n12; they are also appear in Innes, *Creating the Commonwealth*, 120.

4. The challenges inherent in meeting export markets with fish in the early decades of settlement are recounted in Vickers, *Farmers and Fishermen*, 91–142; evidence can also be found in Dow, *Records and Files of the Quarterly Courts*, 2:386–87, 7:305–8. See also George Corwin Account Books, 1651–1662, in George Corwin's Letters, Bills, Ledgers and Day Books, 1651–1684, The Phillips Library, Peabody Essex Museum, Salem, MA.

5. *Journal of John Winthrop*, 27; Johnson, *Johnson's Wonder-Working Providence*, 83; *Roger Clap's Memoirs* (Boston 1731), in Young, *Chronicles of the First Planters*; John Winthrop to Sir Nathanial Rich, 22 May 1634, in Everett Emerson, *Letters from New England*, 115–16.

6. Cronon, *Changes in the Land*, 45; Fulmer Mood, "John Winthrop, Jr. on Indian Corn," *New England Quarterly* 10 (1937): 128; Erhard Rostland, "The Evidence for Use of Fish as Fertilizer in Aboriginal North America," *Journal of Geography* 56 (1957): 222; Lynn Ceci, "Fish, Fertilizer: A Native North American Practice?" *Science* 188 (1975): 26–30; John Pond to William Pond, [ca. 1632], *Winthrop Papers*, 3:19; Johnson, *Johnson's Wonder-Working Providence*, 114; Mood, "John Winthrop, Jr. on Indian Corn," 126; Wood, *New England's Prospect*, ed. Vaughan, 35; Thomas Franklin Waters, *Ipswich in the Massachusetts Bay Colony, 1633–1917*, 2 vols. (Ipswich, MA, 1905–17), 1:75–76.

7. I located twenty-one fishermen in Upham, "Town Records of Salem," 16, 33, 36, 62, 78, 80, 83–83, 88, 92. I confirmed property ownership in these records as well (ibid., 19–27, 37). Jury and grand jury participation, as well as criminal charges, are documented in Dow, *Records and Files of the Quarterly Courts*. For an interpretation that stresses the threat these men posed to traditional Puritan stability, see Vickers, *Farmers and Fishermen*, 91–95; John Winthrop, *History of New England*, 2:326–27; and Waters, *Ipswich in the Massachusetts Bay Colony*, 1:88.

8. *Town Records of Salem, Massachusetts*, 15, 92, 27–28.

9. John Berenton, "Brief and True Relation of the North Part of Virginia, 1602," in *Early English and French Voyages*, ed. Henry S. Burage (New York, 1906), 331; Wood, *New England's Prospect*, ed. Vaughan, 56; *Fourth report of the Record Commissioners of the City of Boston*, 5; *Journal of John Winthrop*, 151; Waters, *Ipswich in the Massachusetts Bay Colony*, 1:12–13; *Records of the town of Cambridge (formerly New-towne) Massachusetts, 1630–1703*, 22.

10. Wood, *New England's Prospect* (1633), in Young, *Chronicles of the First Planters*, 404; Waters, *Ipswich in the Massachusetts Bay Colony*, 1:75–76; *Journal of John Winthrop*, 307; *Roger Clap's Memoirs*, in Young, *Chronicles of the First Planters*, 351.

11. *Roger Clap's Memoirs*, in Young, *Chronicles of the First Planters*, 351; Wood, *New England's Prospect* (1633), in ibid., 409–10. Mention of four large ships in existence in the Massachusetts Bay appears in Young, *Chronicles of the First Planters*, 185n1. They were the

Blessing of the Bay, built in 1631, weighing 30 tons; the *Desire,* built in 1636, weighing 120 tons; a 100-ton ship built by Matthew Craddock; and a 300-ton ship built by Hugh Peter. On shipbuilding, see *Winthrop Papers,* entries for 16, 22 July, 8 August 1631, March and December 1632, and 26 March 1633, 3:45, 47, 54, 56. Further details can be gleaned from John Winthrop to John Winthrop Jr., 6 November 1634, in ibid., 2:125.

12. "Bradford's and Winslow's Journal," in Young, *Chronicles of the First Planters,* 163–64, 167–68; John Noble, ed., *Records of the Court of Assistants of the Colony of the Massachusetts Bay, 1630–1692,* vol. 2 (Boston, 1904), 22.

13. Hubbard, *General History of New England,* in *Proceedings of the Massachusetts Historical Society* 5 (1840): 111; *Journal of John Winthrop,* 307 (a rare case of Virginia trade appears in the entry for 29 August 1634, p. 125). More typical trade for this early period was the trade in alewives, exemplified in James Luxford to John Winthrop, July 1639, *Winthrop Papers,* 4:126. Trade of alewives for wood between Ipswich and Boston is documented in Hugh Peter to John Winthrop, January 1638, ibid., 3:3; references to trading local corn can be found in Hugh Peter to John Winthrop, ibid., 3:13–14.

14. The few studies that deal extensively with the timber trade, like those dealing extensively with the fish trade, do so through a transatlantic lens. See Bailyn, *New England Merchants,* 83; Charles Carroll, *Timber Economy of Puritan New England,* 130; McCusker and Menard, *Economy of British America,* 91–111; Herbert I. Winer, "History of the Great Mountain Forest, Litchfield County, Connecticut" (PhD diss., Yale University, 1951); and Powell, *Puritan Village,* 55–57. Bailyn's still essential overview of the colony's timber production begins in 1641, a full decade after settlement; Carroll's excellent study concentrates on the industry's response to overseas demand after the Great Migration; and McCusker and Menard summarize the scholarship on the industry through the exclusive lens of the staples model.

15. *Note-Book Kept by Thomas Lechford,* 302. More general overviews of early Massachusetts housing can be found in Abbott L. Cummings, *The Framed Houses of Massachusetts Bay, 1625–1675* (Cambridge, 1979); R. G. St. George, "Set Thine House in Order," in *New England Begins: The Seventeenth Century,* vol. 2 (Boston, 1982), 159–351; and Fischer, *Albion's Seed,* 62–67.

16. *Journal of John Winthrop,* 47; Johnson, *Johnson's Wonder-Working Providence,* 321. On building methods, see Allen G. Noble, *Wood, Brick, and Stone: The North American Settlement Landscape,* vol. 1, *Houses* (Amherst, MA, 1984); and Alfred E. Poor, *Colonial Architecture of Cape Cod, Nantucket, and Martha's Vineyard* (New York, 1932).

17. Cronon, *Changes in the Land,* 119; Dorcester Town Records, 2–40; *Second report of the record commissioners of the city of Boston,* 2–58; *Town Records of Salem, Massachusetts,* 84; Carl Bridenbaugh, "Yankee Use and Abuse of the Forest in the Building of New England, 1620–1660," *Proceedings of the Massachusetts Historical Society* 89 (1977): 3–35; John R. Stilgoe, "Pattern on the Land: The Making of a Colonial Landscape, 1633–1800" (PhD diss., Harvard University, 1976), 100–115; Joseph Wood, *New England Village: Creating the North American Landscape* (Baltimore, 1997); Seed, *Ceremonies of Possession;* John Demos, *Entertaining Satan: Witchcraft and the Culture of Early New England* (New York, 1983).

18. Charles Carroll, *Timber Economy of Puritan New England,* 68; Dow, *Records and Files of the Quarterly Courts,* 1:5; Sarah Night, *The Private Journal of a Journey From Boston to New York, in the Year 1704* (Albany, 1865), 26–37, 66–68; W. F. Ganong, "The Voyages of Sieur de Champlain," in *The Works of Samuel de Champlain in Six Volumes,* ed. H. P. Biggar (Toronto,

1922–36), 1:104–5, 338–39; Joseph A. Goldenberg, *Shipbuilding in Colonial America* (Charlottesville, VA, 1976), 93–95. A great deal of information on shipbuilding can be found in George Corwin Account Books, 1663–1672, in George Corwin's Letters, Bills, Ledgers and Day Books, 1651–1684; Philip English Shipping Account Book, 1678–1690, Philip English Shipping Account Books, 1664–1718; and John Higginson Account Book, 1678–1689, FMs H3671, all in The Phillips Library, Peabody Essex Museum.

19. *Journal of John Winthrop*, 81, 98, 92, 132, 119.

20. Innes, *Creating the Commonwealth*, 275; Young, *Chronicles of the First Planters*, 185n1; Charles Carroll, *Timber Economy of Puritan New England*, 70; William Wood, *New England's Prospect* (1633), in Young, *Chronicles of the First Planters*, 394; Goldenberg, *Shipbuilding in Colonial America*, 37; Bernard Bailyn and Lotte Bailyn, *Massachusetts Shipping, 1697–1714: A Statistical Study* (Cambridge, MA, 1959), 1–10.

21. *Early records of the town of Dorchester*, 5, 8, 26, 41; *Town Records of Salem, Massachusetts*, 31, 34; *Records of the Town of Cambridge (formerly New-towne) Massachusetts, 1630–1703*, 34. As these examples suggest, the internal demand for timber remained as strong as that for fish, if not stronger. This factor helped keep production locally focused, as with fish. Equipment limitations in the timber trade, however, were not nearly as inhibiting.

22. *Early records of the town of Dorchester*, 8; *Note-Book Kept by Thomas Lechford*, 412; *Journal of John Winthrop*, 85–86.

23. Virginia DeJohn Anderson, *New England's Generation*, 13 and n2; Elizabeth B. Sumner, *Ancestry and Descendants of James Hensman Colman and Betsy Tobey* (Los Angeles, 1957), 66–67; Thomas Gostlin to John Winthrop Jr., *Winthrop Papers*, 3:124–25; *Note-Book Kept by Thomas Lechford*, 342–44; Charles Boardman Jewson, ed., "Transcript of Three Registers of Passengers from Great Yarmouth to Holland and New England," *Norfolk Record Society Publications* 25 (1954): 30. These sources provide only the slightest hint of the number of "carpenters" who migrated to New England. For one thing, men rarely recorded their occupation. Second, lists that document the transfer of occupation from the Old World to the New are compromised by the fact that New England was a settlement society that demanded a great deal of occupational fluidity. A man with a few carpentry skills back home easily became a "carpenter" in New England.

24. Through a range of financial incentives the General Court joined carpenters and other investors in the effort to build sawmills, a project that cost from £400 to £600 to complete. See Innes, *Creating the Commonwealth*, 303; Shurtleff, *Records of the Governor and Company*, 1:149, 256; Benno M. Forman, "Mill-Sawing in Seventeenth-Century Massachusetts," *Old-Time New England* 60 (1970): 110–30; *Boston town records*, 1:12, 54.

25. Dow, *Records and Files of the Quarterly Courts*, 1:45, 63. Carpenters found themselves at the nexus of many transactions, and they took advantage of this position to generate more opportunities for themselves. They served as market clerks, kept farms, traded locally, and held land.

26. Johnson, *Johnson's Wonder-Working Providence*, 116; *Note-Book Kept by Thomas Lechford*, 92.

4. The Persistence of Tradition

1. Timothy H. Breen and Stephen Foster, "The Puritans' Greatest Achievement: A Study of Social Cohesion in Seventeenth Century Massachusetts," *Journal of American History* 60 (1973): 5–9; Powell, *Puritan Village*, 150–70; Joan Thirsk, "The Family," *Past and Present* 27

(1964): 116–22; Greven, *Four Generations*, 21–72; Martin, *Profits in the Wilderness*, 111–23; Peter N. Carroll, *Puritanism and the Wilderness*, 70; Eric G. Nellis, "Labor and Community in Massachusetts Bay, 1630–1660," *Labor History* 18 (1977).

2. New England's depression is most thoroughly documented, albeit with several interpretive problems, in Gottfried, "First Depression in Massachusetts"; John Winthrop, *Winthrop's Journal*, 2:31; John Tinker to John Winthrop, 28 May 1640, *Winthrop Papers*, 4:251; Shurtleff, *Records of the Governor and Company*, 1:307; and Thomas Hooker to Thomas Shephard, 2 November 1640, Hutchinson Papers, Massachusetts State Archives, Boston. Historians have generally taken these accounts at face value. Echoing Gottfried, Bailyn wrote that the depression "destroyed the embryonic economy of the Puritan Commonwealth." Charles Carroll explained that the economy was "suddenly and dramatically shattered." As I show in this chapter, all of these assessments are overstated. For those Puritans who did go home, see William L. Sache, "The Migration of New Englanders to England, 1640–1660," *American Historical Review* 8 (1948): 251–78.

3. Bailyn, *New England Merchants*, 83–84; *Aspinwall Notoriall Records from 1644–1651* (Boston, 1903), 244–45, 75–76, 380; John Winthrop, *Winthrop's Journal*, 2:248–50; Shurtleff, *Records of the Governor and Company*, 1:82, 87, 100, 106, 130, 152, 171, 173, 188, 215, 246, 253.

4. Bailyn, *New England Merchants*, 85–86; Charles Carroll, *Timber Economy of Puritan New England*, 80–83; John Winthrop, *Winthrop's Journal*, 2:406, 458, 573, 722; Vickers, *Farmers and Fishermen*, 101.

5. An approach that considers the depression in the context of the local economy—specifically, the region's infrastructure—has the added advantage of being more consistent with colonial America's extant records. Historians who examine the seventeenth-century economy using the staples approach are frequently frustrated by a dearth of surviving shipping records. With few exceptions, colonial governments did not start to keep systematic shipping records until the eighteenth century. By contrast, the records required for an infrastructural approach, mainly court and town records, are readily available for seventeenth-century Massachusetts. They heavily inform my interpretation of the depression and, in so doing, paint a clear picture of continuity.

6. Allen, *In English Ways*, 1–10; Joan Thirsk, "Farming Techniques," in Thirsk, *Agrarian History of England and Wales*, 4:192–93; Robert Trow-Smith, *A History of British Livestock Husbandry to 1700* (London, 1700), 16–18; Peter Laslett, *The World We Have Lost: England before the Industrial Age* (New York, 1971), 40–47; Wrightson, *English Society*, 31–36; Christopher Hill, *Change and Continuity in Seventeenth-Century England* (London, 1974), 220–25.

7. Quoted in *Puritans in America: A Narrative Anthology*, ed. Alan Heimart and Andrew Delbanco (Cambridge, MA, 1985), 30–31. The Puritans' emotional reaction toward the depression was a response best summarized in Cotton Mather's idea that "the most concealed, and yet the most violent, of all our passions, usually is that of IDLENESS." Cotton Mather, *Bonifacius: An Essay Upon the Good* (1710), ed. David Levin (Cambridge, MA, 1966), 9.

8. *Journal of John Winthrop*, 684–87. This Marblehead catch is often cited as prima facie evidence that Massachusetts was deeply involved in exportation in the 1640s. Winthrop's use of *afflict*, however, is instructive. Catching £4,000 worth of fish was one thing, but successfully getting it to overseas markets was another. In this case at least, the cost was a 50 percent loss.

9. *Journal of John Winthrop*, 386. Turner's ship was the *St. John*. He bought a quarter-share of it in 1640.

10. The shipbuilding industry remains largely unexamined as a discrete topic, but the following references provide a good starting point: Innes, *Creating the Commonwealth*, 270–79; Goldenberg, *Shipbuilding in Colonial America*, 37; Bailyn and Bailyn, *Massachusetts Shipping*, 100–105; Davis, *Rise of the English Shipping Industry*; and *Journal of John Winthrop*, 384.

11. One major indication that historians have relied on as evidence of a region's immersion into export markets is the presence of what are called top-down linkages. For example, assessing the situation in seventeenth-century Massachusetts, Innes writes: "Along with sawmills and the cod fishery, New England shipyards afforded the region with a rich network of backward (production) and forward (consumption) linkages." These connections, he continues, "allowed local capitalists to invest in sawmills . . . as well as the gristmills constructed in virtually every town of consequence." *Creating the Commonwealth*, 276. Although historians often overstate the impact of such linkages, their central point, best articulated in Albert O. Hirschman's book *The Strategy of Economic Development* (New Haven, CT, 1958), is valid. The following section thus examines Ipswich, Rowley, Lynn, Cambridge, Salem, and Marblehead with the express intention of finding such linkages suggestive of an export transition.

12. The Ipswich information is based on Waters, *Ipswich in the Massachusetts Bay Colony*, 1:21, 77–81; and an examination of the Ipswich Town Records and Land Grants, 1634–1657, held on microfilm at the Ipswich Public Library, Ipswich, MA. The Rowley information comes from Amos Everett Jewett, *Rowley, Massachusetts, 1639–1850* (Rowley, 1946), 176; Town of Rowley Index to Town Records, Rowley Town Hall, Rowley, MA; and Benjamin Mighill and George Blodgett, *The Early Records of the Town of Rowley, Massachusetts, 1639–1672* (Rowley, 1894), 50–80.

13. Thomas Gray, *The Founding of Marblehead* (Baltimore, 1984), 12–16; Vickers, *Farmers and Fishermen*, 91–108; William Hammond Bowden, ed., "Marblehead Town Records," printed in the *Essex Institute Historical Collections* 69 (1933): 211–37.

14. Fischer, *Albion's Seed*, 151–58, shows that the continuity was a continuity not only with settlement habits but also with economic practices inherited from England. See also Allen, *In English Ways*; Samuel Maverick, "A Brief Description of New England and the Severall Towns Therein, Together with the Present Government Thereof," *Proceedings of the Massachusetts Historical Society* 1 (1884–85); Rutman, "Governor Winthrop's Garden Crop"; and Rutman, *Husbandmen of Plymouth*.

15. Bowden, "Marblehead Town Records," 212; Gray, *Founding of Marblehead*, 22–23.

16. Gray, *Founding of Marblehead*, 26–27.

17. Bowden, "Marblehead Town Records," 212–13.

18. Ibid., 210.

19. Mighill and Blodgett, *Early Records of the Town of Rowley*, 52; Jewett, *Rowley, Massachusetts*, 156–57.

20. Mighill and Blodgett, *Early Records of the Town of Rowley*, 33; Jewett, *Rowley, Massachusetts*, 159.

21. Mighill and Blodgett, *Early Records of the Town of Rowley*, 36; Jewett, *Rowley, Massachusetts*, 168–73; Samuel Eliot Morison, *Builders of the Bay Colony* (New York, 1930), 164. Other activities that Rowley settlers continued to practice, according to town records, were extending the common by five miles, forcing homeowners to "improve gates in the com-

mon," making sure that all land "laid out" was "bounded with a stake of stones at each corner," a stake "as big as a man's leg," and hiring eight men "to procure and keep bulls." Town of Rowley Index to Town Records.

22. E. N. Hartley, *Ironworks on the Saugus: The Lynn and Braintree Ventures of the Company of the Ironworks in New England* (Norman, OK, 1957), 44–59; Innes, *Creating the Commonwealth*, 237–71; Alonzo Lewis and James Newell, *History of Lynn* (Boston, 1865), 203–13.

23. Lewis and Newell, *History of Lynn*, 214–23. Sources dealing with slightly later periods but still confirming the continuity of economic behavior include *Records of Ye Towne Meetings of Lyn* (Lynn, MA, 1949); *Vital records of Lynn, Massachusetts, to the end of the year 1849* (Salem, MA, 1905); and *Extracts from the Records of the Town of Lynn* (Lynn, MA, 1856).

24. *Records of the Town of Cambridge, (formerly New-towne) Massachusetts, 1630–1703*, 43–45.

25. Ibid., 57–59, 49, 52–54.

26. Ipswich Town Records and Land Grants, 1634–1657. The records on the Ipswich school are badly torn but comprehensive enough—covering more than one hundred years—to warrant a sustained look.

27. *Town Records of Salem, Massachusetts*, 98–164.

5. Founding Forge

1. Johnson, *Johnson's Wonder Working Providence*, 69–72.

2. The conditions and affects surrounding the end of the Great Migration are explored in Virginia DeJohn Anderson, *New England's Generation*, 200–203; Gottfried, "First Depression in Massachusetts," 655–62; Nicholas Canny, "English Migration," in *Europeans on the Move: Studies on European Migration, 1500–1800*, ed. Canny (Oxford, 1994), 40–41; Margaret Ellen Newell, *From Dependency to Independence*, 54; and McCusker and Menard, *Economy of British America*, 91.

3. Rutman, "Governor Winthrop's Garden Crop." On shipping during this period, see *Aspinwall Notoriall Records*, 385–97, 244–45; references to particular shipments and bills of lading are in *Winthrop Papers*, 5:62. See also John Winthrop, *Winthrop's Journal*, 2:62; and Robert Child to Samuel Hartlib, 24 December 1645, in *Publications of the Colonial Society of Massachusetts* 37 (1959): 52.

4. My analysis of Essex County probate records keeps in mind the warnings made by Gloria L. Main in "Probate Records as a Source for Early American History," *William and Mary Quarterly* 32 (1975). My sample for the figures that follow on grain and beef included one hundred inventories printed in Dow, *Probate Records of Essex County*, vol. 1; see the appendix for a list of the individual inventories, dates recorded, town, and value. On cow ownership, see ibid., 1:212–14. In addition to grain and beef supplies, 76 percent owned pork; 44 percent, cheese or butter; and 36 percent, barley or malt.

5. Cronon, *Changes in the Land*, 34–54; Betty Fussell, "Translating Maize into Corn: The Transformation of America's Native Grain," *Social Science Research* 66 (1999): 58–63; Mood, "John Winthrop, Jr. on Indian Corn," 23.

6. Dow, *Records and Files of the Quarterly Courts*, 2:28, 217–18, 365, 20, 180, 186, 74. Background on economic exchange in a cash-poor environment comes from Michael Merrill, "Cash Is Good to Eat: Self-Sufficiency and Exchange in the Rural Economy of the United States," *Radical History Review* 4 (1977): 42–72; and Shammas, "How Self-Sufficient Was Early America?"

7. On the region's integration into the transatlantic market, see Bailyn, *New England Merchants,* chap. 6; Margaret Ellen Newell, *From Dependency to Independence,* 72–83; Rutman, "Governor Winthrop's Garden Crop," 400; Hunter, *Purchasing Identity in the Atlantic World,* 34–70; McCusker and Menard, *Economy of British America,* 96–99; and Charles Carroll, *Timber Economy of Puritan New England,* 75–87.

8. Susan Geib, "Hammersmith: The Saugus Ironworks as an Example of Early Industrialization," in *New England Begins: The Seventeenth Century,* ed. Jonathan L. Fairbanks and Robert F. Trent, 3 vols. (Boston, 1982), 2:175–201; McCusker and Menard, *Economy of British America,* 96; Bailyn, *New England Merchants,* 61–70; Hartley, *Ironworks on the Saugus.*

9. I base this argument on my analysis of the Lynn Ironworks Papers, 1651–1653, Baker Library, Harvard Business School, Cambridge, MA.

10. Hartley, *Ironworks on the Saugus,* 123.

11. Ibid., 188.

12. Ibid.

13. "Coard Wood is Debitor to Sundry Accts" (1651), 77–86, Lynn Ironworks Papers.

14. Hartley, *Ironworks on the Saugus,* 146.

15. "Coard Wood is Debitor to Sundry Accts," 77–86.

16. Details on the charcoal-making process come from the pamphlet *American Charcoal Making in the Era of the Cold-Blast Furnace,* by Jackson Kemper (Washington, DC, 1987), available at the ironworks site in Saugus, MA. Additional background can be found in Hartley, *Ironworks on the Saugus,* 165–71.

17. "Coard Wood is Debitor to Sundry Accts," 77–86. Hurdles were planks laid across soft ground to provide firm passage.

18. Hartley, *Ironworks on the Saugus,* 147.

19. Ibid., 167n2; "The Ironworks at Hammersmith and Braintree" (1653), 114–21, Lynn Ironworks Papers, which includes a debt for "2 floating shovels" for 10s.

20. Hartley, *Ironworks on the Saugus,* 148–49; "Bogg Mine Is Debiter to Sundry Accts." (1651), 87–88, Lynn Ironworks Papers.

21. See Hartley, *Ironworks on the Saugus,* 167. Winthrop makes a reference to this "rock mine" in *Winthrop Papers,* 5:239. The account for the mine is in "Rock Mine Is Debiter to Sundry Disbursements" (1651), 89, Lynn Ironworks Papers. Some archaeological evidence indicates that the company may initially have imported limestone, only later to rely exclusively on the local igneous rock.

22. "Rock Mine Is Debiter to Sundry Disbursements," 89.

23. "Servants appertayning to Mr. John Becx, Mr. Frost, Mr. Joshua Foote and Company of London merchants being to the Ironworks as debitter" (n.d.), 97–102, Lynn Ironworks Papers.

24. "Scotts Being at the Ironworks appartayning to the aforementioned Mr. John Becx" (1651), 103–7, ibid.; "The Farme at Lynn app. to Mr. John Becx" (1651), 108–13, ibid.

25. "Servants, appartayning unto the Company are Debittor unto Sundry accts." (1653), 150, ibid.

26. "Sundry Sums in Reference to the Workes " (n.d.), 90–96, ibid.

27. "The Ironworks at Hammersmith and Braintree," 114–21.

28. "To the Account of Bar Iron Making," Lynn Ironworks Papers; "The Ironworks at Hammersmith and Braintree," 114–21.

29. "The Farme at Lynn"; "Sundry Sums in Reference to the Workes."

30. "To the Account of Bar Iron Making."

31. "Scotts Being at the Ironworks appartayning to the aforementioned Mr. John Becx" (1651), 103–7; "Servants appertayning to Mr. John Becx, Mr. Frost, Mr. Joshua Foote."

32. "To the Account of Bar Iron Making"; "The Farme at Lynn."

33. "Sundry Sums in Reference to the Workes"; "The Farme at Lynn."

34. "The Ironworks at Hammersmith and Braintree," 114–21.

35. "To the Account of Bar Iron Making."

36. Ibid.

37. "The Ironworks at Hammersmith and Braintree," 114–21.

38. Ibid.

39. "The Farme at Lynn"; "Sundry Sums in Reference to the Workes."

6. The Provincialism of Young George Corwin

1. For background information on Corwin, see Hunter, *Purchasing Identity in the Atlantic World*, 41–48; Richard Gildrie, *Salem, Massachusetts, 1626–1683: A Covenant Community* (Charlottesville, VA, 1975), 103–7; and Sidney J. Perley, *History of Salem, Massachusetts*, vol. 2 (Salem, 1929), 221.

2. Josiah Child, *A New Discourse of Trade* (London, 1804), 198–202; Richard Vines, quoted in Margaret Ellen Newell, *From Dependency to Independence*, 81.

3. McCusker and Menard, *Economy of British America*, 97.

4. Bailyn, *New England Merchants*, 139–43; Greene, *Pursuits of Happiness*, 62; Bushman, *From Puritan to Yankee*.

5. George Corwin account sample, 1651–56, MS 445 in George Corwin Account Books, 1652–1684, in George Corwin's Letters, Bills, Ledgers and Day Books, 1651–1684; accounts of Benjamin Balch (February 1652–January 1655) and Mr. Norrice (November 1653–March 1655), ibid., 30, 55.

6. Accounts of John Leach (March–November 1653), Thomas Gordon (February 1652–September 1653), and John Beckett (September–February 1655), ibid., 31–32.

7. George Corwin account sample, 1653–56; accounts of Nathanial Putnam (September 1655–March 1656), Joseph Jencks (December 1652–January 1653), and Elias Stileman (August 1653–July 1654), George Corwin Account Books, 1651–1653, in George Corwin's Letters, Bills, Ledgers and Day Books, 1651–1684, 2, 62.

8. Philip English Shipping Account Books, 1664–1718, MS 11; Cheever, "Some Remarks on the Commerce of Salem, from 1626 to 1741, with a Sketch of Philip English," 72; David Konig, "A New Look at the Essex 'French': Ethnic Tensions in Seventeenth-Century Essex County, Massachusetts," ibid. 110 (1974): 174; Bailyn, *New England Merchants*, 144.

9. On fishing and wood supplies, see Philip English Shipping Account Books, 1664–1718, MS 11, 54, 151, 154, 156; and Vickers, *Farmers and Fishermen*, 159, table 5.

10. Philip English Shipping Account Books, 1664–1718.

11. Bailyn, *New England Merchants*, 143.

7. Economic Continuity and Its Contents

1. Virginia DeJohn Anderson, *New England's Generation*, 191–201; Harry S. Stout, *The New England Soul: Preaching and Religious Culture in Colonial New England* (New York, 1986), 88–96; Robert G. Pope, *Halfway Covenant*; Allen, *In English Ways*, 223–29; Greven, *Four Generations*, 103–24.

2. Ministers are quoted in Bailyn, *New England Merchants*, 141–42. See also Virginia DeJohn Anderson, *New England's Generation*, 195–200; and Staloff, "Where Religion and Profit Jump Together." The ministers, however, may have protested too much. While merchants stood out as the obvious culprits in the region's perceived decline, these same men often used their wealth to strengthen instead of challenging congregational bonds. The costs of printing and distributing sermons, repairing and building meetinghouses, and paying clerical salaries, to name just a few, were willingly absorbed by merchants enjoying newfound commercial wealth. "Without the economic resources provided by a vigorous economy," explains one historian who has studied this connection, "the Puritan movement in America would have died out rapidly." See Staloff, "Where Religion and Profit Jump Together," 10. Even when the connections between profit and piety were less conspicuous, they often served to intensify rather than diminish Puritan mores. The emerging merchant class in Marblehead and Gloucester, for example, demonstrated a concerted effort to preserve "inherited beliefs and values" in an inverse proportion to their push into the commercial world. When the ministers' words of warning are not taken at face value, there is much to suggest that the supposedly inextricable link between the downfall of traditionalism and the rise of overseas commercialism was in fact a chimerical one.

3. Harrison Ellery and Charles Pickering Bowditch, *The Pickering Genealogy*, vol. 1 (privately printed, 1897), 44–46.

4. Account of John Hovey, John Pickering Account Book, 1684–1716, fp1, 96, The Phillips Library, Peabody Essex Museum, 96.

5. Account of Eleazer Keafer, ibid., 106.

6. Accounts of John Harvey, Manassah Marsten, John Neale, and Ephriam Kempton, John Pickering Account Book.

7. Accounts of Ingersoll and Manassah Marsten, ibid.

8. Account of Frances Faulkner, John Barnard Account Book, [ca. 1702]–1708, Fam. MSS B2598, The Phillips Library, Peabody Essex Museum.

9. Accounts of Job Tyler (22 June 1703) and Joseph Lovejoy (1699), ibid.

10. Accounts of Nathanial Stevens, Joseph Parker, and William Andel, ibid.

11. Background on Burnham comes from "Deed from John Burnham Sr. to John Burnham Tertious," 1 March 1694, in Essex Society of Genealogists, *Essex County Deeds, 1639–1678* (Bowie, MD, 2003), bk. 10, pp. 23–25; Elizabeth Puckett Martin, *Deacon John Burnham of Ipswich and Ebenezer Martin of Rehobeth, Massachusetts and Some of Their Descendants* (Baltimore, 1987); Roderick H. Martin, *The Burnham Family Genealogical Records of the Descendants of the Four Emigrants of the Name Who Were Among the Early Settlers in America* (New Britain, CT, 1869); and Thomas Franklin Waters, *Ipswich in the Massachusetts Bay Colony, 1633–1700* (Ipswich, MA, 1905).

12. Accounts of Nathanial Perkins (28 March 1700–11 December 1704) and Isaac Perkins (11 July 1698–5 May 1705), John Burnham Account Book, 1698–1700, FMs B9663, The Phillips Library, Peabody Essex Museum.

13. Accounts of John Whipple (17 November 1697, 11 June 1698), Nathanial Rust (10 February 1703–27 October 1705), Thomas Perrin (10 May 1693–9 May 1694), and Isaac Littlehale (17 June 1692–15 May 1694), ibid.

14. John Burnham Account Book.

15. Douglas R. McManis, *Colonial New England: A Historical Geography* (New York, 1975), 128–29; Innes, *Creating the Commonwealth*, 260–62; Hartley, *Ironworks on the Saugus*, 276.

16. Richard Hobart Account Book, 1699–1701, FMs H681, entry for 23 December 1699, The Phillips Library, Peabody Essex Museum.

17. Richard Hobart Account Book, 1699–1701. One labor transaction did not list the cost, and none included a date. The only people he noted hiring labor from were a "Mr. Parsons" and a "Henry T."

18. Ibid., 29 May 170[4?]. Hobart records being away in Boston for seven days and assesses that he lost £1 1s. in his own labor during his absence.

19. Ibid., entries for 22 February and 25 May, year not specified, and for 25 June 1699.

20. Hobart's clients are difficult to identify because he preceded their last names with the generic "Mr." rather than a first name. However, he had a habit of listing the town from which a client came only if the client was not from Salisbury. Most of the time, then, towns are not mentioned, and we may assume that they lived in Salisbury. When towns are listed, we find him doing business in Boston, Neponsett, Newbury, and, on one occasion, Weathersfield, Connecticut.

21. Richard Hobart Account Book, 15 August (£9 6s.), 17 August (£3), 30 June 1699 (£1).

22. Ibid., 3 June 1699 (£4), August 1700 (£20), 23 October 1699 (£5), 30 June 1699 (£1).

23. Ibid., 4 November 1699.

24. Ibid., undated entry.

25. Ibid., 29 May 1701.

26. Hobart practiced mixed farming in addition to working as a blacksmith. A 1682 assessment reveals that he owned five cows, three yearlings, one horse, one pig, two houses (one of them his shop), ten sheep, eight acres of meadow ground, two acres of broken ground, and six acres of pasture. See Dow, *Records and Files of the Quarterly Courts*, 8:390.

27. Jacob Adams Account Book sample, 1675–76, 2, from Jacob Adams Account Book, 1673–1693, Baker Library, Harvard Business School.

28. "The Account Book of Jacob Adams of Newbury Mass., and Suffield, Conn," typescript attached to the Jacob Adams Account Book, 1673–1693, 10–11.

29. Jacob Adams Account Book sample, 1675–76, 3, 5, 6, 15.

30. Ibid., 11–13.

31. Ibid., 1, 2, 7, 10, 13, 16.

32. Ibid., 1.

33. Ibid., 14.

34. Ibid., 7, 9, 11.

35. Biographical sketch of Adams accompanying "Account Book of Jacob Adams of Newbury Mass., and Suffield Conn," 12.

8. The Hidden Benefits of Local Trade

1. John Pickering Account Book; John Burnham Account Book; John Barnard Account Book.

2. Account of Eleazer Keafer, John Pickering Account Book, 96.

3. Account of Ephriam Kempton, ibid., 106.

4. Accounts of William Harris, John Neale, and Charles Macarter, ibid., 146, 28, 126.

5. Accounts of John Trenchman and John Harvey, ibid.

6. Accounts of Mr. Coswell,, Abraham Martin, Joseph Marshall, and Jeremiah Buckman, John Burnham Account Book.

7. Accounts of John and William Haskell (2 March 1706) and Andrew (26 March 1705), ibid.

8. Accounts of Ephriam Kempton and John Harvey, John Barnard Account Book.

9. Accounts of Robert Annable (September 1705, 24 May 1706) and John Burnham, ibid.

10. Account of Samuel Giddings (24 March 1703, 11 Nov. 1704), ibid.

11. Account of William Giddings (2 August 1705), ibid.

12. Account of Frances Faulkner, John Barnard Account Book.

13. Accounts of William Blunt (1702) and Henry Chandler (1700), ibid.

14. Account of Hooker Osgood, ibid.

15. Accounts of Mr. Foster (3 July 1704) and Nathanial Perkins (27 September 1704), John Burnham Account Book; Frances Faulkner (1703–4), John Barnard Account Book; Mr. Taley (17, 23 March 1681), John Flint Account Book, 1679–1684, FMs F624, The Phillips Library, Peabody Essex Museum.

16. Accounts of Abraham Martin (5 September 1705), John Burnham Account Book; Frances Faulkner (1704), Ezekial Osgood (1703), Mr. West (1689), Benjamin Coker (1703), John Barnard Account Book; Richard Hobart Account Book; Manassah Marsten (1684–86), John Pickering Account Book.

17. Accounts of Frances Faulkner, Stephen Barnard (1705), Henry Chandler (1700), Thomas Johnson (1699), Nat Lovejoy (1702), John Johnson (1699), and John Barker (1699), John Burnham Account Book.

18. Accounts of Eleazer Keafer and George Ingersoll, John Pickering Account Book, 106, 116; and Alice Faulkner, John Barnard Account Book.

19. Accounts of John Marsten and Samual Brown, John Pickering Account Book, 136, 37; and John Johnson, John Barnard Account Book.

20. Accounts of Deliverance Parkman and John Harvey, John Pickering Account Book, 26, 106.

21. Accounts of William Cogswell (10 March 1705), John and William Haskell (9 May 1702), Jonathan Low (13 May 1701), and Nathanial Perkins (5 June 1704), John Burnham Account Book.

22. Accounts of John Neale, William Pickering, Samual Brown, and John Harvey, John Pickering Account Book, 146, 28, 27, 106.

23. Accounts of Alice Faulkner and John Ingalls, John Barnard Account Book.

24. Accounts of Capt. John Price (1695) and Goodman Bointon (1697), ibid.

25. Accounts of Manassah Marsten, John Harvey, and Joseph Boyce, John Pickering Account Book, 126, 106, 156, 166.

26. Accounts of Frances and Alice Faulkner, Stephen Barnard, and George Abbott, John Barnard Account Book; and Jeremiah Buckman and Robert Annable, John Burnham Account Book.

27. Margaret Ellen Newell, *From Dependency to Independence*, 86.

28. Helpful literature on labor arrangements in England and New England includes Daniel Vickers, "Working the Fields in a Developing Economy: Essex County, Massachusetts, 1630–1675," in *Work and Labor in Early America*, ed. Stephen Innes (Chapel Hill, NC,

1988); Keith Thomas, "Work and Leisure in Pre-Industrial Society," *Past and Present* 27 (1964); D. C. Colemen, "Labour in the English Economy in the Seventeenth Century," *Economic History Review,* 2nd ser., 8 (1956); Eric G. Nellis, "Communities of Workers: Free Labor in Provincial Massachusetts, 1690–1765" (PhD diss., University of British Columbia, 1979); Innes, *Labor in a New Land;* and Laslett, *World We Have Lost.*

29. Vickers, *Farmers and Fishermen,* 64.

30. Ibid.

31. Accounts of Ephriam Kempton, John Marsten, and Joseph Boyce, John Pickering Account Book.

32. Accounts of Joseph Marshall and John Burnham's sons, John Burnham Account Book.

33. Accounts of Alice Faulkner, Steven Branard, John Parker, Moses Tyler, and John Granger, John Barnard Account Book.

34. John Burnham Account Book.

35. Accounts of Steven Branard, Samual Fry, Joseph Parker, and Thomas Chandler, John Barnard Account Book.

36. Accounts of the Cogswells, Fosters, and Giddingses, John Burnham Account Book.

37. Laurel Thatcher Ulrich, *Good Wives: Image and Reality in the Lives of Women in Northern New England, 1650–1750* (New York, 1980), 35–50.

38. Account of Eleazer Keafer, John Pickering Account Book.

39. Accounts of John Russell, John Burnham Account Book; and Mary Coker and John Price, John Barnard Account Book.

40. Accounts of Alice Faulkner and Frances Faulkner, John Barnard Account Book.

9. Back to Business as Usual in the Bay Colony

1. Timothy H. Breen, "Persistent Localism: English Social Change and the Shaping of New England Institutions," *William and Mary Quarterly* 32 (1975): 4. On the continuity of Puritan cultural and economic habits in Massachusetts, see Fischer, *Albion's Seed,* 13–206; Carl Bridenbaugh, *Vexed and Troubled Englishmen, 1590–1642* (New York, 1968); David Cressy, *Birth, Marriage, and Death: Ritual, Religion, and the Life Cycle in Tudor and Stuart England* (New York, 1997); Cressy, *Coming Over;* Thompson, *Mobility and Migration;* Allen, *In English Ways;* and George Lee Haskins, *Law and Authority in Early Massachusetts: A Study in Tradition and Design* (New York, 1960), 163–68. On the persistence of "persistent localism" into the next century, see Richard Maxwell Brown, "Back Country Rebellions and the Homestead Ethic in America, 1740–1799," in *Tradition, Conflict, and Modernization: Perspectives on the American Revolution,* ed. Richard Maxwell Brown and Don E. Fehrenbacher (New York, 1977), 76–79; and Margaret Ellen Newell, *From Dependency to Independence,* 24–35.

2. Breen and Foster, "Puritans' Greatest Achievement," 9; Powell, *Puritan Village;* Greven, *Four Generations,* 40–102; John Demos, *A Little Commonwealth: Family Life in Plymouth Colony* (New York, 1970); Edmund S. Morgan, *The Puritan Family: Religion and Domestic Relations in Seventeenth-Century New England* (New York, 1966), 66–86; Vickers, "Competency and Competition," 3–4; Edward M. Cook Jr., *Fathers of the Towns: Leadership and Community Structure in Eighteenth Century New England* (Baltimore, 1976); David Konig, *Law and Society in Puritan Massachusetts, Essex County, 1629–1692* (Chapel Hill, NC,

1979); Mary Beth Norton, *Founding Mothers and Fathers: Gendered Power and the Forming of American Society* (New York, 1996), 113–27. For works supporting the idea that familial structure was a continuation from England, see Lawrence Stone, *The Family, Sex, and Marriage in England, 1500–1800* (New York, 1977); Ralph Houlbrooke, *The English Family, 1450–1700* (New York, 1984); and Susan Amussen, *An Ordered Society: Gender and Class in Early Modern England* (Oxford, 1988).

3. Dow, *Records and Files of the Quarterly Courts*, 8:250–53.

4. Ibid., 7:161–62.

5. Ibid., 8:322.

6. Ibid., 8:423. Town of Rowley Index to Town Records, 3.

7. Dow, *Records and Files of the Quarterly Courts*, 7:275, 163, 188, 192, 171; 8:180, 374.

8. Ibid., 7:115.

9. Account of John Newman (4 March 1681–3 November 1682), John Flint Account Book.

10. Account of Bartholomew Gedney (9 June–14 December 1682), ibid.

11. Account of George Deane (1 March 1682–7 June 1684), ibid.

12. Account of Thomas Newell (2 June 1681), ibid.

13. Dow, *Records and Files of the Quarterly Courts*, 6:373, 313; 7:27, 197; 8:143, 128, 345.

14. Inventory of the estate of George Booth, in ibid., 8:364.

15. Dow, *Records and Files of the Quarterly Courts*, 8:154.

16. Ibid.

17. J. de L. Mann, *The Cloth Industry in the West of England from 1640 to 1880* (Oxford, 1971), 290–96.

18. John Pearson Account Book sample, 1675–76, from John Pearson Account Book, 1674–1799, Pearson Family Papers, Baker Library, Harvard Business School.

19. Ibid. Interestingly, Pearson did not manipulate prices in order to encourage operation at full capacity. His records, in fact, provide no evidence of the incentives he may have used to concentrate his business.

20. Ibid., 116–17. On hard cash in Massachusetts, see Benjamin A. Hicklin, "'Crying Up the Coin': Specie Accumulation in Seventeenth-Century Maritime Massachusetts" (paper, Southwestern Social Science Association Annual Conference, San Antonio, TX, 15 April 2006).

21. John Pearson Account Book sample, 227.

22. Ibid., 5 April, 31 March 1685.

23. Ibid., 16, 20 March 1685; Dow, *Records and Files of the Quarterly Courts*, 7:216.

10. Merchant Anxiety and the Local Economy

1. The following references are only a reflective sample of the extensive literature written from this perspective: Jacob Price, "What Did Merchants Do? Reflections on British Overseas Trade, 1660–1790," *Journal of Economic History* 49 (1989): 267–84; idem, "A Note on the Value of Colonial Exports of Shipping," ibid. 36 (1976): 704–24; idem, *Capital and Credit in British Overseas Trade: The View from the Chesapeake* (Cambridge, MA, 1980); Phyllis Deane and W. A. Cole, *British Economic Growth, 1688–1789* (Cambridge, 1962); Ralph A. Davis, "English Foreign Trade, 1700–1774," *Economic History Review*, 2nd ser., 15 (December 1962): 285–303.

2. Account of Theodore Atkinson, "Merchandise received from on board the ship 'Elinor and Christian' for the acct. of Mr. William Gibbs of Barbados," and "Merchandise for acct. of Mr. William Gibbs received from aboard sundry vessells, from Barbados, is debtor," in Robert Gibbs Business Records, 1659–1708, Miscellaneous MSS, box 2, folders 12 and 13, American Antiquarian Society, Worcester, MA.

3. "Mr. Robert Gibbs, merchant is dr . . . baggs of cloth woole shipped by John ? from Bilbao," ibid.

4. "Isaac Woodbury and Co., DR, 1680," and "Joseph Phippany and Co., DR, 1680," John Higginson Account Book, 69–70, 72–73.

5. "John Higginson, DR, by frait of the 2 hh fish" (in undated entry); "Goods Taken on bord the slupe" included "3 hh for Mr. Higginson and 2hh for Mr. Higgenson" (in 1694 entry), both in Samual Ingersoll Account Book, 1685–1695, The Phillips Library, Peabody Essex Museum.

6. Accounts of Tobias Carter, Samual Wakefield, and Richard Friend, John Higginson Account Book, 101, 100, 99.

7. "Goods landed" (n.d), Samual Ingersoll Account Book, 1685–1715, The Phillips Library, Peabody Essex Museum.

8. Accounts of Goody Seaver (6 March 1675), Margaret Tomkins (7 April 1692), and Goodman Langon (n.d.), Robert Gibbs General Store Account Book, 1669–1708, American Antiquarian Society, Worcester, MA.

9. "Mr. Maules own evidence as clerk of the market vs. Elizabeth Haskett" (23 March 1705), Thomas Maule Account Book, 1681–1701, FP 1, fol. 134, The Phillips Library, Peabody Essex Museum.

10. Accounts of John Raymond (1 June 1681–3 November 1682), Joseph Reed (4–27 May 1681), and John Simpson (11 October 1681), John Higginson Account Book, 101, 100, 104.

11. Entry for 15 June 1692, Samual Ingersoll Account Book, 1685–1715.

12. Philip English to John Pilgrim, 28 January 1695, Philip English Ship Papers, 1651–1736, box 1, folder 2, The Phillips Library, Peabody Essex Museum.

13. Dan King to Phillip English, 8 October 1688, ibid., box 1, folder 4.

14. John Seale to Phillip English, 15 March 1704, ibid.

15. Seale to English, 31 March 1707, ibid., box 1, folder 3.

16. Sampson Sheafe to Jonathan Corwin, 4 September 1688, Business Papers, 1669–1711, Jonathan Corwin Papers, box 1, folder 6, The Phillips Library, Peabody Essex Museum.

17. William Hollingsworth to his mother, 19 September 1689, Hollingsworth Family Papers, 1679–1700, box 1, folder 1, The Phillips Library, Peabody Essex Museum.

18. My thinking on this matter has been influenced by an older body of scholarship dealing with the development of the railroad in the nineteenth-century United States. Traditionally, economic historians have portrayed the railroad as a mode of transport that replaced the intricate canal system that Americans had build throughout the East and the Midwest. A more nuanced interpretation, however, argues that the canal and the railroad actually complemented each other for a period of about twenty years and that this cooperation was critical to the railroads' taking off to become the region's single most efficient form of transportation. See George R. Taylor, *The Transportation Revolution, 1815–1860* (New

York, 1951); and Albert Fishlow, *American Railroads and the Transformation of the Antebellum Economy* (Cambridge, MA, 1965).

19. Accounts of Joseph Roade (19 March 1680–5 April 1681), John Trask of Beverly (30 January 1679–6 April 1681), John Clifford (12 February 1679–28 November 1682), and Joseph Phippany Jr. (10 February 1679–25 July 1681), and "My Cart and Horse, DR." (May 1680–"winter 1680"), John Higginson Account Book, 65–67.

20. Accounts of Goodman Seaver (19 July 1673), David Flint (n.d.), Goodman Landin (n.d.), Goody Hacker (16 March 1700), Gilbert Cole (May 1676), Goody Weborn (n.d.), and Goody Peale (n.d.), Robert Gibbs General Store Account Book.

21. Works endorsing the greater-opportunity view include Demos, *Little Commonwealth;* and Roger Thompson, *Women in Stuart England and America: A Comparative Study* (Boston, 1974). Challenging it are Mary Beth Norton, *Liberty's Daughters: The Revolutionary Experience for American Women* (Boston, 1980); and Marylynn Salmon, *Women and the Law of Property in Early America* (Chapel Hill, NC, 1986).

22. Accounts of Goody Spring (n.d.), Goody Seaver (19 September 1674), and Goody Courser (n.d.), Robert Gibbs General Store Account Book.

23. Accounts of John Hornbry (3 August 1667), Richard Smith (23 September 1669), Wally Hornbart (1667), Avery Bullsher (1666), Cornbury (n.d.), John Whipple (12 July 1669), and William Brown (n.d.), Philip English Shipping Account Books, 1664–1718, box 17, vol. 1.

24. Accounts of John Pickering (1680) and John Baylor and Co. (9 August 1680), John Higginson Account Book, 88, 2.

25. "Goods landed in my store" (22 June 1692), Samual Ingersoll Account Book, 1685–1715.

26. Ibid.

11. The Local Basis of International Trade

1. The application of traditional economic models—which tend to favor measurements of input and output—to historical development often overlook not only shipping but also the provisioning of those ships as an essential input. While considering the entire colonial economy as a measure of trade balance, John McCusker and Russell Menard note, "The carrying trade as an earner of credits in the balance of payments was an important alternative strategy to the export of commodities." Many historians, they argue, "believe it will prove upon further investigation to have been important enough . . . to create a surplus." McCusker and Menard, *Economy of British America,* 93. Although the question of trade balance remains incidental to the issue at hand, it does encourage us to look at an activity that was essential to export activity: provisioning.

2. "Landed for Secretary, 1688," Samual Ingersoll Account Book, 1685–1715, 3.

3. "What the men should have . . ." ([1698?]), Samual Ingersoll Account Book, 1685–1715.

4. Provisioning entries for *Little General,* ibid., passim.

5. See entries for the *Repair* (20 April 1702), the *Dragon* (n.d.), and the *Susanna* (10 April 1690), Philip English Shipping Account Books, 1664–1718, box 1, folders 1, 2, and 1.

6. "Invoice of Goods Laden on Bord the Ketch Friendship" (October–November 1679), "Nicolas Legrave on a fishing on Ketch John and Thomas" (1681), and "John Swazy and Co.

on a fishing voyage in the Ketch Dolphin" (1681), John Higginson Account Book, fols. 39, 99, 98.

7. "Ketch James Bonaventure, 1686–1689," "Ship, Salem,. 1696," and "Speedwell, 1699," all in Jonathan Corwin Papers, box 1, folder 9.

8. Provisioning entries for *Little General,* "Goods from Mr. Lolley," "Goods from Mr. Allen," and "My owne vendor," Samual Ingersoll Account Book, 1685–1715.

9. "Invoice of Goods Laden on Bord the Ketch Friendship" (October–November 1679); "Nicolas Legrave on a fishing on Ketch John and Thomas" (1681); "John Swasy and Co. on a fishing voyage in the Ketch Dolphin" (1681); and accounts of John Raymond (1 June 1681–3 September 1682), William Bowditch (18 April–29 September 1681), Benjamin Small (n.d.), Henry Henrick (9 March 1680–8 July 1681), and Timothy Lindall (27–29 February 1680), John Higginson Account Book, 50, 99, 98, 101, 101, 97, 93.

10. "Ketch James Bonaventure, 1686–1689," and account of Edward Littlefield (7 October 1679), Business Papers, in Jonathan Corwin Papers, box 1, folders 9 and 6, respectively.

11. Accounts of Thomas Woodbury (15 November 1670), Humphry Woodbury (1664), Job Holyard (4 March 1669), and William Hombart (1667), Philip English Shipping Account Books, 1664–1718, box 17, vol. 1.

12. "Ketch, Swallow, 1654–1690/1" (14 June 1687), "Speedwell, 1699," and "Ship, Salem, 1696," all in Jonathan Corwin Papers, box 1, folder 9.

13. "The New Ketch called the Swan" (10 February 1680) and "Ketch Dolphin, dr." (2 February 1680), John Higginson Account Book, fols. 78, 79.

14. "Deed of sale" (24 September 1691), "Mr. Cornbury" (n.d.), and "bill of Mr. Barton" (1691), Philip English Shipping Account Books, 1664–1718, box 1, folder 4, vol. 1, and folder 2.

15. James E. McWilliams, "Brewing Beer in Massachusetts Bay, 1630–1690," *New England Quarterly* 1 (1998): 543–69.

16. "Bill, Sept 6, 1686," John . . . [illegible] to Capt. John Price, 17 October 1687, "receipt" (18 April 1688), "bill" (n.d.), "bill" (31 October 1689), "receipt" (5 December 1689), and William Bowditch to John Price, 15 August 1689, all in Hollingsworth Family Papers, box 1, folder 1.

17. *Susanna,* 1688–89, English Family Papers, box 1, folder 3, The Phillips Library, Peabody Essex Museum.

18. The single existing study on the seventeenth-century fishing trade is Vickers, *Farmers and Fishermen.* Vickers is primarily concerned with demonstrating the ways in which merchants secured labor for their fishing voyages. His analysis, as thorough as it is on this point, reveals little about the overall structure of the fishing industry.

19. "An account of fish received in 1669," Robert Gibbs Business Records, box 2, folder 14.

20. Ibid.

21. "Bill, William Hathorne to Isaac Woodbury" (1704), English Family Papers, box 1, folder 5.

22. Accounts of Edward Homan (February 1700), William Leach (11 November 1670), Thomas Cromwell (n.d.), and Cornbury (1667), Philip English Shipping Account Books, 1664–1718.

23. "Repair, 1887/88," ibid, box 1, folder 1.

24. Entry for 10 June 1680, Business Papers, Jonathan Corwin Papers, box 1, folder 6.

25. Entries for 12 March–16 August 1686, ibid.

26. Entry for 15 June 1687, ibid.

27. Entries for 15 June, 27 August 1687, 23 April 1686, ibid.

28. "Isaac Woodbury and Co., DR., 1680," John Higginson Account Book, fols. 69–70.

29. "Joseph Phippany and Co, DR., 1680," ibid., fol. 72.

30. "Joseph Phippany and Co. Acct., 1681," fol. 97.

31. Entries for August 1692, 16 July 1694, and 29 February 1695, Samual Ingersoll Account Book, 1685–1715.

32. Accounts of John Pickering (31 December 1680–26 December 1681), Richard Flander (22 January–11 February 1680), and John Trask (29 July–13 August 1681), John Higginson Account Book, fols. 88, 90, 100.

33. Entry for August 1692, Samual Ingersoll Account Book, 1685–1715.

34. Accounts of William Henfield (25 March–17 December 1681), John Trask (29 July–13 August 1681), Ezekial Wallers (5 April 1681–5 February 1682), William Dodge (18 May–19 November 1681), and John Beckett (2 January–6 February 1691), John Higginson Account Book.

35. "Goodes landed in my store (1692)" and entry for August 1692, Samual Ingersoll Account Book, 1685–1715.

36. Accounts of Jeremiah Neale and Thomas Ramont, Jacob Pudetor Account Book, 4, 2, The Phillips Library, Peabody Essex Museum.

37. "Landed for Secretary" (1688), 3, and entries for 11 July 1692 and 5 April 1695, Samual Ingersoll Account Book, 1685–1715.

38. "Boston, NE" (2 August 1677) and entry for 20 June 1681, both in Business Papers, Jonathan Corwin Papers, box 1, folder 6.

39. "John Simpson's bill of work," 5 March 1685, Capt. George Corwin Papers, 1641–1685, George Corwin Account Books, box 1, folder 1, in George Corwin's Letters, Bills, Ledgers and Day Books, 1651–1684.

40. Accounts of Mrs. Elizabeth Turner (29 August 1682) and Benjamin Small (1 April 1681), John Higginson Account Book, fols. 86, 95.

41. Accounts of Ezekial Giles (May 1701) and "John Kimball's wife" (February 1688), Robert Gibbs General Store Account Book.

42. Robert Gibbs Business Records, box 2, folder 14.

43. Account of Theodore Atkinson, ibid., box 2, folder 12.

44. Cape Porpoise River Mill Falls Papers, 1658–1700, in Jonathan Corwin Papers, box 1, folder 8, 1, 2, 11, 16.

45. Accounts of William Deane (26 June 1675), Robert Gibbs General Store Account Book; and Henry Dearing, Robert Gibbs Business Records, box 2, folder 14.

46. Joseph Stover to Jonathan Corwin, 4 July 1682, 25 November 1679, and 28 September 1679, all in Cape Porpoise River Mill Falls Papers.

47. "Provisions left in Landlord Stovers Custody," 42, ibid.

48. Stover to Jonathan Corwin, 17 November 1680, and accounts of Seaburn Bradrook, 11, and Mr. Austin, 1, all in ibid.

49. Stover to Jonathan Corwin, 11 February 1679, "Things for the Mills to be sent to Edward Littlefield," and "Things Necessary to be Down at the Mills," all in ibid.

Epilogue

1. Heyrman, *Commerce and Culture*, 62–63; Bailyn, *New England Merchants*, 196–97.

2. John Gould Account Book, 1697–1733, Gould Family Papers, The Philips Library, Salem, MA.

3. Ibid., MSS 233, 118–21.

4. Ibid., 46–49.

Index

Italicized page numbers refer to illustrations, while the letter t following a page number denotes a table.

Index

Index

Index

Index

Index